Abstracts of the
TESTAMENTARY PROCEEDINGS
of the
PREROGATIVE COURT OF MARYLAND

Volume VI: 1686–1689, 1692-1693

Libers: 13 (Folios 433–519),
14, 14A, and 15A

by
V. L. Skinner, Jr.

CLEARFIELD

Printed for
Clearfield Company, Inc., by
Genealogical Publishing Co., Inc.
Baltimore, Maryland
2006

International Standard Book Number: 0-8063-5308-2

Made in the United States of America

INTRODUCTION

Purpose of the Prerogative Court.

The Prerogative Court was the central point for probate for Provincial Maryland. It was mirrored after the Prerogative Court of Canterbury. There was a judge as well as clerk(s) of the court. Initially, all probate was brought directly to the Prerogative Court, located in the Provincial Capital. As the Province became more populous, all documents were still to be filed with the Prerogative Court; however, administration of probate was delegated to the various county courts. Even so, there are documents only in the Prerogative Court and not in the appropriate county, and vice versa.

Documents filed in the Prerogative Court.

The following documents were filed in the Prerogative Court: administration bond, will, inventory, administration accounts, and final balances. The testamentary proceedings contain the administration bond and the docket for the court. If the administrator is lax in filing documents, then a summons is also recorded.

Equity Court

The Prerogative Court was also the court for equity cases--resolution of disputes over the settlement and distribution of an estate. The case was brought before the judge and could take several years to resolve. Often depositions were taken and recorded in the minutes.

Notes on the Abstraction.

1. The left hand column contains the liber/folio number. The folio numbers are presented just as they appear in the actual document, e.g., 32a, 78½.

2. The right hand column contains the abstraction text.

3. Various libers specify a particular session for the Prerogative Court, e.g., 1678; or, September Court 1742. This information is presented as "Court Session:" followed by the

appropriate session. Should no session have been specified, then the phrase "no date" is used.

4. An ellipsis (...) is used to indicate a continuation of the previous information, but no relevant genealogical information is present.

5. The following symbols are used in the abstraction:
    ?   difficult to read.
    #   pounds of tobacco.
    !   [sic].

Abbreviations.

The following abbreviations have been used throughout this abstraction:

AA — Anne Arundel Co.
ACC — Accomac Co.
BA — Baltimore Co.
CE — Cecil Co.
CH — Charles Co.
CR — Caroline Co.
CV — Calvert Co.
dbn — de bonis non
DE — Delaware
DO — Dorchester Co.
ENG — England
FR — Frederick Co.
g — gentleman
HA — Harford Co.
IRE — Ireland
KE — Kent Co. MD
KEDE — Kent Co. DE
LaC — letters ad colligendum (for temporary collection & preservation of assets)
LoA — letters of administration
MA — Massachusetts
MD — Maryland
MO — Montgomery Co.
NE — New England
NEI — "non est inventar" (not found)
NY — New York
NYC — New York City
p — planter
PA — Pennsylvania
PG — Prince George's Co.
PoA — power of attorney
QA — Queen Anne's Co.
SM — St. Mary's Co.
SMC — St. Mary's City
SO — Somerset Co.
TA — Talbot Co.
VA — Virginia
WA — Washington Co.
WO — Worcester Co.

This volume is a continuation of the series, covering 1686 to July 1689, and then June 1692 to 1693. From July 1689 to June 1692, the Prerogative Court did not function because of the Glorious Revolution. When the Court reconvened in June 1692, direction was given to the Registrar to instruct the various counties to bring in the various probate documents that they had obtained, and to provide a list of outstanding estates.

Court Session: 1686

13:433 29 November. Exhibited bond of William
Dare administrator of Francis Fry.
Security: George Oldfeild (CE).

Moses Jones exhibited his accounts on
estate of James Wheeler (CH).

Edward Jones (CE) exhibited oath of John
Hiland & Samuel Wheeler, appraisers of
John Cammell (CE).

Exhibited will of John Taylor (DO),
proved before Henry Hooper (g).

Richard Ladd (g, CV) exhibited oath of
Richard Pollard administrator of William
Gamball (CV). Securities (CV): John
Hollins, George Seelings. Also
exhibited oath of Nathaniel Dare & Isaac
Baker, appraisers. Also exhibited
inventory of said Richard Gamball.

30 November. James Rounds (g, SO)
exhibited oath of Thomas Pointer & John
Smock, appraisers of Richard Hill. Also
exhibited will, proved before said
Round.

13:434 Exhibited will of Augustine Harman
Bohemiah, proved before Mr. William
Dare.

Exhibited will of Thomas Gerrard (SM),
proved before Capt. James Bowling (SM).

Mr. Edward Jones (CE) exhibited oath of
William Dare (CE) administrator of
Edward Fry.

Exhibited bond of Sarah Bartlett
administratrix of Ralph Bartlett (CH).
Security: Richard Boughton (CH).

Exhibited inventory of Richard Jones
(CH), by appraisers Thomas Craxton &
Robert Benson.

Exhibited will of William Walton (SO),
proved before John Osbourne (SO).

Hance Hanson (g, KE) exhibited oath of Mr. John Hinson & Charles Tilden administrators of Morgan Williams (KE), sworn September 1686. Securities (KE): Edward Sweatnam, Elias King. Also exhibited oath of Allexander Walters & Francis Barnes, appraisers sworn same day.

13:435 Also exhibited inventory.

Edward Beedle (g, BA) exhibited oath of Miles Gibson administrator of John Yeo (BA), sworn 5 June 1686. Securities (BA): James Phillips, Thomas Richardson. Also exhibited oath of Thomas Hedge & James Phillips, appraisers sworn same day. Also exhibited inventory.

Exhibited additional inventory of Maj. Thomas Trueman (CV), by appraisers Ninian Beale & Thomas Ellis.

Exhibited inventory of Mrs. Mary Trueman (CV), by appraisers Ninian Beale & Thomas Gant.

Exhibited inventory of Robert Evans (TA), by appraisers Thomas Robins & William Bexsley.

William Rosewell (SM) vs. estate of Dr. Patrick Innes. Caveat exhibited.

13:436 1 December. Exhibited inventory of John Clarke (SM), by appraisers Richard Edlen & John Compton. Mr. Joseph Pile (SM) exhibited oath of Richard Edlen & John Compton, appraisers of John Clarke. Also exhibited oath of Ann Clarke executrix.

2 December. Exhibited inventory of Henry Bennitt (AA), by appraisers James Morray & Walter Carr. Also exhibited bond of Abraham Clark administrator. Securities (AA): Walter Carr, James Morray.

6 December. Exhibited bond of John Godsgrace (CV) administrator of James Godsgrace. Securities (CV): John Chittam, Thomas Robinson. Thomas Tasker

Court Session: 1686

(g, CV) exhibited oath of Edward Hurlock
& John Keatch, appraisers. Also
exhibited inventory.

29 November!. Exhibited will of Robert
Skinner (CV), proved before Thomas
Brooke (g).

5 January. Exhibited will of Arthur
Storer (CV), constituting Ann Skinner &
Martha Greenfeild executrices. Said
Skinner & Greenfeild were granted
administration. Appraisers: Thomas
Gant, Thomas Holladay. Thomas Brooke
(g) to administer oath.

13:437   Exhibited will of Robert Skinner (CV),
proved before Thomas Brooke (g). Ann
Skinner exhibited that no executor was
named. Said Ann was granted
administration. Appraisers: Thomas
Holladay, Joseph Letchworth. Thomas
Brooke (g) to administer oath.

Thomas Greenfeild (CV) exhibited will of
William Trueman (CV), constituting him
executor. Said Greenfeild was granted
administration. Appraisers: Thomas
Gant, Thomas Holladay. Thomas Brook (g)
to administer oath.

6 January. Richard Keene & Edm. Dennis
exhibited that they can find no will in
papers of Dr. Patrick Innes
(chirurgeon, CV). Date: 6 December
1686. Hugh Hopewell exhibited accounts
on said estate. Mentions: William
Sargison, Timothy Keene. Amount: #7494.
13:438   Mentions: William Rosewell. Copy of LoA
to said Hopewell, as principle creditor.
Mr. John Griggs to administer oath.

27 January!. John Magruther (CV)
administrator of his brother James
Magruther exhibited accounts.

20 January. Mrs. Elisabeth Anketill
widow of Francis Anketill was granted
administration on his estate.
13:439   Appraisers (SM): Capt. Thomas Courtney,
Thomas Miles. Maj. Nicholas Sewall to
administer oath.

3 February. Exhibited oath of Hugh
Hopewell (CV) administrator of Patrick
Innes. Securities (CV): Francis Hill,
Richard Keen. Also exhibited oath of
Edmond Dennis & Dr. (N), appraisers.

7 February. Gourny Crowe &
Philladelphia Rawlings widow of John
Rawlings (DO) were granted
administration on his estate.
Appraisers: Michael Basey, Edward
Newton.

Elisabeth Mitchell (SM) widow of John
Mitchell (SM) was granted administration
on his estate. Security: Edward Morgan
(SM). Appraisers: John Evans, John
Wade. Kenelme Cheseldyn to administer
oath.

13:440 8 February. Thomas Crowder (CV)
exhibited additional accounts on estate
of William Kent.

9 February. William Harris was granted
administration on estate of John Roult,
as principle creditor. Appraisers:
George Browne, Benjamin Ricaud. John
Hinson (KE) to administer oath.

21 February. Summons to Richard
Charlett, Robert Dove, & James Bigger
regarding estate of James Nutthall. Mr.
Sprigg to deliver.

13:441 11 February. James Bigger summoned.
Mentions: orphan of James Nutthall.

12 February. George Parker (g) on
behalf of Madam Ursula Burges widow of
Col. William Burges exhibited his will,
constituting her executrix. Mr. Thomas
Tench (AA) or Thomas Knighton (AA) to
prove said will. Said Ursula was
granted administration.

Maj. Nicholas Gassaway to examine
accounts of Thomas Dryfeild (AA)
administrator of William Fisher.

William Holland (g, CV) was granted
administration on estate of Richard

Hosier (CV), as principle creditor.
Appraisers: William Parker, Francis
Burkfaire (?). Francis Hutchins (g) to
administer oath.

13:442 George Parker procurator for Lydia
Conant (AA) widow of Robert Conant was
granted administration on his estate.
She cannot travel to SM. Thomas
Knighton (g) to administer oath.

Maj. Nicholas Gassaway & Thomas
Knighton to examine accounts of Thomas
Tench & his wife Margaret (AA) on estate
of Nathan Smith.

14 February. John Waters (AA) & Richard
Gottee (AA) executors of Thomas Pratt
(AA) were granted administration on his
estate.

Benjamine Cottman (SO) executor of
Samuel Simms (SO) was granted
administration on his estate.

Exhibited inventory of Jonathon Squire
(SM), by appraisers John Tennison &
Thomas Mosely.

13:443 Exhibited inventory of Edward Jones
(SM), by appraisers Henry Laurence &
Thomas Hebb.

David Browne petitioned for LoA on
estate of Dr. Allexander Innes. Date:
10 December 1686 Somerset Co. Said
Browne was granted administration.
Appraisers: Capt. Henry Smith, Capt.
Roger Woolford (SO) to administer oath.

17 February. William Nicholls
(merchant, CV) was granted
administration on estate of William
Wallis (taylor, CV), as principle
creditor. Appraisers: John Sunderland,
Marke Clare. Mr. Basill Warring (g,
CV) to administer oath.

13:444 22 February. Elisabeth Anketill (SM)
administratrix of Francis Anketill
petitioned for Thomas Courtney & Thomas
Miles be sworn as appraisers.

Court Session: 1686

Henry Lewis & his wife Abigall executrix
of Robert Thomas exhibited second
accounts.

Joseph Pile (SM) executor of Bartholomew
Piggott (SM) exhibited accounts.

John Sorbourough (AA) who married Jane
relict & executrix of William Mitchell
(AA) was granted administration on his
estate. Appraisers: James Orwick,
William Fergason. Mr. Edward Burges

13:445   23 February. John Scott (CV) who
married relict & executrix of Thomas
Sterling exhibited 1st accounts.

Exhibited inventory of Dr. Patrick
Innes, by appraisers Edm. Dennis &
Samuell Wythens.

Michael Taney (CV) was granted
administration on estate of Joseph
Rycutt (CV), as principle creditor.
Mentions: Capt. Ladd, Paul & John Hogan,
Charles Harrington, John Sewell, Mathew
Lewis. Security: John Powell (SM).
Appraisers: Henry Trueman, Thomas
Arnall. Roger Brooke to administer
oath.

13:446   Elenor Sprigg for orphans of Ja. Nuthall
vs. Anthony Underwood (g) procurator
for James Bigger & ux. Elioner Sprigg
(CV) petitioned on behalf of orphan
children of her brother James Nuthall
(CV). Mentions: bill from estate of
Joseph Frye (CV), James Bigger, servant
man, eldest son of dec'd.
13:447   Said Underwood was granted continuance.
•   Richard Charlett (CV), age 40,
deposed. Mentioned: (N) Hitchcock
(merchant, London).
13:448   ...
•   Robert Dove (CV), age 50, deposed.

Letter from Nicholas Bayard, Esq.
(mayor, NYC): Mary Hoggon (spinster, of
competent age, NYC) deposed
13:449   that she knew Mr. Alexander Innes
(clerke, NYC) & his brother Mr. Patrick
Innes (MD, now dec'd) over past 10 years

Court Session: 1686

& had seen them several times at her
mother's house on Rudeland in Fanchurch
St. & other places in London. Also,
that 3 or 4 years since, said Patrick
went to MD & she knew of several letters
to Thomas Simpson (Loathbury). Date: 10
January 1686. Ruling: Said Alexander
was granted administration dbn on estate
of his brother Patrick. Administration
to Hugh Hopewell, Jr. was revoked.
13:450   Securities: James Macall, John Scott (g,
CV).

24 February. Anthony Neale (CH)
executor of James Neale (g, CH)
exhibited 1st accounts. Continuance was
granted.

James Bigger (CV) summoned to render
accounts & inventory on estate of James
Nutthall.

Sheriff (CV) to summon Richard Hill (CV)
to testify on behalf of orphans of James
Nuthall vs. James Bigger.

25 February. Edward Larrimore exhibited
additional accounts on estate of Thomas
Shelton, but he did not take oath.

John Hall (BA) & Sarah relict of James
Collyer (BA) were granted administration
on his estate. Appraisers: Moses
Groome, Michaell Judd. Miles Gibson (g)
to administer oath.

13:451   Mary Gunnery relict of Benjamin Gunnery
(BA) was granted administration on his
estate. Appraisers: Moses Groome,
Michael Judd. Miles Gibson to
administer oath.

26 February. Exhibited will of John
Sunderland (AA), proved before Capt.
Richard Hill (g, AA).

Richard Cloude (SM) was granted
continuance to render accounts on estate
of John Gouldsmith.

Elisabeth Girling relict of Richard
Girling (TA) was granted administration

on his estate. Appraisers: John
Whittington, Thomas Anderson. George
Robins to administer oath.

13:452   Exhibited will of Peter Ingo (CE),
constituting Mathew Dellahay executor.
William Dare to prove said will. Said
Dellahay was granted administration.
Appraisers: Gasperus Herman, Thomas
Smith. Said Dare to administer oath.

Richard Beard (AA) exhibited accounts on
estate of Daniel Taylor.

Robert Doyne (g, CH) to prove will of
John Ward (CH), per request of Dameras
Ward widow.

Thomas Tench & his wife Margrett
executrix of Nathan Smith (AA) exhibited
accounts.

28 February. Richard Willhouse (DO)
administrator of Richard Dawson
exhibited accounts.

Benjamin Capill (AA) one of executors of
Thomas Parsons (AA) exhibited accounts.

13:453   1 March. Ann Jones (BA) widow of Daniel
Jones exhibited his will, constituting
here executrix. John Boring (g, BA) to
prove said will. Said Ann was granted
administration. Appraisers: Anthony
Demondidier, John Carrington. Said
Boring to administer oath.

Exhibited will of John Kemp (BA),
constituting Sarah Wickell (alias Sarah
Kemp) executrix. John Boring (g) to
prove said will. Said Wickell was
granted administration. Appraisers:
Anthony Demondidier, John Carrington.
Said Boring to administer oath.

George Parker (g) for Elisabeth Hunton
widow of Mordecay Hunton (CV) exhibited
his will, constituting her executrix.
She is unable to travel to SM. Thomas
Tasker (g) to prove said will. Said
Elisabeth was granted administration.
Appraisers: Basill Wareing, John Broome.

Court Session: 1686

Said Tasker to administer oath.

13:454 Jane Cary (SO) relict & executrix of
Thomas Cary (SO) exhibited his will.
William Brereton (g) to prove said will.
Said Jane was granted administration.
Appraisers: John Panther, Cornelius
Johnson. Said Brereton to administer
oath.

Exhibited will of Thomas Impey (TA),
constituting widow Deborah Impey
executrix. James Murphy to prove said
will. Said Deborah was granted
administration. Appraisers: James
Sedgwick, John Newman. Said Murphy to
administer oath.

Exhibited will of Peter Parsons (SO);
however, no executor was cited. William
Brereton (g) to prove said will. Mary
(widow) was granted administration.
Appraisers: Stephen Luffe, Benjamin
Cottman. Said Brereton to administer
oath.

Exhibited will of Henry Staples (TA),
constituting widow Ann Staples
executrix. Symon Wilmore (g) to prove
said will. Said Ann was granted
administration. Appraisers: Daniel
Norris, William Thomas. Said Wilmore to
administer oath.

2 March. Richard Woolman son of Alice
Woolman (TA) was granted administration
on her estate. Thomas Smithson (g) to
administer oath.

13:455 Henry Costin (TA) administrator of
George Buxton exhibited accounts.
Continuance was granted.

Mr. John Griggs (CV) to administer oath
to Nicholas Page & Richard Keene,
appraisers of Dr. Patrick Innes.

Hugh Hopewell, Jr. (CV) swore that he
gave a just inventory of estate of Dr.
Patrick Innes & delivered such to Mr.
Alexander Innes who now has
administration.

Court Session: 1686

Frances Young (TA) widow of William
Young (TA) was granted administration on
his estate. Appraisers: John Serjeant,
Phillip Hoskins. Mr. Henry Coursey to
administer oath.

3 March. William Elgate son & heir of
William Elgate (SO) was granted
administration on his estate.
Appraisers: Capt. John Winder, James
Weatherly. William Brereton (g) to
administer oath.

Mrs. Elisabeth Coursey exhibited
accounts on estate of Maj. William
Coursey (TA). Mentions items
disallowed: payment to William Coursey
(heir), payment to William Coursy.

13:456 4 March. Marmaduke Semmes (p, SM) &
Abraham Rhodes (p, SM) exhibited that
James Bourne (chirurgeon, SM, dec'd) was
possessed of considerable estate, made a
nuncupative will, constituting Richard
Thompson & Robert Morehouse executors.
Said Morehouse renounced administration.
Said Thompson was granted
administration. Security: said Semmes.
Said Thompson took possession of the
estate & has left the Province,
intending to defraud creditors. John
Addison is attorney for said Thompson.
13:457 Sheriff (SM) to summon said Addison.

Robert Carvile (g) for George Uty (BA)
heir of Col. Nathaniell Uty petitioned
for search of bond of Elisabeth Uty on
said estate.

Michael Miller for Thomas Joce (KE) was
granted administration on estate of
Thomas Parker (KE), as principle
creditor. Appraisers: William True,
Thomas Piner. Daniel Norris (g) to
administer oath.

13:458 William Frisby (g, KE) to administer
oath to Richard Lowder surviving
executor of William Fawson regarding
accounts.

Court Session: 1686

Maj. Joseph Wicks (KE) was granted continuance on estate of Benjamin Randall.

5 March. Clement Hill exhibited oath of Mr. Alexander Innes administrator of Dr. Patrick Innis.

Sheriff (SM) exhibited summons to John Addison. Mr. John Addison exhibited accounts on estate of Dr. James Bourne.

Gertrude relict of John Cropper exhibited that in 1670, she & the dec'd were married in Accomac, VA. She lived with him for 6 or 7 years & had several children, who are living. At that time, said John, through the "aparements" of Rhoda Faucett, "betooke himself unlawfully to her company". Said John moved to SO with said Rhoda & lived in adultery,

13:459 for about 10 years, having several base children. Said John died November last, seized of several tracts of land in the Province & goods & chattels bequeathed to his base children & made said Rhoda executrix. Petition that the estate be secured & inventoried & she to provide evidence. Date: 2 March 1686. Ruling: granted.

13:460 William Whittington attested to validity of said petition. Date: 4 March 1686. Justices (SO) to summon Rhoda Faucett & to deliver goods & chattels.

13:461 Probate of will to be suspended. Sheriff (SO) to summon Gertrude Cropper & Rhoda Faucett.

13:462 Col. William Stevens & 2 others empowered to act. Date: 9 March 1686.

Mr. Robert Carvile to receive a copy of bond of Elisabeth Uty on estate of Col. Nathaniel Uty, per request of George Uty heir.

(N) Burford petitioned for:
• will of Lawrence Hoskins to be proved. Appraisers: Ralph Smith, Joseph Cornell.
• LoA to Jane Pembrooke relict of John Pembrooke (CH). Appraisers:

Cleborne Lomax, Alexander Smith.
- LoA to Mary Bayly relict of John Bayly (CH). Appraisers: Henry Hardy, Richard Ashman.
- Said Burford & Capt. Humphry Warren to examine accounts of Peter Carr & estate of Nathaniel Veining.

9 March. Thomas Burford (CH) to prove will of Lawrence Hoskins. Rebeccah Tyer (CH) executrix was granted administration. Appraisers: Ralph Smith, Joseph Cornell. Said Burford to administer oath.

13:463 Jane Pembrooke widow of John Pembrooke (CH), was granted administration on his estate. Appraisers: Cleborne Lomax, Alexander Smith. Said Burford to administer oath.

Mary Bayly widow of John Bayly (CH) was granted administration on his estate. Appraisers: Henry Hardy, Richard Ashman. Said Burford to administer oath.

Thomas Burford, Esq. & Capt. Humphry Warren to examine accounts of Peter Carr & of Nathaniel Veining & to take oath of Rebeccah Tyre executrix of James Tyre (CH) executor of said Carr & administrator of said Veining.

10 March. Clement Hill, Esq. was granted administration on estate of Anthony Murty (SM).

12 March. William Dent petitioned for Meverell Hulse executor of James Peart (CV).
13:464 Col. Henry Jowles (g, CV) to prove said will. Said Hulse was granted administration. Appraisers: James Keech, Richard Southerne. Said Jowles to administer oath.

11 March. Meverell Hulse (CH) administrator of (N) Hatteraile was granted dismissal.

16 March. George Burges (AA) exhibited will of Francis Stockett (AA), written

in Latin, constituting (N) executor who
is also dec'd, as are witnesses. Said
Burges was granted administration.
Appraisers: Dr. Woolfran Hunt, Nicholas
Nicholson. Mr. Henry Dawson to
administer oath.

13:465 18 March. John Kerke (DO) son & heir of
John Kerke (DO) was granted
administration on his estate.
Appraisers: Alexander Fisher, Peter
Stoakes. Bartholomew Ennalls to
administer oath.

19 March. John Kerke (SO) administrator
of Edward Furlong (SO) exhibited
accounts. Continuance was granted.

Exhibited bond of Dr. John Ottridge
administrator of Dr. John Porter
(Bristoll). Securities (KE): Hance
Hanson, William Harris. John Hinson (g,
KE) exhibited oath of John Ottridge
administrator of John Porter (ENG).
Signed: John Hynson.

Ann Dennis executrix of Thomas Banks was
ordered to pay Maj. Nicholas Sewall
guardian of Charles Beckwith son of
George Beckwith his portion.

13:466 Said John Hinson further exhibited oath
of William Harris & Charles Hynson,
appraisers of said Porter, sworn same
day.

Said Hinson exhibited will of James
Ringold, proved. Also exhibited oath of
Mary Ringold executrix, sworn 28
September last. Also exhibited oath of
Daniel Norris & Phillip Davis,
appraisers sworn same day.

William Brereton (g, SO) exhibited oath
of Thomas Cocks & Isaac Noble,
appraisers of William Stevens.

Capt. Richard Hill (AA) exhibited will
of James Sumerland (AA), proved.

21 March. Exhibited inventory of John
Tillyard (BA), by appraisers Arthur

Taylor & Robert Love.

Exhibited inventory of James Miller (KE), by appraisers George Greene & John Carter.

13:467 Exhibited bond of Elisabeth Guess administratrix of George Guess (CH). Security: John Gray (CH).

Isaac Winchester exhibited oath of Mathew Ereckson & William Temple, appraisers of Thomas Browne (KE), sworn 14 September 1686. Also exhibited bond of Edward James administrator. Securities (KE): William Temple, Mathew Ereckson. Also exhibited inventory.

Richard Ladd (g, CV) exhibited oath of William Harris administrator of Henry & Ann Harris. Securities: James Cranford, Alexander Frazer. Also exhibited oath of William Taylor & Thomas Harris, appraisers. Also exhibited inventory.

13:468 Exhibited inventory of Francis Swinfenn (CV), by appraisers Capt. Ninian Beale (CV) & Thomas Holladay (CV).

Miles Gibson (g, BA) exhibited will of John Tillyard, proved. Also exhibited oath of Abraham Taylor & Robert Love, appraisers. Also exhibited inventory.

Exhibited bond of Richard Swetnam (TA) administrator of Edward Hardgrave. Securities: John Stanely, Nicholas Hackett.

James Murphy (g, TA) exhibited oath of MM John Newman & Lawrence Knowles, appraisers of Richard Medcalfe (merchant, York, ENG), sworn 29 December 1686. Also exhibited inventory.

Sheriff (CV) to summon Richard Brightwell & Richard Southerne administrators of Mary Trueman to show cause why they should not pay the proportional share to Mary, Elisabeth, Ann, & Catherine Cooksey children of Phillip Cooksey & his wife Elisabeth (dec'd) eldest sister of said Trueman.

13:469 22 March. Francis Hutchins (g, CV) exhibited oath of Jane Buttram administratrix of Nicholas Buttram. Securities (CV): George Young, William Williams. Also exhibited oath of Hezekiah Bussey & George Bussey, appraisers.

23 March. Exhibited inventory of Dr. John Porter (Bristoll), by appraisers William Harris & Charles Hinson.

24 March. Exhibited will of Thomas Burford, proved before Col. Henry Darnall.

Court Session: 1687

25 March. Ann Burford (CH) relict & executrix of Thomas Burford, Esq. was granted administration on his estate. Appraisers: Capt. Humphry Warren, William Dent. Col. Edward Pye (CH) to administer oath.

13:470 Sheriff (SM) to summon William Gwither executor of Nicholas Gwither (SM) to render additional inventory, per Richard Smithson.

Sheriff (CV) to summon Ann Dennis (alias Ann Bankes) executrix of Thomas Bankes to render inventory.

Sheriff (CV) to summon Richard Smith & his wife Barbara executrix of John Rousby executor of Christopher Rousby, Esq. to render inventory on both estates.

To: Ann Dennis (alias Ann Bankes, CV) widow & executrix of Thomas Bankes (CV). There remains a portion due Charles Beckwith son of George Beckwith (CV, dec'd). He is of full age to choose a guardian & chose Maj. Nicholas Sewall (CV).

13:471 John Ottridge (merchant, Bristoll) administrator of Dr. John Porter

(Bristoll) exhibited accounts. Said Ottridge is attorney for Sarah Porter relict. Mentions: children. Clerk to send

13:472 accounts of hogsheads of tobacco shipped to ENG: 27902. Signed: John Ottridge. Date: 24 March 1686/7. Accounts of goods left in hand of Richard Jones

13:473 overseer of plantation on Chester River of Mrs. Sarah Porter. Date: 8 March 1686/7. Mentions: 4 English servants, 1 Negro. Witnesses: Hance Hanson, William Glanvile.

13:474 Amount: #40060.

29 March. Exhibited inventory of Henry Adams (CH), by appraisers Daniel Mason & Robert Goodrick.

Elisabeth Donn widow & executrix of Obadiah Donn (SM) has remarried & she & her now husband embezzle said estate.

13:475 Justices (SM) to summon them & take sufficient security.

Elisabeth Baker (SMC) relict of John Baker (g, SMC) was granted administration on his estate. Securities (SMC): Thomas Grunwin, John Llewellin.

7 April. Mary Bayly was granted administration on estate of John Bayly (CH) & Thomas Burford Esq. was to administer oath. Said Burford is dec'd. Appraisers: Henry Hardy, Richard Ashman. Capt. Humphry Warren to administer oath.

Robert Doyne (g, CH) & Capt. Humphry Warren (g, CH) to examine accounts of Rebeccah Tyer widow & executrix of James Tyer executor of Peter Carr & administrator of Nathaniel Veining.

13:476 Rebeccah Tyer (CH) widow & executrix of James Tyer petitioned for Robert Doyne (g, CH) to prove will & administer oath.

Mrs. Rebeccah Tyer executrix of Lawrence Hoskins (CH) petitioned for Robert Doyne to prove said will &

administer oath.

Capt. David Browne (SO) exhibited will of Archibald Ereskin (SO), constituting him executor. William Brereton to prove said will. Said Browne was granted administration. Said Brereton to administer oath.

James Heath was appointed Registrar.

13:477 List of Records of the Office:
- Testamentary Proceedings: #1: 1637, 1638, 1639, 1640; #2: 1657; #3: 1658, 1659; #4: 1660, 1661; #5: 1662, 1663; #6: 1664, 1665; #7: 1665, 1666; #8: 1666, 1667, 1668; #9: 1668, 1669; #10: 1670, 1671, 1672, 1673, 1674; #11: 1674, 1675; #12: 1675, 1676, 1677, 1678; #13: 1675; #14: 1676; #15: 1677; #16: 1678; #17: 1679; #18: 1680; #19: 1681; #20: 1682; #21: 1682, 1683, 1684, 1685, 1686, 1687.
- Wills & Inventories: #A: 1670; #B: 1670, 1671, 1672, 1673, 1674; #C&PC: 1673, 1674, 1675.
- Wills: #A: 1676, 1677; #B: 1678; #C: 1679; #D: 1680; #E: 1681; #F: 1682; #G: 1682, 1683, 1684, 1685, 1686, 1687.
- Inventories & Accounts: #I: 1674, 1675; #II: 1676; #III: 1676, 1677; #IV: 1677; #V: 1678; #VI: 1679; #VII: 1680; #VIII: 1681; #IX: 1682 (4 books); #X: 1683, 1684, 1685, 1686; #XI: 1686, 1687.

13:478 George Parker for Robert Proctor vs. estate of Michael Cusick. Caveat exhibited.

11 April. Jane Pembrooke relict of John Pembrooke (CH) was granted administration on his estate. Thomas Burford was to administer oath, but is dec'd. Capt. William Barton to administer oath. Dec'd was much indebted to Phillip Lynes.

12 April. Henry Coursey, Jr. exhibited will of William Young. Frances Young

relict was granted administration on his estate. Date: 18 March 1686.

13:479 Administration to said Frances revoked. Said Coursey to prove will & administer oath.

Exhibited will of Col. William Burges (AA), proved before Thomas Tench by William Elridge, John Harrison, & John Edwards (witnesses). Date: 19 February 1686/7.

William Whittington petitioned for summons for: John Sterry who married Sarah only daughter of John Piake (SO) vs. William Hearne who married relict of said Piake.

18 April. Mark Richardson (BA) exhibited will of Joanna Gouldsmith (BA), constituting Susanna wife of said Mark executrix. Mr. Edward Beedle to prove said will. Said Susanna was granted administration. Appraisers: James Phillips, George Goldsmith. Said Beedle to administer oath.

LoA received for William Elgate, Jr. However, there is no John Wetherly nor John Bennitt in the County.

13:480 Appraisers: Capt. John Winder, Mr. James Wetherly. Send by Col. Stevens or Mr. Fran. Jenkins. Signed: William Brerton. Date: 7 April 1687 at Wiccocomico.

26 April. George Parker for Ann Dennis (CV) relict & executrix of Thomas Bankes (CV) was granted continuance.

Thomas Tench (AA) exhibited oath of Ursula Burges executrix of Col. William Burges.

Col. Henry Jowles (CV) exhibited oath of Samuell & Frances Warcup executrix of Thomas Darcy (alias Thomas Matchett). Also exhibited oath of Louis Lonally & Gabriell Burnham, appraisers.

27 April. Exhibited will of Rowland Williams (CE), constituting Richard

Edmunds, Jr. executor. Said Edmunds was granted administration. James Wroth to administer oath.

Cornelius Comegys (KE) exhibited will of Henry Hozier, proved.

29 April. Exhibited will of Joseph Everett (KE), constituting relict Penelope executrix. Daniel Norris to prove said will. Said Penelope was granted administration. Appraisers: Thomas Piner, William True. Said Norris to administer oath.

13:481 Maj. Nicholas Sewall, Mr. George Parker, & Mr. Michaell Taney executors of Edmund Dennis (CV) have refused executorship & therefore the concerns of Thomas Bankes (CV). [A relict of said Dennis & relict & executrix of said Bankes.] Said 3 are to take all papers of said Dennis & Bankes into custody & to render accounts.

Exhibited will of Obadiah How (CV); however no executor was cited. Col. Henry Jowles to prove said will. Joseph How was granted administration on his estate, as next of kin. Appraisers: James Keetch, Cor. Watkinson. Said Jowles to administer oath.

William Shertcliff administrator of Joseph Harding (SM) was granted quietus est.

Exhibited will of Peter Parsons, proved before William Brereton (SO). Also exhibited bond of Mary Parsons. Securities: Thomas Relfe, William Robinson.
13:482 Also exhibited oath of said Mary. Also exhibited oath of William Robinson & Thomas Ralph, appraisers. Also exhibited inventory.

Exhibited will of Thomas Cary. Cornelius Johnson, one of the appraisers, is dec'd. Jane Cary executrix petitioned for Mr. Thomas Hobbs.

Exhibited will of Cornelius Johnson
(SO), constituting William Jones, Jr.
executor. William Brereton to prove
said will. Said Jones was granted
administration. Appraisers: George
Betts, John Panter. Said Brereton to
administer oath.

Exhibited will of Samuell Seon, proved
before William Brereton. Also exhibited
inventory.

William Harris (KE) administrator of
John Rolt exhibited inventory.

Exhibited inventory of Samuell
Pilesworth.

Exhibited will of William Young (KE),
constituting relict Hannah executrix.
Charles Tilden to prove said will. Said
Hannah was granted administration. Said
Tilden to administer oath.

13:483 Exhibited will of Henry Parker (TA),
constituting Daniell Walker, Sr.
executor. Thomas Smithson to prove said
will. Said Walker was granted
administration. Said Smithson to
administer oath.

Exhibited will of Francis Carpenter
(DO), constituting William Thomas
executor. Jacob Loockerman to prove
said will. Said Thomas was granted
administration. Said Loockerman to
administer oath.

Exhibited bond of Cornelius Comegys
administrator of Richard Grey.
Securities: Daniell Norris, Thomas
Piner. Also exhibited inventory.

Exhibited bond of Thomas Joce
administrator of Thomas Parker.
Appraisers: Thomas Piner, William Deane.
Also exhibited inventory.

Exhibited bond of George Green
administrator of Henry Naish.
Securities: Cornelius Comegys, John
Gilvert. Also exhibited inventory.

Court Session: 1687

Exhibited will of Daniel Jones (BA), proved by Mathew Hudson & Wolfran Hunt (witnesses) before John Boring. Also exhibited inventory.

Exhibited will of John Kemp (BA), proved before John Boring. Also exhibited inventory.

William Legg (KE) administrator of John Dobbs exhibited accounts. Continuance was granted.

13:484 Exhibited will of James Peart (CV), proved before Col. Henry Jowles.

30 April. Thomas Deakins administrator of Henry Hanson (SM) exhibited accounts. Continuance was granted.

Clement Hill, Esq. for Mr. Richard Gardiner was obliged to pay orphan of (N) Delahay. Mentions: "Crackbourne's Purchase".

3 May. Exhibited will of Hendrick Matson (CE), proved before Nicholas Allome.

7 May. Exhibited inventory of William Trueman (CV).

Exhibited inventory of Arthur Scorer (CV).

9 May. David Blaney was granted administration on estate of Symon Harris (TA), on behalf of orphans & as greatest creditor. Appraisers: William Finey, John Dams. George Robotham to administer oath.

10 May. Exhibited will of Robert King (TA), constituting John King executor. Maj. Petter Sayer to prove said will. Said John was granted administration. Said Sayer to administer oath.

13:485 11 May. Rose widow of Dennis Odwine (CV) was granted administration on his estate. Appraisers: John Fenwick, John Sewall. Richard Fenwick to administer oath.

Thomas Grunwin for Richard Bishop
brother & heir of William Bishop (TA)
petitioned for Nicholas Clouds & Thomas
Seward executors to render accounts.

12 May. Renewal of summons to Justices
(SO) for (N) Cropper & (N) Faucett.

17 May. Phillip Lynes (SM) vs. estate
of Edmond Dennis (CV). Caveat
exhibited. Mentions: Ann Dennis
(widow).

13:486 19 May. Exhibited inventory of Dennis
Odwine (CV).

Exhibited will of Edward Smith, Jr.
(SO), constituting Edward Wale &
Nathaniel Innis executors. Col.
William Stevens to prove said will.
Said Wale was granted administration.
Appraisers: John Smocke, Rob. Keyte.
Said Stevens to administer oath.

Exhibited will of Rory Patrick (alias
Roger Patrick, SO), constituting widow
Ann Patrick executrix. Col. William
Stevens to prove said will. Said Ann
was granted administration. Appraisers:
(N) Peart, Samuell Hopkins. Said
Stevens to administer oath.

Exhibited will of Capt. John Osborne
(SO), constituting widow Attalanta
Osborne executrix. Col. William
Stevens to prove said will. Said
Attalanta was granted administration.
Appraisers: (N) Peart, Samuell Hopkins.
Said Stevens to administer oath.

Exhibited will of Alexander Williams
(SO), constituting Charles Ratcliff &
Thomas Pointer executors. Col. William
Stevens to prove said will. Said
Ratcliff & Pointer were granted
administration. Appraisers: (N) Peart,
Samuell Hopkins. Said Stevens to
administer oath.

Court Session: 1687

Col. William Stevens to examine accounts of Gilbert Hamilton administrator of Hierome Batty.

Exhibited inventory of John Rousby (CV).

13:487 Exhibited will of Mordicay Hunton (CV), proved before Thomas Tasker. Also exhibited oath of Elisabeth Hunton executrix.

Exhibited will of Nathaniell Ashcombe (CV), proved by George Gamball, John Henning, & William Gooding (witnesses).

Exhibited inventory of Hierome Batty (SO). Also exhibited bond of Gilbert Hamilton administrator. Securities: Thomas Finwick, Thomas Jones.

Exhibited will of Henry Bishop, Sr. (SO), proved before Col. William Stevens. Also exhibited oath of Ann Bishop executrix. Also exhibited oath of Mathew Scarborow & Samuel Hopkins, appraisers.

Col. Stevens exhibited will of Randall Revell (SO), proved. Also exhibited oath of Katharine Revell executrix. Also exhibited oath of Robert King & John King, appraisers.

Exhibited additional inventory of Capt. Thomas Walker.

Exhibited inventory of John Clark (SO). Col. William Stevens exhibited oath of Gilbert Hamilton administrator of Jeorome. Also exhibited oath of Richard Farewell & Sam. Cooy, appraisers.

13:488 21 May. Nathaniell Dare administrator of Thomas & Ann Cleverly (CV) exhibited accounts. Quietus est was granted.

23 May. Elisabeth Baker (SMC) widow & administratrix of John Baker petitioned for alterations: Securities: Thomas Courtney, James Cullen. Appraisers: Thomas Grunwin, John Llewellin. Garret Vansweringen exhibited oaths.

Court Session: 1687

25 May. Henry Hanslap to administer
oath to Henry Ridly, Thomas Knighton, &
Marun Duvall, Sr., appraisers of Col.
William Burges (AA).

Henry Hanslap exhibited oath of John
Edwards administrator of James Mitchell
(AA). Securities: John Grey, John
Powell. Also exhibited oath of Walter
Phelps & Benjamin Evans, appraisers.
Also exhibited inventory.

Thomas Knighton exhibited oath of Lydia
Conant administratrix of Robert Conant
(AA). Securities: Samuell Garland, Abel
Browne. Also exhibited oath of John
Sollers & Robert Gower, appraisers.
Also exhibited inventory.

13:489   Exhibited will of Thomas Pratt (TA),
proved before Henry Hanslapp. Also
exhibited inventory.

26 May. Henry Hanslapp (AA) exhibited
accounts on estate of Samuel Wheeler
(AA).

30 May. Exhibited will of Humphry
Nicholls (CE), constituting Jacob
Devilliard executor. Nicholas Allume to
prove said will. Said Devilliard was
granted administration. Appraisers:
Andrew Clement, Henry Rigge. Said
Allume to administer oath.

Exhibited inventory of William Sinclere.

Elisabeth Baker (SMC) petitioned for
Phillip Lynes (SM) administrator of
William Smithson (DO) to render
inventory.

1 June. Exhibited inventory of Thomas
Bankes (CV).

4 June. Exhibited inventory of Maj.
James Ringold (KE).

Michael Miller for Thomas Hicks (KE)
exhibited will of Edward Hamon (KE),
constituting widow Ann executrix. Said
Ann is since dec'd & orphans are in

custody of said Hicks. Charles Tilden
to prove said will. Said Hicks was
granted administration. Said Tilden to
administer oath.

13:490   6 June.   Baker Brookes son & heir of
Baker Brookes (CV) vs. Henry Brent &
his wife Ann relict of said elder
Brookes. Libel exhibited.

7 June. Sheriff (CV) to summon James
Bigger to answer libel on behalf of
orphans of James Nutthall.

8 June. Exhibited inventory of John
Bayly (CH).

15 June. Richard Bowen executor of
Robert Stanly (CV) exhibited accounts.
Continuance was granted.

William Lyle executor of Phillip Jones
exhibited accounts.

Michaell Taney exhibited accounts on
estate of Joseph Ricaut.

17 June. Jane Mansell (SM) widow of
Vincent Mansell was granted
administration on his estate. Said Jane
cannot travel as she is poor & a charge
of children. Said Jane was also granted
administration on estate of her brother
Justinian Tennison (SM). Mentions:
Thomas Dillon, (N) Darnall (brother &
sister to said Hill).

13:491   Exhibited bond of Mary Bayly
administratrix of John Bayly.
Securities: Joseph Cornell, Richard
Smith. Humphry Warren exhibited oath of
said Mary. Also exhibited oath of Henry
Hardy & Richard Ashman, appraisers.

Exhibited inventory of James Tyre (CH).

Exhibited will of John Ward, proved
before Robert Doyne.

18 June. Miles Gibson (BA) exhibited
oath of Mary Gundry administratrix of
Benjamin Gundry (BA). Securities: John

Thomas, Mary Stansby. Also exhibited oath of Moses Grome & Michaell Judd, appraisers. Also exhibited inventory.

Said Gibson exhibited oath of John Hall & his wife Sarah Hall administrators of John Collyer (BA). Securities: Thomas Scudamore, Nicholas Johnson. Also exhibited oath of Moses Grome & Michaell Judd, appraisers. Also exhibited inventory.

James Phillips was granted administration on estate of John Mould (BA), as greatest creditor. Appraisers: John Walston, George Goldsmith. Ed. Bedle to administer oath.

13:492 Robert Carvile procurator for Mary, Elisabeth, Katherine, & Ann Cooksey children of Phillip Cooksey (CV) vs. Anthony Underwood for Richard Brightwell & Richard Southern administrators of Mary Trueman. Libel exhibited.

20 June. John Hollen petitioned that Sumer Adams left him & Samuell Heydon overseers to care for his children. The youngest son was bound out to said Heydon. Said Adams's son does not desire administration on his estate. Samuell Heydon was granted administration on estate of Sumer Adams (SO). Appraisers: Stephen Luff, Stephen Cannon. James Dashield to administer oath.

22 June. Ann Hargness (CH) exhibited accounts on estate of William Hargness.

Clement Hill exhibited oath of John Bullock & John Mansell & Jary Tennison, appraisers of Vincent Mansell & of Justinian Tennison, Jr.
13:493 Securities: John Tennison, Justinian Tennison.

30 June. William Barton exhibited oath of Jane Pembrooke (alias Jane Bracher) administratrix of John Pembrooke (CH). Securities: John Bracher, Cleborn Lomax. Also exhibited oath of Cleborne Lomax &

Court Session: 1687

Alexander Smith, appraisers. Also
exhibited inventory.

4 July. William Dent exhibited
inventory of estate of Mr. Mordicay
Hunton (CV). Mentions: Mr. Hugh Ellis
married the widow. Date: 13 June 1687.

Thomas Smithson (TA) exhibited oath of
Richard Woolman administratrix of Alice
Woolman (TA). Securities: James Scott,
Christopher Santee. Also exhibited oath
of James Scott & Christopher Santee,
appraisers.

6 July. Exhibited inventory of Alice
Woolman.

13:494   8 July. Exhibited will of Robert Potts
(CH); however, no executor was cited.
Robert Doyne to prove said will. Jane
Lindsey relict was granted
administration. Appraisers: Nicholas
Cooper, Christopher Breames. Said Doyne
to administer oath.

Exhibited additional inventory of Col.
Phillomen Lloyd (TA).

Exhibited inventories of:
• Henry & Ann Harris (CV). Date: 21
  March 1686.
• Richard Hosier (CV). Date: 26 April
  1687.
• Edward Hargrave (TA). Date: 26
  April 1687.
• John Stephens (TA). Date: 26 April
  1687.
• Anthony Murty (SM). Date: 25 May
  1687.

Exhibited bond of M. Miller
administrator of James Miller.
Securities: Elias King, Morgan Jones.

Exhibited bond of William Holland
administrator of Richard Hozier.
Securities: William Parker, Ja.
Crandford.

Priscilla Manning relict of John Taylor
(DO) exhibited accounts.

Robert Orme & Richard Thornbury administrators of Mathew Axon & administrators of Richard Bedworth exhibited accounts, sworn before Thomas Tench.

Exhibited will of Thomas Thorn (KE), proved before William Harris on 26 April 1687.

Exhibited will of Stephen Keddy (KE), proved before Cornelius Comegys on 28 April 1687.

13:495   Henry Hanslapp (AA) exhibited oath of John Waters & Richard Gottee executors of Thomas Pratt (AA). Also exhibited oath of Walter Carr & Benjamin Capell, appraisers.

Henry Jowles (CV) exhibited oath of Meverell Hulse executor of James Peart. Also exhibited oath of James Keetch & Richard Southern, appraisers.

Nicholas Allome (CE) exhibited oath of Mathias Mattison executor of Henrick Mattison (CE). Also exhibited oath of William Ward & Henry Rigg, appraisers.

John Boring (BA) exhibited oath of Anthony Demondidier & John Carrington, appraisers of John Kemp (BA).

Said Boring exhibited oath of Anthony Demondidier & John Carrington, appraisers of David Jones (BA).

12 July. George Parker procurator for Rebeckah Lytfoot widow of Thomas Lytfoot exhibited his will. George Ashman to prove said will. Said Rebeckah was granted administration. Appraisers: Christopher Guist, John Thomas. Said Ashman to administer oath.

Robert Proctor (AA River) was granted administration dbn on estate of Michaell Cusacke, as chief creditor. Former administrator Fran. Stockett is dec'd. Said Robert cannot travel to SMC. Appraisers: John Gather, Richard Jones.

Court Session: 1687

Maj. Edward Dorsey to administer oath.

13:496 16 July. Exhibited will of Thomas Jackson (merchant, SMC), proved.

18 July. Robert Fraizer administrator of Dennis Hurly (SM) exhibited accounts. Estate is overpaid. Quietus est was granted.

Samuell Chamberlain administrator of Thomas Wright (SM) exhibited accounts. Continuance was granted.

James Lewis & his wife Katharine executrix of Edmond Townhill (AA) exhibited accounts, proved before Col. William Burges.

19 July. Edward Bedell (BA) exhibited oath of Col. George Wells administrator of Nicholas Browne (BA). Securities: Richard Edmonds, George Goldsmith. Also exhibited oath of George Goldsmith & Richard Edmonds, appraisers. Also exhibited inventory.

20 July. Anthony Underwood (SM) exhibited will of Thomas Jackson (SMC), proved, constituting Margrett Jackson executrix. However, if she did not come to the Province, said Underwood was to be constituted executor. Said Margrett has not come.

13:497 Said Underwood was granted administration. Appraisers: Garratt Vansweringen, James Cullen. John Llewellin (g) to administer oath. [estate of Thomas Jackson (SMC) granted to Anthony Underwood who married Margrett Jackson.]

13:498 Also exhibited bond. Securities: Thomas Grunwin, Thomas Beal. John Llewellin (g, SMC) exhibited oath of Anthony Underwood executor. Also exhibited oath of Garratt Vansweringen & James Cullen, appraisers.

Exhibited inventory of Francis Anketill (SM).

27 July. Exhibited will of Archibald
Ereskin (SO), proved. Also exhibited
inventory.

13:499 William Brereton (SO) exhibited oath of
Capt. David Brown executor. Also
exhibited oath of Samuell Hopkins &
Henry Morgan, appraisers.

Exhibited bond of David Brown
administrator of Alexander Innes (SO).
Security: John Brown. Also exhibited
inventory.

Exhibited inventory of Thomas Proffitt
(SO).

Exhibited inventory of Richard Hill
(SO).

Exhibited inventory of William Bishop
(SO).

Exhibited inventory of Randall Revell
(SO).

Col. William Stevens exhibited that
William Turvile & William Brown moved to
VA. Therefore, said Stevens exhibited
oath of Samuell Hopkins & John Smock,
appraisers of Thomas Proffitt, in their
stead. Date: 16 November 1686.

28 July. At request of Joseph Grey,
sheriff (SO) to summon Thomas Jones (SO)
& his wife Jane late wife of Thomas Grey
to answer libel of said Joseph.

Sheriff (SO) to summon William Hearne to
answer libel of John Sterry.

13:500 Elinor Stapelfort widow of Raymond
Stapelfort (DO) petitioned for joint
administration with her son Charles
Stapelfort. Ruling: granted. Exhibited
will; however, no executor was cited.
Henry Hooper to prove said will.
Appraisers: James Moore, William
Shenton. Said Hooper to administer
oath.

William Brereton (SO) exhibited oath of
William Elgate, Jr. administrator of

Court Session: 1687

William Elgate, Sr. Securities: James
Wetherly, Edward Bennitt. Also
exhibited oath of Capt. John Winder &
Mr. James Wetherly, appraisers. Also
exhibited inventory.

30 July. Richard Fenwick (CV) exhibited
oath of Rose Odwine administratrix of
Dennis Odwine (CV). Securities: John
Fenwick, John Sewall. Also exhibited
oath of John Sewall & John Fenwick,
appraisers. Also exhibited additional
inventory of said Dennis Odain.

13:501 Thomas Tasker (CV) to examine accounts
of John Chittam administrator of Dorothy
Williams.

1 August. Exhibited bond of John Kerk
administrator of John Kerk (DO).
Securities: Henry Howard, John Edwards.
Also exhibited inventory.

Exhibited will of Edward Haman (KE),
proved. Charles Tilden exhibited oath
of Thomas Hicks administrator.
Securities: John Bowles, Edward Fry.
Also exhibited oath of John Bowles &
William Thomas, appraisers. Also
exhibited inventory.

John Hynson exhibited oath of William
Harris administrator of John Rolt (KE).
Securities: Hans Hanson, Charles Hynson.
Also exhibited oath of George Browne &
Benjamin Ricaud, appraisers.

Exhibited will of William Young (KE).
Charles Tilden exhibited oath of Hannah
Young (alias Hannah Howard) executrix.
Also exhibited oath of Edward Beck &
John Willis, appraisers.

Exhibited inventory of Thomas Jackson
(merchant, SMC).

13:502 Exhibited inventory of Justinian
Tennison (SM).

Exhibited inventory of Nicholas Buttram
(CV).

Court Session: 1687

Exhibited inventory of Dorothy King (CV).

Exhibited inventory of Vincent Mansell (SM).

Exhibited inventory of Walter Bounsell (TA).

Exhibited additional inventory of Mordicey Hunton (CV).

Exhibited will of Laurence Hoskins, proved. Also exhibited inventory.

John Hynson & Charles Tilden administrators of Morgan Williams (KE) exhibited accounts.

William Thomas administrator of James Lesson (KE) exhibited accounts.

Jerimiah Sheredine & his wife Jane widow of Nicholas Buttrum (CV) exhibited accounts.

David Parsons administrator of Humphry Jones (SM) exhibited accounts, sworn before Clement Hill.

13:503 2 August. Samuell Bourn administrator of Dorothy King (CV) exhibited accounts. Continuance was granted.

Cate McDonnell administrator of Hugh Hanlon (CV) was granted continuance.

Charles Tilden executor of Samuell Pilesworth (KE) exhibited accounts. Continuance was granted.

Gilbert Hamilton administrator of Hierome Batty (SO) exhibited accounts, sworn before Col. William Stevens.

Sheriff (CV) exhibited summons to Henry Brent & his wife Ann administrators of Baker Brooke, Esq. Also exhibited summons to James Bigger.

Sheriff (SM) exhibited summons to Phillip Lynes.

Court Session: 1687

Sheriff (KE) exhibited summons to
Nicholas Clouds & Thomas Seward.

Capt. Richard Ladd executor of Fran.
Swinfen (CV) exhibited accounts.
Continuance was granted.

Christopher Beanes administrator of
Richard Crackbourn (CV) exhibited
accounts.

James Biscoe & his wife Sarah relict &
administratrix of Charles Priest (SM)
were granted continuance. Mentions:
orphans.

13:504   John Turner who married relict &
executrix of Richard James (AA)
exhibited accounts. Continuance was
granted.

George Newman administrator of George
Newman (CH) exhibited additional
accounts.

Thomas Dante administrator of Peter
Milles (SM) was granted continuance.

John Hance & his wife Mary
administratrix of Christopher Kellett
(CV) exhibited accounts. Continuance
was granted.

Richard Jenkins executor of James Rumsey
(CV) exhibited account. Estate is
overpaid. Quietus est was granted.

Ann Hopewell relict & administratrix of
Francis Hopewell (CV) exhibited that her
husband was not in debt & she is a poor
widow. Dismissal was granted.

William Smith administrator of John &
Elisabeth Hunt (CV) exhibited accounts.

Abigail Simons executrix of John Shankes
(SM) was granted continuance.

Abigail Symons exhibited additional
inventory on estate of George Yeedon
(SM).

Richard Bishop vs. Robert Carvile
procurator for Nicholas Cloud & Thomas
Seward executors of William Bishop.
Said Carvile appeared.

13:505 Anthony Underwood procurator for Richard
Smithson vs. Robert Carvile procurator
for William Guither. Libel exhibited.

Sheriff (TA) exhibited summons to
Nicholas Clouds & Thomas Seward.

3 August. Exhibited inventory of Thomas
Burford (CH).

George Newman (CH) exhibited receipt
from Henry Giffords (CH) & his wife
Elisabeth daughter of Thomas Gibson (CH,
dec'd). Said Newman was executor of
said Gibson. Date: 22 December.
Witnesses: George Sutten, David Davis.
Also exhibited receipt from Thomas
Gibson, Jr. son of said Thomas. Date: 1
August 1687. Witness: Rand. Brandt.

13:506 Exhibited additional inventory of Thomas
& Ann Cleverly (CV).

Henry Coursey, Jr. to summon Margrett
Peterson to render accounts on estate of
her husband. Mentions: (N) Swetnam, (N)
Comegys, Herbert Knot. Date: 25 July
1687.

George Parker for Col. Thomas Taillor
vs. estate of Thomas Hedge (BA). Caveat
exhibited.

George Parker for self & Mordecay Hunton
administrators of Thomas Cosden (CV)
exhibited accounts.

John Kirke administrator of Edward
Furlong (SO) exhibited accounts.
Continuance was granted.

13:507 John Hodson (DO) administrator of James
Agg was granted continuance.

Henry Lewis & his wife Abigail executrix
of Rob. Thomas (SM) exhibited that there
is no further accounting, except what

remained for the orphans. Dismissal was granted.

James Pattison administrator of James Watkins (SM) was granted continuance.

Said Pattison administrator of Edward Ward (SM) was granted continuance.

John Sykes (SM) exhibited accounts on estate of Robert Hudson (SM).

Richard Keen vs. Joseph Edloe executor of Dr. Edward Molines. Answer to libel exhibited. Said Edloe exhibited accounts.

Summons to procurator of Nicholas Clouds et. al. executors of (N) Bishop to render accounts.

George Newman executor of Thomas Gibson (CH) exhibited accounts.

4 August. Hugh Gill & his wife Margarett executrix of Francis Holland exhibited
13:508 that said Margarett is unable to travel to SMC because of age & sickness. Thomas Knighton (g, AA) to examine accounts.

Henry Brent & his wife Ann widow of Baker Brooke (CV) exhibited accounts. Continuance was granted.

Anthony Underwood procurator for Richard Bishop vs. Robert Carvile procurator for Nicholas Clouds & Thomas Seward executors of William Bishop (TA). Libel exhibited.

Per request of Phillip Lynes one of creditors of Edmond Dennis (CV, dec'd) [Richard Dudson (SM)], Ann widow was summoned to accept or renounce administration.

Sheriff (CV) to summon Gabriell Burnham one of appraisers of Thomas Matchett (alias Thomas Darcy) to return inventory.

Court Session: 1687

Robert Carvile for creditors of Richard Chilman (SM, dec'd) petitioned for administration dbn. Gerard Sly was granted such. Securities: Phillip Lynes, Nicholas Clouds.

Kenelme Cheseldyn administrator of Jonathon Squire (SM) was granted continuance.

13:509 Phillip Lynes administrator of William Smithson (DO) petitioned for new appraisers: William Hill, John Pollard.

Children of (N) Cooksey vs. Richard Southern & Richard Brightwell administrators of Mary Trueman (CV). Said Southern & Brightwell resummoned; they did not appear.

Orphans of James Nutthall vs. James Bigger. Did not appear. Resummoned.

Stephen Luff (SO) exhibited LoA from William Archbishop of Canterbury. [Section in Latin.] Date: 2 January 1685. Signed: Thomas Welham (Reg.). Witnesses: William Cox, Richard Hassell.
13:510 Also: Richard Moore (g, Mells, SO) who married Elisabeth widow & administratrix of Edward Watkins (mariner, Bristoll) exhibited PoA to Stephen Luff (merchant, Monokin River).
13:511 Witnesses: William Cox, Joseph Luffe, John Eiorne. Witnesses (ENG): Stephen Luffe, Sr., Thomas Morris. Said Luff was granted administration on estate of said Watkins, for use of said Moore, et. al. Capt. David Brown to take bond.

Nehemiah Blakiston & George Layfeild attorneys for Gerrard Sly (dec'd) summoned to answer Robert Carvile administrator dbn of Richard Chilman.

Sheriff (CE) to summon Samuell Wheeler administrator of Alexander Nash to render further accounts.

Per Richard Bishop (TA), sheriff (TA) to summon Walter Jones, (N) Read, Andrew Evans, & Henry Green to testify in suit

vs. Nicholas Clouds, et. al. executors
of William Bishop. Also sheriff (KE) to
summon Daniell Norris to testify.

13:512 5 August. Col. Stevens petitioned.
Date: 23 July 1687 Pocomoke.
- Mrs. Sarah White (widow) summoned
  to render accounts. Family is sick
  & herself not well. Weather is hot.
- Jane Wallace (widow) summoned to
  render accounts. She is very
  "antient" woman & now very sick.
- Also exhibited accounts of Gilbert
  Hamilton administrator of Hierom
  Batty.
Widow White was granted continuance.
Col. Stevens to examine accounts of
widow Wallace.

13:513 John Godsgrace (CV) administrator of
Alice Goldson was granted continuance.

Nicholas Clouds for self & Thomas Seward
executors of William Bishop (TA)
exhibited accounts.

16 August. Sheriff (CH) to summon
George Pounsey & his wife Mary relict of
John Boswell to answer the
administration.

20 August. Exhibited will of Henry
Parker (TA), proved. Also exhibited
inventory. Thomas Smithson exhibited
oath of Daniell Walker executor. Also
exhibited oath of Thomas Mountford &
Peter Dodd, appraisers.

22 August. Per Richard Bishop (TA),
sheriff (TA) to summon Robert Macklyn &
John Gribble to testify in suit vs.
Nicholas Clouds & Thomas Seward
executors of William Bishop (TA).

13:514 29 August. Mr. Luke Gardiner exhibited
renunciation of Katharine Benson relict
of Hugh Benson (SM), recommending the
petitioner's brother Richard. Date: 15
August 1687. Witness: Clement Hill.
Said Luke was granted administration for
Mr. Richard Gardiner, as greatest
creditor. Appraisers: Richard Newman,

John Bright.

> 30 August. John Wright (CV) was granted administration on estate of his wife Mary Appraisers: John Read, William Read. Mr. Richard Fenwick to administer oath.

13:515 Exhibited will of Sumer Adams (SO), proved. Also exhibited inventory. James Dashiell exhibited oath of Stephen Luffe & Stephen Cannon, appraisers.

> 1 September. Exhibited will of Thomas Emerson (TA), proved. Also exhibited inventory. George Robotham exhibited oath of Katharine Emerson executrix. Also exhibited oath of William Finey & Andrew Abbington, appraisers.

> Exhibited will of John Shipwas (SO), constituting Abraham Heath executor. William Brereton to prove said will. Said Heath was granted administration. Appraisers: William Harper, Richard Chambers. Said Brereton to administer oath.

> Exhibited inventory of Symon Harris.

> Exhibited inventory of William Cooke (TA).

> Exhibited inventory of Thomas Stevenson (TA).

> Henry Hanslapp exhibited oath of George Burges administrator of Francis Stockett. Also exhibited oath of Dr. Woolfran Hunt & Nicholas Nicholson, appraisers.

> Exhibited will of Thomas Stevenson (TA), proved. George Robotham exhibited oath of John Brown executor. Also exhibited oath of William Finey & Andrew Abbington, appraisers.

13:516 Col. George Wells (BA) exhibited that Capt. Johnson administrator of Nicholas Brown, who died by drowning, disposed of the estate as quickly as possible, & of

another freeman who lived with said
Brown & also drowned. Also a petition
for Letters ad Colligendum on estate of
Richard Willen, whose estate Capt.
Johnson has entered upon unlawfully.
Ruling: no letters.

Exhibited bond of Joseph Everett (KE).
Securities: Thomas Pinner, Phillip
Everett.

Exhibited bond of Samuell Heydon
administrator of Somer Adams.
Securities: John Panther, Thomas
Holbrook.

Exhibited bond of David Blaney
administrator of Symon Harris (TA).
Securities: Andrew Price, William
Colleton.

Exhibited bond of John Thrift
administrator of William Cooke.
Securities: John Pooley, Thomas Roe.

Exhibited bond of George Burges
administrator of Francis Stockett (AA).
Securities: Thomas Plumer, John Gray.

12 September. Exhibited inventory of
George Guest (CH), by appraisers John
Gray & William Mosse.

13:517   Susanna Busy administratrix of Paul Busy
(CV) exhibited accounts. Continuance
was granted.

Thomason Viney administratrix of Henry
Viney (CV) exhibited accounts.
Continuance was granted.

John Dossett & Jonathon Goosey executors
of Thomas Atwell (CV) exhibited
accounts.

Richard Bowen executor of Robert Stanly
(CV) exhibited additional accounts.

George Bussey administrator of John King
(CV) was granted continuance.

Jacob Hallett administrator of Jerimiah Hansliff (AA) exhibited accounts.

Exhibited inventory of Thomas Matchett (alias Thomas Darcy), by appraiser Gabriell Burnham.

Thomas Pennington administrator of Robert Tyler (AA) exhibited accounts.

Abraham Clark (CV) administrator of Henry Bennitt (AA) was granted continuance.

Edmond Howe (CV) administrator of Edward Fletcher (CV) was granted continuance.

13:518   Exhibited bond of William Thomas administrator of Robert Lundin (TA). Securities: Rice Evans, George Collison. Exhibited inventory of Robert Lundin. James Murphy (TA) exhibited oath of administrator.

13 September. Exhibited inventory of Robert Skinner (CV).

Exhibited will of Robert King (TA), proved. Also exhibited inventory. Maj. Peter Sayer exhibited oaths.

Alice Smith widow of Thomas Smith (CV) exhibited that her conscience would not permit her to take oath as executrix. She will send her sons to next court to exhibit receipts for their portions of their father's estate, he dying clear of debt.

Maj. Sayer (TA) exhibited summons to Walter Jones, Andrew Evans, & Henry Green.

Isaack Calke (CE) exhibited that he was very sick for a long time & is still dangerously ill. Date: 7 September 1687. Continuance was granted.

13:519   Nicholas Dorrell who married Chatherine relict & administratrix of Andrew Peterson (CE) exhibited accounts.

Court Session: 1687

Exhibited will of Thomas Daniell (DO), proved. Also exhibited inventory.

Martin Mugenburgh executor of Isaack Daniel (CE) exhibited accounts.

Sheriff (CH) exhibited summons to George Pounsy.

Sheriff (CV) exhibited summons to Richard Brightwell & Richard Southern to answer Cooksey's children; James Bigger to answer orphans of (N) Nutthall.

John Bean who married relict & executrix of Thomas Gerrard (SM) administrator of Timothy Richardson was granted continuance on estate of said Richardson.

Exhibited inventory of Thomas Gerrard (SM).

14:1   13 September. Richard Haseldyn (TA) who married widow of Francis Brooke was granted administration on his estate. (Col. Philemon Lloyd was to have administered oath, but died.) Appraisers: James Scott, Josias Crouch. Thomas Smithson (TA) to administer oath.

Administrators of Richard Chilman vs. George Layfeild attorney for Gerrard Sly. Said Layfeild appeared and renounced attorneyship.

Joseph Gray vs. Robert Carvile procurator for Thomas Jones & his wife Ann (SO). Answer exhibited.

Col. George Wells (BA) exhibited accounts on estate of Simon Dakins (BA).

Exhibited additional inventory of John Probart (CH). Maj. John Wheeler administrator exhibited accounts.

Jane Duncon (AA), now wife of William Ferguson, relict of Patrick Duncon was summoned to render accounts. Date: 2 September 1687. Continuance was granted.

Court Session: 1687

14:2   Mattias Mattison executor of Henry
Mattison exhibited inventory.
Continuance was granted.

Daniell Phillips (CV) administrator of
Richard Hewson exhibited accounts.

William Dossey administrator of John
Dossey (DO) exhibited additional
accounts.

Samuell Warcupp & his wife Fran.
executrix of Thomas Matchett (alias
Thomas Darcy, CV) exhibited accounts.

Exhibited bond of Anthony Chilcot
administrator of Margrett Harper (DO).
Securities: John Edwards, Edmond
Branock.

Exhibited inventory of Richard Girling.
Also exhibited bond of Elisabeth Girling
administratrix. Securities: Thomas
Anderson, John Whittington.

Nicholas Allom exhibited oath of Jacob
Devillyard executor of Humphry Nicholls
(CE). Also exhibited oath of Henry
Rigges & Andrew Clement, appraisers.
Also exhibited inventory.

Exhibited will of Zachary Thompson (TA),
proved.

George Robotham exhibited oath of
Richard Swetnam & Andrew Abington,
appraisers of Robert Noble.

Exhibited will of Raymond Stapelford
(DO), proved. Also exhibited inventory.
Henry Hooper exhibited oath of
appraisers. Also exhibited bond of
Eleanor Stapelfort & Charles Stapelfort,
administrators. Securities: William
Robson, John Phillips.

14:3   Exhibited will of Roger Wedill (TA),
constituting Mary Wedill relict
executrix. Mr. Henry Coursey, Jr. to
prove said will, & administer oath.

Page 42

Court Session: 1687

Maj. Edward Dorsey (AA) exhibited oath
of Robert Proctor administrator of
Michael Cusack (AA). Security: Andrew
Norwood. Also exhibited oath of John
Gather & Richard Jones, appraisers.
Also exhibited inventory.

14 September. Ann Bonnman widow of
William Bonnman (TA) was granted
administration on his estate.
Appraisers: John Chaires, Richard Jones.
Henry Coursey, Jr. (TA) to administer
oath.

Exhibited will of John Viner (TA),
constituting Josias Crouch executor.
Capt. James Murphy to prove said will.
Said Crouch was granted administration.
Said Murphy to administer oath.

Richard Bishop (TA) petitioned for
sheriff (SM) to summon John Gribble &
Robert Macklyn to testify against
Nicholas Clouds & (N) Seward.

16 September. Col. George Wells
administrator of Nicholas Brown who
married Ann administratrix of Dennis
Inglish (BA) exhibited accounts on
estate of said Inglish.

17 September. John Stanly (TA) was
granted administration on estate of
Miles Thornton (TA), as greatest
creditor. Appraisers: James Bishop,
Rob. Bryan. Edward Mann to administer
oath.

John Skipper administrator of John
Snowden (SM) exhibited additional
accounts.

Anguish Murrah who married relict &
executrix of Thomas Daniell (DO)
exhibited accounts.

14:4 Exhibited inventory of John Cockerill
(CE). Also exhibited bond of Richard
Simpers who married Ann relict.
Securities: Richard Whitton, William
Mansfeild. William Dare exhibited oath
of said Ann.

Exhibited will of Peter Jegon (CE), proved.

<u>17 September</u>. Samuell Creyker & his wife Mary relict of George Sealy (DO) exhibited accounts.

Joseph Spernon & his wife Alice relict & administratrix of Thomas Hinton (CE) exhibited additional accounts.

Robert Brightwell & Richard Southern (CV) exhibited answer to libel of children of Phillip Cookesey.

William Dare administrator of Thomas & Mary Long (TA) exhibited accounts.

Robert Macklyn one of orphans of Robert Macklyn (p, TA, dec'd) petitioned that he was an infant at his father's death. William Bishop & Mathew Ward administered said estate for petitioner & his brother Richard Macklyn. Soon after, said Ward died. Petitioner was age 17 in 1680, & determined that surviving administrator William Bishop has wasted the estate. LoA to said Bishop were revoked & granted to petitioner. Petitioner demanded an account from said Bishop.

14:5 Said Bishop never gave any accounting. Said Bishop died in 1684, constituting Thomas Seward & Nicholas Clouds executors. Petitioner has requested accounts, but no results. Nicholas Clouds summoned.

Richard Swetnam administrator of John Steevens (TA) exhibited accounts.

<u>20 September</u>. Exhibited will of Thomas Cooper (KE), constituting Richard Jones executor. Capt. Henry Laurence to prove said will. Said Jones was granted administration. Appraisers: Valentine Southern, Christopher Grangier. Said Laurence to administer oath.

Per Richard Bishop, sheriff (SM) to summon Col. Vincent Lowe, Griffith Jones, & Michaell Miller in suit against

Court Session: 1687

Nicholas Clouds & (N) Seward.

Ebenezar Blakiston administrator of
Thomas James (CE) exhibited accounts.

Exhibited will of Andres Clements (CE),
constituting his son Andres executor.
George Stevens to prove said will. Said
Andres the younger was granted
administration. Appraisers: Griffith
Cock, Henry Riggs. Said Stevens to
administer oath.

22 September. Exhibited will of Richard
Pettybone (AA), constituting Isaack
Pettybone & Joseph Pettybone executors.
Nicholas Greenbury to prove said will.
Said executors were granted
administration. Appraisers: Humphry
Boone, Robert Eagle. Said Greenbury to
administer oath.

Mabell Offly exhibited that she is very
old & sickly & cannot travel to Office.
There are no debts & estate of her
husband is small. Mr. Thomas Smithson
to examine accounts.

14:6   Charles Pine administrator of James
Denton (BA) exhibited accounts. Francis
Watkinson to examine additional
accounts.

Daniell Longman administrator of Richard
Arnold (AA) exhibited accounts.

Dorothy Musgrove widow of Cuthbert
Musgrove (CH) was granted administration
on his estate. Robert Doyne to
administer oath.

George Pownsey who married Mary relict
of John Boswell (CH) was granted
administration on his estate. Robert
Doyne to administer oath.

Richard Smith & his wife Barbara
executrix of John Rousby (CV) were
granted continuance. Said Smith was
summoned to render inventory on estate
of Christopher Rousby (CV), for whom
said John was executor. Said

Page 45

Christopher's estate is imbedded in that of said John.

Shery Wansey executor of Joseph Sone (DO) was granted continuance.

Martha Wamsley received renewed quietus est on her husband's estate, per William Dare.

14:7   Thomas Jones administrator of Daniell Wine (BA) exhibited accounts.

Henry Green administrator of Albert Jonson (TA) exhibited accounts.

Widow of Maj. William Coursey exhibited additional accounts.

23 September. Benjamin Williams administrator of James Philks (AA) exhibited accounts.

Exhibited inventory of Henry Hickson (CH).

Frances Collins widow of Thomas Collins (TA) was granted administration on his estate. Appraisers: John Kennemont, Daniell Walker. Maj. Peter Sayer to administer oath.

Exhibited will of John Osborne (SO), proved. Col. William Stevens exhibited oath of Attalanta Osborne executrix.

Exhibited will of Edward Smith, Jr. (SO), proved. Col. William Stevens exhibited oath of Edward Wale & Nathaniell Innis executors.

Exhibited will of Alexander Williams (SO), proved. Col. William Stevens exhibited oath of Charles Ratcliff & Thomas Pointer executors.

Exhibited will of Rory Patrick (alias Roger Patrick, SO), proved. Col. William Stevens exhibited oath of Ann Patrick executrix.

Court Session: 1687

24 September. Miles Gibson
administrator of John Yeo (BA) exhibited
accounts.

Robert Carvile procurator for Nicholas
Clouds & (N) Seward exhibited answer to
libel of Richard Bishop.

14:8 Suit to be heard next Monday.

Sheriff (CE) with Mr. Wroth to examine
papers of Maj. Edward Inglish (dec'd) &
to take those concerning cause between
said Inglish & (N) Harmer. Capt. Pierce
to continue overseeing the plantation.
• Michaell Miller, age 44, deposed
   that the deponent did lee a
   procuration in custody of Mr.
   Ebenezar Blackiston from Timothy
   Harmer to prosecute Maj. Edward
   Inglish.

William York (BA) petitioned that he &
James Collier in May 1686 made accounts.
Said Collyer died March last. Deponent
is deputed by Capt. John Waterton the
first in the will of Mr. John Waterton
& Mr. James Collier his brother.
Executor came from PA in June last.
Petitioner was granted continuance.
Edward Collier (heir to said James,
Philadelphia) carried away all papers.

14:9 Continuance was granted.

Thomas Smithson (TA) to administer oath
to Sarah Hall on accounts of estate of
James Hall.

Gabriell Parratt executor of John Smith
(AA) exhibited accounts. Estate is
overpaid.

28 September. Anthony Underwood
procurator for Richard Bishop (TA) vs.
Nicholas Clouds & Thomas Seward
executors of William Bishop (TA). Libel
exhibited. Ruling: Maj. Peter Sayer to
examine various persons in Clouds'
account of alleged payments. Maj. Sayer
is also to take possession of certain
chattel.

14:10 Robert Macklyn vs. Nicholas Clouds one
of executors of William Bishop (TA).
Continuance was granted. [cf. f. 4.]

1 October. John Wyet & his wife Sarah
executrix of Thomas Jones (KE)
petitioned for Daniell Norris to examine
accounts.

18 October. Margrett Jackson widow &
relict of Thomas Jackson (SM) exhibited
will, constituting her executrix. Said
Margrett was granted administration, &
LoA to Anthony Underwood revoked.
14:11 Garrat Vansweringen (SMC) to administer
oath.

19 October. Exhibited will of Daniell
Carnell (TA), constituting relict
Deborah Carnell & Edward Pollard
executors. Edward Man (TA) to prove
said will. Said Deborah & Pollard were
granted administration. Appraisers:
Thomas Robins, John Stanly.

24 October. William Brereton exhibited
oath of Jane Cary executrix of Thomas
Cary (SO). Also exhibited oath of John
Panther & Thomas Hobbs, appraisers.
Also exhibited will, proved. Also
exhibited inventory.

James Murrey (AA) was granted
administration on estate of George Lee
(AA), as chief creditor. Appraisers:
Thomas Morgan, John Scott. Thomas
Knighton (g) to administer oath.

Samuell Cluely & his wife Elisabeth
relict of William Marshall (p, CV) were
granted administration on his estate.
Appraisers: George Coate, Robert Wood.
Mr. George Lingan (CV) to administer
oath.

Robert Cagge who married widow of Mark
Child petitioned for administration on
his estate. Appraisers: John Arden,
William Wilkinson. Date: 8 October
1687.
14:12 Said Robert was granted administration
on estate of said Mark Child (BA). John

Court Session: 1687

Boring to administer oath.

29 October. Gilbert Clarke exhibited will of Mr. Hugh Marshall, who died at his house in his seasoning, constituting Mr. Edward Napper executor. Said Napper is also in his seasoning. Date: 26 October 1687. Capt. Humphry Warren (CH) to prove said will. Said Clarke was granted administration. Appraisers: MM Anthony Neale, William Hatton. Said Warren to administer oath.

Sarah Bishop relict of Henry Bishop (SO) was granted administration on his estate. Appraisers: John Smock, William Richardson. Edmund Howard to administer oath.

4 November. John Dekreyker was granted administration on estate of Robert Wright (CH). Appraisers: John Stanbery, John Ratcliff. John Courts to administer oath.

Elisabeth McDowell widow of Henry McDowell (CV) was granted administration on his estate. Appraisers: Thomas Purnell, Isaack Baker. John Griggs to administer oath.

14:13 Richard Thompson executor of James Bourn exhibited accounts.

Exhibited will of John Meconikin (KE), constituting his son John Meconikin executor. Said son was granted administration. Appraisers: Alexander Waters, Louis Merriday. Christopher Goodhand to administer oath.

5 November. Exhibited inventory of John Mitchell (SM).

7 November. Robert Carvile procurator for James Mills (BA) executor of Samuel Boston vs. Thomas James & his wife Sarah administratrix of Giles Stevens (BA). Libel exhibited. Also said Carvile exhibited libel against said Thomas James & his wife Sarah administratrix of said Stevens

Page 49

administrator of Samuel Tracy as before.

Thomas Brooke for self & his mother petitioned that Robert Trevant (CV) died at his house last March, with a will constituting said Brooke executor. Said Brooke does not intend to administer the estate. Date: 3 November 1687. Richard Marsham to prove said will. Hugh Stone was granted administration, as greatest creditor. Appraisers: Richard Marsham, Richard Brightwell. Said Brooke to administer oath.

14:14 Elisabeth Ellis widow of Peter Ellis (BA) renounced administration on his estate. His estate is inconsiderable. Witnesses: James Mills, Mary Thrift. Daniell Laurence was granted administration, as greatest creditor. Appraisers: MM Edward Bedle, George Goldsmith. Col. George Wells to administer oath. Witness: James Milles.

12 November. Clement Hill, Esq. for Mary Johnson widow of John Johnson (SM) exhibited his will, constituting her executrix, witnessed by John Vaudry, et.al. Joseph Pile to prove said will. Said Mary was granted administration. Appraisers: Thomas Carvile, John Long. Said Pile to administer oath.

14:15 Rebeccah Tyer executrix of James Tyer (CH) administrator of Nathaniell Verin (CH) exhibited accounts on said Verin's estate, proved before Clement Hill, Esq.

15 November. Kenelm Cheseldyn petitioned:
* Mrs. Mary Ashcom widow of Nathaniell Ashcom (CV) for administration on his estate. Mr. Lad to administer oath.
* Also said Mary for administration on estate of her brother Samuell Ashcom, for use of her children: Mary, Nathaniell, Elisabeth, John Ashcom. They are next-of-kin & minors. Appraisers (CV): Samuell Bourn, Thomas Parslow.
Date: 20 October 1687. Will constituted

said Mary & Charles Ashcom (brother of
dec'd) executors. Said Charles is
absent from the Province. Said Mary was
granted sole administration on estate of
both said Nathaniell & said Samuell
Capt. Richard Ladd to administer oath.

19 November. Exhibited will of Thomas
Lytfoot (BA), proved before George
Ashcom (BA).

14:16   21 November. Exhibited inventory of
Francis Stockett (AA).

29 November. William Brereton (SO)
exhibited oath of William Jones executor
of Cornelius Johnson (SO). Also
exhibited oath of John Panther & George
Betts, appraisers. Also exhibited will
proved & inventory.

William Brereton exhibited oath of
Abraham Heath executor of John Shipway
(SO). Also exhibited oath of William
Harper & Richard Betts, appraisers.
Also exhibited will proved & inventory.

Kato McDonnell administrator of Hugh
Hanlon (CV) exhibited accounts.

Thomas Whitchally who married Jane
relict & executrix of John Fanning (CH)
exhibited additional accounts.

Capt. Richard Ladd executor of Francis
Swinfen (CV) exhibited additional
accounts.

30 November. Humphry Warren (CH)
exhibited oath of Edward Naper executor
of Hugh Marshall (CH). Also exhibited
oath of Anthony Neale & William Hatton,
appraisers.

John Courts (CH) exhibited oath of John
deKreyker administrator of Robert Wright
(CH). Securities: Rich. Beaumont,
Richard Newton. Also exhibited oath of
John Stanberry & John Ratcliff,
appraisers.

14:17 Exhibited will of Edward Smith (SO), constituting widow Anne Smith executrix. Col. William Stevens to prove said will. Said Anne was granted administration. Appraisers: John Smock, William Richardson. Said Stevens to administer oath.

1 December. Theophilus Keyton who married widow of John Buck (AA) was granted administration on his estate. Appraisers: Philip Howard, John Gather. Maj. Edward Dorsey to administer oath.

Walter Phelps who married sister & only heiress of George Benson (AA) was granted administration on his estate. Appraisers: John Grey, John Edwards. Capt. Edward Burges to administer oath.

Exhibited will of Richard Gardener (g, SM), constituting Col. Henry Darnall, Clement Hill, Esq., & Luke Gardiner executors. Said Darnall has renounced administration. Said Hill & Luke Gardiner were granted administration.

3 December. Anthony Underwood procurator for Richard Sweatnam vs. estate of Thomas Mountford (TA). Caveat exhibited.

John Bean who married Ann Gerrard relict & executrix of Thomas Gerrard (SM) administrator of Timothy Richardson was granted continuance on said Richardson's estate.

Edmund How administrator of Edward Fletcher (CV) was granted continuance.

Exhibited will of Thomas Davies (TA), constituting James Saywell executor. William Combes to prove said will. Said Saywell was granted administration. Appraisers: William Winterson, Francis Harrison. Said Combes to administer oath.

14:18 William Kennerly (DO) exhibited verbal will of William Tike (DO), bequeathing all to said Kennerly. Dr. John Brookes

Court Session: 1687

(DO) to prove said will.

5 December. John Pursell administrator of Simon Stevens (TA) exhibited accounts. Continuance was granted.

6 December. George Lingan to examine additional accounts of Susanna Busy (CV) administratrix of Paul Busy (CV).

Ann Dennis widow of Edmond Dennis (CV) renounced administration on his estate.

Edmond Stow who married Jane relict of John King (CV) exhibited accounts. Continuance was granted.

John Mountfort brother & heir of Thomas Mountfort (TA) was granted administration on his estate. Anthony Underwood on behalf of Richard Sweatnam did not object. Appraisers: John Stanly, William Eastgate. James Murphy to administer oath.

Exhibited will of Richard Bennison (AA), constituting his widow Susanna Bennison executrix. Capt. Nicholas Greenbury to prove said will. Said Susanna was granted administration. Appraisers: Robert Eagle, James Orick. Said Greenbury to administer oath.

Exhibited will of Richard Gardiner (SM), proved before Col. Henry Darnall.

14:19 John Mountfort exhibited letter from John Edmondson regarding said Mountfort's administration on estate of his brother Thomas Mountfort (TA). Security: said Edmondson. George Robins to administer oath.

Exhibited inventory of Hugh Abell (DO).

Maj. Peter Sayer exhibited accounts of William Bishop (dec'd) at Nicholas Clouds.

14:20 Nehemiah Blakiston (SM) vs. estate of Reme Lefar (SM). Caveat exhibited.

Page 53

Court Session: 1687

7 December. Elisabeth Murphy relict of
Nicholas Murphy (TA) was granted
administration on his estate.
Appraisers: William Finey, John Hacker.
George Robotham to administer oath.

8 December. John Strawbridge & his wife
Honora administratrix of William Furnice
(SO) petitioned for Col. William
Stevens to examine accounts. Said
Honora is not able to travel.

Exhibited inventory of Timothy
Richardson (SM).

Exhibited will of William Young (TA),
proved before Henry Coursey, Jr. Also
exhibited inventory.

Nicholas Greenbury (AA) exhibited oath
of Isaack & Joseph Petybone executors of
Richard Pettybone (AA). Also exhibited
oath of Humphry Boone & Robert Eagle,
appraisers. Also exhibited will,
proved.

Clement Hill, Esq. & Luke Gardiner
executors of Richard Gardiner (SM)
petitioned for exemplification.
14:21   Will was proved before Henry Darnall on
1 December 1687 by William Dent, & on 3
December 1687 by William Langworth &
Thomas Mattenly.

9 December. Richard Bishop brother &
heir of William Bishop (TA) vs. Thomas
Seward & Nicholas Clouds executors of
said Bishop.
14:22   Mentions: "Tippings Plantation" to said
Seward, land formerly seated by Walter
Jones to said Clouds, "Bishopston" to
said Clouds. Residue to (equally):
Richard Bishop, Sr., Richard Bishop,
Jr., William Bishop, said Clouds, & said
Seward. At time of said William's
decease, said Richard lived in Colliton
Rawly parish, County Devon, ENG.
14:23   William Dent procurator for defendants.
14:24   Mentions: Walter Jones, Nicholas Clouds,
Richard Chafe, Michaell Seward, Thomas
Seward, Jr.
14:25   Anthony Underwood procurator for

Page 54

Court Session: 1687

plaintiff. Robert Carvile procurator
for defendants.
- Robert Macklyn, age 25, deposed that
  he was bound for Nicholas Clouds to
  Thomas Seward.
- Andrew Evans deposed that at the
  house of Henry Green, said Evans
  gave said Clouds discharge for a
  bill. Mentions: wife of said Evans.
- Walter Jones, age 45, deposed.
- Griffeth Jones, age 40, deposed

14:26 ...
    that he & Richard Sweatnam were
greatest creditors. Mentions: Rob.
Ellis, Mr. Robert Smith, said
Seward said that said Clouds was a
"rogue", Mrs. Hemsley widow of Mr.
Hemsley.

14:27 ...
- John Greeble deposed that Seward
  said that Clouds had destroyed &
  converted to his own private account
  a considerable amount of the estate.
- Col. Vincent Lowe deposed.
  Mentions: Robert Smith.
Maj. Peter Sayer (TA) inquiry.
14:28 Ruling: defendants have not fulfilled
the will. Defendants are guilty of
conniving & embezzling, & fraud in the
accounts. Defendants are excluded from
executorship. Richard Bishop, Sr. was
granted administration dbn.

14:29 Henry Brent & his wife Ann executrix of
Baker Brooke, Esq. (CV) exhibited
additional accounts.

Philip Lynes (SM) was granted
administration on estate of Robert
Langly (BA), as principle creditor.
Appraisers: George Goldsmith, Richard
Edmonds. Col. George Wells to
administer oath.

10 December. Nicholas Clouds one of
executors of William Bishop (TA) was
granted continuance.

Ann Harquest administratrix of William
Harquest (CH) was granted quietus est.

Page 55

Exhibited will of Henry Kennit (KE), constituting John Weeks & William Pickett executors. Said Pickett (KE) was renounced administration. Date: 17 October 1687. Appraisers: Richard Lowder, William Brereton. Mentions: dec'd has lawful wife & several legitimate children in ENG, &

14:30 his will leaves all to a base son by one Dorothy Noble (a common harlot).

William Inglish brother of Maj. Edward Inglish (CE) was granted administration on his estate. Securities: Michaell Miller, Nicholas Clouds. Appraisers: George Brown, Walter Tally. Giddon Gwndry to administer oath.

Sarah Porter (Bristoll) widow of John Porter (MD) petitioned that her husband's estate was committed to John Okridge for her. Said Sarah approves the inventory & accounts. Date: 9 September 1687. Witnesses: Richard Garrett, Richard Hasell, William Cox, Jos. Sander.

14:31 Joseph Saunders exhibited LoA & PoA. [Paragraph in Latin.] Thomas Otridge, Jr. (fuller, Tellisford, County Somerset) brother & administrator of John Otridge (chirurgeon, Bristoll) gave PoA to Joseph Saunders (merchant, Bristoll).

14:32 Date: 22 August 1687. Witnesses: John Hall, Thobias Garland, Thomas Shitup. Joseph Saunders was granted administration for use of said Thomas. Maj. Peter Sayer to administer oath.

George Gundry (CE) to prove will of James Fish.

23 December. Jane French exhibited her renunciation as administratrix of estate of Robert French (AA). James Wareing was granted administration, as principle creditor. Appraisers: Robert Lockwood, Samuell Garland. Thomas Knighton to administer oath.

31 December. John Bennit (Clifts, CV) was granted administration on estate of

Court Session: 1687

William Willymott, who died at house of
James Badcock (Clifts), as greatest
creditor.

14:33   Appraisers: Marke Clare, Thomas Crowder.
Mr. Bazill Warren to administer oath.

3 January. Exhibited will of Robert Lee
(SM), constituting Col. Henry Darnall
executor. Said Darnall was granted
administration. Appraisers: Garrett
Vansweringen, Thomas Beal.

Exhibited will of Bryan Crowly (SM),
constituting Ann Crowly executrix. John
Dent to prove said will. Said Ann was
granted administration. Appraisers:
Giles Wilson, Henry Noris. Said Dent to
administer oath.

4 January. John McDowell son & heir of
William McDowell (CV) vs. Daniel Evans
& his wife Mary relict & administratrix
of said William. Summons to render
accounts.

Exhibited will of Robert Lee (SM),
proved before Col. William Digges.
Said Digges exhibited oath of executrix.

5 January. Exhibited inventory of
Edward Smith (SO), by appraisers John
Smocke & Robert Cade.

Exhibited inventory of Alexander
Williams (SO), by appraisers Bryan Paert
& Samuell Hopkins.

Exhibited additional inventory of Maj.
James Ringole, by appraisers Daniell
Norris & Philip Dafes.

9 January. Exhibited inventory of
Robert Lee (SM), by appraisers Gar.
Vansweringen & Thomas Beale.

14:34   Mary Hackett widow of Nicholas Hackett
renounced administration on his estate,
recommending John Edmondson, as greatest
creditor. Date: 3 September 1687.
Witnesses: Daniell Doneuan, John Glouer.
John Edmondson petitioned for William
Rodeney to administer on estate of

Nicholas Hacket, & for Thomas Stratton
to administer on estate of Edmond
Gibbons. Date: 3 December 1687.
William Rodeney exhibited will of said
Nicholas, constituting said Mary
executrix. Said Rodeney was granted
administration. George Robins to
administer oath.

10 January. Exhibited will of Ben.
Smith (CE), but no executor was named.
Rebeckah Smith relict was granted
administration. Appraisers: Matt.
Matteson, Henry Riggs.

Elisabeth Solesbury widow of John
Sallesbury (KE) petitioned that Josias
Lanham be granted administration on his
estate, as principle creditor. Date: 23
November 1687. Witnesses: George
Thompson, Benjamin Ricaud.
14:35   Josias Lanham (KE) petitioned that said
estate is small. Said Lanham was
granted administration. Appraisers:
Morgan Jones, William Hodges. John
Hinson to administer oath.

Elisabeth Hatton (TA) widow of Samuell
Hatton (TA) was granted administration
on his estate. She is unable to travel
to SM. Appraisers: Thomas Bowdle,
Richard More. William Combes to
administer oath.

Exhibited will of John Walker (TA), but
no executor was named. Mr. Henry
Coursey, Jr. to prove said will.
Margrett Walker relict was granted
administration. Appraisers: Thomas
Bruff, Henry Price. Said Coursey to
administer oath.

14:36   Mr. George Plowden for Henry Dryden was
granted administration on estate of his
servant Robert Dorne (d. 2 February
last). From: Thomas Blanfoard, 7
January 1687. Richard Marcham (CV) to
administer oath.

13 January. Anthony Underwood
procurator for Jonah Wingfield & his
wife Sarah & Eleanor Hooper to answer

Court Session: 1687

libel of William Chapline (SO). ["Nil"
is written in the margin.]

Anthony Underwood procurator for William
Chapline vs. Jonah Wingfield & his wife
Sarah & Eleanor Hooper (CV) to answer
libel.

16 January. Jos. Chew (AA) exhibited
will of Francis Holland (AA),
constituting his widow Sarah executrix.
Said Sarah is also dec'd, leaving only 1
daughter by said Holland, who she
committed to the charge of said Chew.
• John Harris, John Booth, & Samuell
  Holliday deposed that Mrs. Sarah
  Holland widow of Francis Holland
  (AA) left her child to her cousin
  Joseph Chew.
14:37 Said Chew was granted administration on
estates of both Francis & Sarah.
Appraisers: John Chaspell, Benjamin
Serman.

18 January. John Griggs (CV) exhibited
oath of Elisabeth Mackdowell
administratrix of Henry MDowell (CV).
Security: John Hambleton, John Watmore.
Also exhibited was oath of Thomas
Purnell & Isaack Baker, appraisers.
John Griggs to prove will of Elisabeth
Mackdowell (CV).

Jane French relict of Robert French
(cooper, AA) renounced administration on
his estate, recommending James Warringe
(planter, AA), as greatest creditor,
before Thomas Knighton (AA). Witnesses:
Thomas Knighton, Elisabeth Knighton.

Jane Mansell (SM) widow of Vincent
Mansell (SM) was granted administration
on his estate, but died soon thereafter.
Justinian Tennison, Sr., father of said
Jane, was granted administration, on
behalf of orphans. Clement Hill, Esq.
to administer oath.

14:38 19 January. Said Justinian, Sr. was
also granted administration on estate of
Justinian Tennison, Jr.

Page 59

Court Session: 1687

Thomas Mitchell administrator of Edward
Abbott (CH) exhibited accounts.

20 January. John Harrison who married
relict & executrix of Thomas Baker (CH)
exhibited additional accounts.

24 January. Exhibited will of Elisabeth
Mackdowell (CV), proved before John
Griggs. Also exhibited oath of John
Hambleton executor. Also exhibited oath
of Isaack Baker & Thomas Purnell,
appraisers.

Exhibited will of John Johnson (SM),
proved before Joseph Pile.

Clement Hill petitioned for LoA for Mary
Stratford widow of Joseph Stratford
(SM). Appraisers: MM William Roswell,
William Langworth. Date: 19 January
1687.

14:39 Said Mary was granted administration.

Capt. John Osborne was to prove will of
William Walton, but did not accomplish
it. Sam. Hopkins to prove said will &
administer oath to Rebecah Walton widow
& executrix.

26 January. Clement Hill petitioned for
LoA for widow, now wife of Daniel Jones,
on estate of Dennis Huscula (SM). Date:
24 January 1687. Robert Green & Francis
Green renounced administration on estate
of said Denis Husculaw. Date: 12
December 1687. Witnesses: Henry Ball,
John Mikles. Daniel Jones was granted
administration, in right of his wife.
Appraisers: Marmaduck Simes, Richard
Eddlin.

14:40 27 January. Mr. George Parker for
Elisabeth Freeman relict & executrix of
Robert Freeman exhibited will. Basill
Waring to prove said will. Said
Elisabeth was granted administration.
Appraisers: John Leach, John Chetham.
Said Waring to administer oath.

George Green (KE) was granted
administration on estate of George

Hasfurt (KE). Appraisers: Mich. Miller, (N) Spear. William Harris to administer oath.

28 January. Sam. Hopkins to receive LoA on estate of Edward Smith (SO). Col. William Stevens died before the same was executed.

Edmund Howard to examine accounts of John Strawbridge & his wife Honora administratrix of William Furnace, formerly to Col. William Stevens.

Exhibited will of Col. William Stevens, Esq. (SO), constituting his widow Elisabeth executrix. Said Elisabeth was granted administration. Appraisers: Thomas Jones, William Planner. Robert King to administer oath.

1 February. Petition for (N) Hill to administer oath on estate of Reme LeFarr. Petitioner is very sick. Signed: Ne. Blakiston. Date: 18 January 1687. Appraisers (neighbors): John Haskins, James Simmons. Said Blakiston was granted administration on estate of Reme LeFeuer (SM). Appraisers: John Hoskins, James Simons. Clement Hill to administer oath.

2 February. Thomas Laurence (AA) son of Benjamin Laurence (AA) exhibited his will, constituting him & Thomas Smith (in ENG) executors. Witnesses live in ENG. Said Thomas Laurence was granted administration. Appraisers: Daniell Longman, John Watkins.

3 February. Robert Carvile for Cornelius Comegys administrator of (N) Broadrib was granted continuance.

Thomas Long for Abigall Scudamore relict of Mr. Thomas Scudamore (BA) was granted administration on his estate. Appraisers: MM John Boring, Francis Watkins. Col. Darnall to administer oath. Also cited was summons to Thomas James & his wife Sarah at libel of James Mills Tordy. Date: 3 December.

Court Session: 1687

14:42 Anthony Underwood for John Mackdowell
vs. John Hambleton executor of
Elisabeth Mackdowell. Libel exhibited
by John brother of Henry Mackdowell.

Robert Carvile for William Aldron (TA)
attorney of Grace Goddard vs. Ann
pretended wife of Thomas Goddard
(chirurgeon, dec'd). Ruling: said Grace
is lawful widow.

Exhibited will of Giles Blizzard (CH),
constituting his widow Mary executrix.
Said Mary was granted administration.
Appraisers: Sam. Jefferson, John Hynson.
Col. Edward Pye to administer oath.

4 February. Exhibited will of Samuell
Rhamsey (CV), but no executor was named.
Thomas Price who married his widow
Elisabeth was granted administration.
Appraisers: Mich. Swift, John Stone.
Col. Henry Jowles to administer oath.

6 February. Thomas Nelson for sheriff
(CV) to summon Robert Wood, Edward
Kinsley, & Thomas Stevens to prove will
of William Marshall. Said Nelson is a
legatee.

14:43 Luke Gardiner in right of his brother
Richard Gardiner (in ENG) was granted
administration on estate of Hugh Benson
(SM), as greatest creditor. Said
Richard is now dec'd. Clement Hill &
said Luke, as executors of said Richard,
were granted administration on estate of
said Hugh.

8 February. Thomas Bouman (merchant,
London) was granted administration on
estate of Roger Baker (CV), as next of
kin. Said Thomas is his sister's son.
Appraisers: Capt. Thomas Clegatt, John
Turner. John Griggs to administer oath.

11 February. Clement Hill exhibited:
• petition of those who are requesting
administration on estate of Dennis
Huscula cannot find security.
Mentions: children of dec'd. Capt.
John Bowling & Mr. Thomas Mudd were

Page 62

granted administration. Appraisers:
MM Richard Edelin, Marmaduck Semme.
Capt. Joseph Pile or Mr. William
Boarman to administer oath.

- inventory of John Johnson.
exhibited bond of widow Stratford.
Mentions: Justinian Tennison, Sr.
Date: 8 February 1687.

14:44   Clement Hill exhibited oath of MM
William Rosewell & William Langworth,
appraisers of Joseph Stratford (SM),
sworn 18 January 1687. Also oath of
widow & administratrix. Securities:
William Rosewell, John Dash.

Said Hill also exhibited that Mr.
Joseph Pile is to administer oath to
Justinian Tennison, Sr. administrator of
Vincent Mansell & administrator of
Justinian Tennison, Jr.

Exhibited inventory of John Johnson
(SM), by appraisers Thomas Carvile &
John Long.

Henry Lowe petitioned for Mr. Grunwin &
said Lowe's mother (N) Loyd to
administer estate of Edward Inman (TA).
Said Hen. Maria Loyd was granted
administration, as greatest creditor.
Maj. Sayer to administer oath.

Ann Sulivan widow of Dennis Sulivan (SM)
was granted administration on his
estate. Appraisers: William Guither,
Thomas Griffin. James Pattison to
administer oath.

Petition for Mr. Henry Coursey to
summon Frances Yongue executrix of
William Yongue (TA) to examine accounts
& for her to render accounts on estate
of Francis Parsons (her husband was
administrator). She is a very poor
widow with 8 children & cannot travel.
Petition also to summon Edward Tomlins
to render accounts on estate of

14:45   Nathaniell Reed (TA). Appraisers:
Thomas Bruf, Henry Price. Mr. Coursey
(g) to administer oath. Date: 25
November 1687. Signed: Robert Smith.

Henry Coursey, Jr. to examine accounts of Frances Young executrix of William Young & her accounts of estate of Francis Parsons (said William was administrator).

Henry Coursey, Jr. to examine accounts of Edward Tomlins administrator of Nathaniell Read (TA).

Robert Carvile procurator for Elianor Sprigg on behalf of orphans of James Nuthall (CV) vs. James Bigger (CV). Sheriff (CV) to attach said Bigger.

14 February. Anthony Underwood administrator of Thomas Jackson (SM) exhibited accounts.

16 February. John Salesbury was granted administration on estate of Elianor Waller (DO), as greatest creditor. Appraisers: Michael Bussy, Badia King. Bartholomew Ennals to administer oath.

Elisabeth Chesly relict of William Marshall was summoned to render accounts.

Joseph Willson (Hunting Creeke, CV) brother of John Willson (CV) was granted administration on his estate. Mr. John Craycroft (CV) to administer oath. [cf. f. 47.]

14:46   Exhibited will of John Edmondson (TA), proved. George Robins exhibited oath of William Ridgeaway, one of the witnesses.

Mary Omely exhibited the receipt for herself & 3 children from estate of Bryand Omely. Date: 16 April 1685. Witnesses: Thomas Mountfort, James Ragley. Sworn before George Robins on 21 December 1687. Susanna Omely exhibited receipt for her portion from estate of Bryand Omely. Date: 16 April 1685. Witnesses: Thomas Mount, James Ragley. Sworn before George Robins on 21 December 1687. Isabella Omely exhibited same; sworn same day.

14:47   Thomas Hughs petitioned for Joseph
Wilson (Hunting Creeke, CV) brother to
John Wilson (CV, dec'd) for LoA on his
estate. Appraisers: John Leatch, Henry
Cox. Said Joseph was granted
administration. Appraisers: John Leach,
Henry Cox. Mr. John Craycrofft (CV) to
administer oath.

Exhibited will of Henry Symons (AA),
constituting his widow Elisabeth Battee
executrix. Maj. Nicholas Gassaway to
prove said will. Said Battee was
granted administration. Appraisers:
John Gresham, James Saunders. Said
Gassaway to administer oath.

17 February. Exhibited inventory of
Richard Pettybone (AA), by appraisers
Humphry Boone & Robert Eagle.

At request of James Bigger, Thomas
Lawsson, John Nelson, & Michaell
Catterton were summoned at suit of
Elianor Sprigg on behalf of orphans of
James Nuthall vs. said Bigger.

14:48   Exhibited inventory of Owen Newen (CH),
by appraisers Richard Boughton & John
Gorley.

Exhibited inventory of Elisabeth
Mackdowell (CV), by appraisers Thomas
Purnell & Isaack Baker.

27 February. Exhibited will of Richard
Bennison (AA), proved before Capt.
Nicholas Greenbury. Also exhibited was
oath of Susanna Bennison executrix.
Also exhibited was oath of Robert Eagle
& James Orruck, appraisers.

Anthony Underwood procurator for Anthony
Drew & his wife Mary Ann one of
daughters of George Uty (BA) vs. Mark
Richardson & his wife Susanna executrix
of said Uty. Libel & summons exhibited.

1 March. Elisabeth Herman widow of
Ephraim Herman (CE) was granted
administration on his estate.
Appraisers: Nathaniell Dare, Edward

Court Session: 1687

Jones. Nathaniel Garrat

Richard Thompson administrator of James
Bourne (SM) exhibited additional
accounts.

John Griggs exhibited oath of Thomas
Bowman administrator of Roger Baker.
Also exhibited oath of Thomas Clegatt &
John Turnell, appraisers.

3 March. Anthony Underwood procurator
for John Mackdowell vs. John Hambleton
(CV). Libel exhibited.

Exhibited will of John Cole (SM), proved
by Elias Beach & John Wilkes (2 of
witnesses). Also exhibited was bond of
Richard Bentham administrator.
Securities: William Guyther, Elias
Beach. Also exhibited was oath of
Thomas Grunwin & William Guyther,
appraisers.

14:49   6 March. Joseph Piles (SM) exhibited
oath of Justinian Tennison, Sr.
administrator of Justinian Tennison, Jr.
(SM) & administrator of Vincent Mansell
(SM). Securities: Oliver Burch, Abraham
Price. Also exhibited was oath of
Thomas Stonestreet & Abraham Price,
appraisers for both estates. Also
exhibited inventory for both estates.

Robert Carvile for Eleanor Sprigg on
behalf of orphans of James Nuthall (CV)
vs. James Bigger. Said Bigger to
produce an account from William Hiccah
(London) & an account of the estate.

Sheriff (CV) exhibited summons to John
Hambleton to answer libel of John
Mackdowell.

Sheriff (TA) exhibited summons to Ann
pretended wife of Thomas Goddard to
answer libel of William Alldrant
attorney of Grace Goddard widow of said
Thomas
14:50   Anthony Underwood for Ann Goddard (TA)
petitioned for Robert Carvile procurator
for William Alldran to exhibit libel.

Court Session: 1687

Ann Dennis executrix of Thomas Bankes
(CV) was granted continuance. Also,
said Ann exhibited that one of the
appraisers is dec'd, & that there is an
additional inventory. New appraiser
(with John Evans): Hugh Hopewell. John
Griggs to administer oath.

Edward Man exhibited inventory of
Richard Bayly, by appraisers Mr. John
Standy & William Wincoer, sworn on 19
(N) 1684. Amount: £369.10.4. Bondsmen:
Capt. Murfye, Henry Newman (long since
gone southward). Exhibited oath of Mr.
Thomas Robins & Robert Bryant,
appraisers of Rachell Baily, sworn 24
April 1685. Also exhibited oath of John
Baily administrator of said Rachell,
sworn same day. Bondsmen: James
Derumple, John Eason. Date: 26 February
1687.

Exhibited inventory of Joseph Stratford
(SM), by appraisers William Roswell &
William Langworth.

Clement Hill exhibited oath of John
Haskins & James Simmons, appraisers of
Rene Lefeuer (SM).
14:51   Also exhibited bond of Nehea. Blackiston
administrator. Securities: John
Haskins, John Seamons.

Michaell Taney (sheriff) exhibited the
attachment for James Bigger "not served
for that the said Bigger willfully keeps
out of the way that he could not be
taken".

Exhibited will of Obadiah How (CV),
proved before Col. Henry Jowles, by
John Ashbe, James Wickes, & Francis
Warcup (witnesses).
• Robert Wood, age 30, deposed that he
wrote the will of William Marshall
(CV) who bequeathed land to his son
Thomas & to Thomas Nelson. Date: 6
March.
• Thomas Stevens, age 28, deposed that
he was a witness to said will.

14:52 8 March. Bartholomew Ennalls exhibited oath of John Salsbury administrator of Elloner Waller (DO). Securities: Richard Adams, Edward Willin.

9 March. Exhibited will of Seaborn Battee (AA), proved before Maj. Nicholas Gasaway, by Wolfran Hunt, Richard Wigg, & Henry Hanslop (witnesses). Also exhibited oath of Elisabeth Battee executrix & widow. Also exhibited oath of John Gresham & James Saunders, appraisers.

12 March. Ann Luct (alias Ann Young) relict of Thomas Cosden (CV) petitioned that she is not worth £5 "in forma pauperis". Robert Carvile & Kenelm Cheseldin assigned as attorneys for her.

Clement Hill, Esq. executor of Stephen Murty (SM) exhibited accounts.

15 March. Exhibited will of Nicholas Cole (SM), proved before Col. Henry Darnall. Also exhibited oath of Thomas Guither executor. Also exhibited oath of Thomas Griffin & Richard Bartam, appraisers.

16 March. Henry Denton was granted administration on estate of John Edwards (SM), as greatest creditor. Appraisers: Richard Tull, John Powell. Garrat Vansweringen to administer oath.

17 March. Anthony Underwood petitioned for Ursula Burges (AA) executrix of William Burges executor of Nicholas Painter regarding accounts of said Painter.

14:53 James Thompson partner to Andrew Clarke (CH) was granted administration on his estate, as greatest creditor. Appraisers: William Hutchins, Robert Midleton. Maj. Wheeler to administer oath.

M. Miller petitioned:
- George Browne (KE) is dec'd, as is his wife. Anthony Allexander

Court Session: 1687

brother-in-law to said George was
granted administration on their
estates, as next of kin, on behalf
of his nephews. Appraisers: Mr.
William Deane, Benjamin Ricaud. Mr.
William Harris to administer oath.

- Appraisers of Maj. Inglish had not
  signed the inventory, & one of them
  is dec'd, i. e., George Browne. New
  appraiser: William Deane. Mr.
  William Harris to administer oath.
  Administrator: Mr. William Inglish.
- Exhibited will of Thomas Seaward
  (KE), whose executrix married
  Griffith Jones. Said Jones who
  married Lucy Seward executrix of
  Thomas Seward was granted
  administration. Appraisers: Josias
  Lanham, Thomas Smith. Mr. John
  Hynson to administer oath.

Cornelius Comegys was granted
administration on estate of William
Latropp (KE), as greatest creditor.
Appraisers: Thomas Piner, Edward Fry.
Daniell Norris to administer oath.

14:54   19 March. Exhibited inventory of
Nicholas Cole (SM), by appraisers Thomas
Griffin & Richard Benton.

20 March. Exhibited will of Humphry
Emerton (AA), constituting his widow
Jone executrix. Capt. Henry Hanslap to
prove said will, & administer oath.

23 March. Exhibited inventory of John
Edwards (SM), by appraisers Richard Tull
& John Powell.

Court Session: 1688

26 March. Exhibited inventory of John
Cole (SM), by appraisers Thomas Grunwin
& William Guytor.

John Boring (BA) exhibited oath of
Robert Cagge administrator of Mark Child
(BA). Securities: John Arden, William
Wilkinson. Also exhibited oath of John
Harden & William Wilkinson, appraisers.
Also exhibited inventory, by appraisers

Court Session: 1688

John Arden & William Wilkinson.

29 March. Exhibited will of John Sinick
(AA), constituting his relict Susanna
executrix. Col. Thomas Taylor to
administer oath.

Basill Wareing (CV) exhibited oath of
John Bennitt administrator of William
Willymott (CV). Securities: John
Benitt, John Russell. Also exhibited
oath of Mark Clare & Thomas Crowder,
appraisers. Also exhibited inventory of
William Willimot, by appraisers Thomas
Crouder & Marke Clare.

14:55   Robert Carvile procurator for Ann
Leisett relict of Thomas Cosden, vs.
George Parker & Mordecay Hunton.
Petition exhibited.

Robert Carvile procurator for Ann
Goddard (London) vs. Grace Goddard
(alias Grace Coppper). Libel exhibited.

31 March. Margrett Golash widow of John
Golash (CV) exhibited his will, but no
executor was named. Said Margrett was
granted administration. Appraisers:
Robert Done, Joseph Fry. Richard
Marsham (CV) to administer oath.

Margrett King widow of William King (CV)
was granted administration on his
estate. Appraisers: John Evans, Hugh
Hopewell. John Griggs to administer
oath.

William Digges was granted
administration on estate of John Rapier
(SM), as greatest creditor. Appraisers:
John Lewellin, Thomas Grunwin.

2 April. Exhibited will of John Miller
(SM), constituting Maj. John Campell
executor. Said will is proved.
Appraisers: William Husband, John
Armsworth. Col. Henry Darnall to
administer oath.

14:56   William Combes exhibited will of Thomas
Davis (TA), proved by oath of John Pope,

Court Session: 1688

John Aldridge, & Sarah Bartlet
(witnesses) Also exhibited oath of James
Sewell executor. Also exhibited oath of
William Wintersel & Frances Harrison,
appraisers. Also exhibited inventory.

Exhibited bond of Col. William Digges
administrator of John Rapier (SM).
Security: Thomas Grunwin.

Richard Pollard who married Mary
administratrix of William Gambell (CH)
exhibited accounts.

Thomas Lindsey who married Jane relict
of Richard Jones (CH) was granted
continuance.

William Combes (TA) exhibited oath of
Elisabeth Hatton administratrix of
Samuell Hatton (TA). Securities: John
Wyner, Richard Turner. Also exhibited
oath of Thomas Bowdle & Richard Moore,
appraisers. Also exhibited inventory,
by appraisers Thomas Bowdell & Richard
More.

3 April. Mary Higgins executrix of
Michael Higgins (CV) was granted
continuance.

14:57   William Radney administrator of Nicholas
Hackett was granted continuance.

John Turner & his wife Elianor executrix
of Richard James (AA) exhibited
additional accounts.

John Hans who married relict &
administratrix of Christopher Kellett
was granted continuance.

Exhibited additional inventory of Thomas
Banks (CV), by appraisers John Evans &
Hugh Hopewell. John Griggs exhibited
oath of said Hopewell.

Robert Yates & his wife Rebeckah
executrix of James Tyer (CH) & executrix
of Peter Carr (CH) exhibited accounts on
estate of said Carr.

Page 71

Court Session: 1688

Ann Denis relict & executrix of Thomas Bankes (CV) exhibited accounts. Continuance was granted.

Exhibited inventory of Thomas Cooper (KE), by appraisers Vallentine Suthern & Christopher Ranger.

Col. Henry Jowles (CV) exhibited accounts of Richard Jenkins who married Ann executrix of William Graves (CV).

14:58 Shery Warmsey administrator of Joseph Jones (DO) was granted continuance.

Robert Carvile for William Elgate "als Jane Mahenney & als".

Nicholas Allom (CE) exhibited will of Benjamin Smith (CE), proved by Martha Callahan & Terlo. Flanagan (witnesses). Also exhibited oath of Rebeckah Smith administratrix. Also exhibited oath of Matthias Mattson & Henry Riggs, appraisers. Also exhibited inventory.

Exhibited bond of Thomas Bowman administrator of Roger Baker (CV). Securities: Richard Smith, Jr., Robert Burman.

Robert Carvile procurator for Rachell Mackall vs. Ph. Clarke & his wife Hannagh administratrix of George Macall. Libel exhibited.

Sent by G. Busser, Tommesin Vine petitioned that she has been very sick. Date: 27 March 1688. Continuance was granted.

Exhibited inventory of Roger Patrick (SO), by appraisers Bryan Paert & Samuell Hopkins.

14:59 Samuell Hopkins (SO) exhibited will of William Walton (SO), proved by (N) Whittington & William Cord (witnesses). Also exhibited oath of Rebeckah Carroll executrix. Also exhibited oath of Matth. Scarbrough & John Townsen, appraisers. Also exhibited inventory.

Court Session: 1688

Samuell Hopkins (SO) exhibited will of
Edward Smith (SO), proved by James
Round, Michaell Howard, & Mary Oman
(witnesses) Also exhibited oath of Ann
Smith executrix. Also exhibited oath of
John Smock & William Richardson,
appraisers.

Exhibited inventory of David Johnson
(TA), by appraisers William Finney &
John Davis.

Thomas Knighton (AA) exhibited will of
Francis Holland (AA), proved by Samuell
Hollyday, Lidia Conant, & John Thomson
(witnesses). Also exhibited oath of
John Chappell & Benjamin Scrivener,
appraisers. Also exhibited bond of
Joseph Chew administrator. Securities:
Samuell Chew, Ann Chew.

John Godsgrace administrator of James
Godsgrace (CV) exhibited accounts.
Continuance was granted.

14:60   William Harrys exhibited oath of George
Greene administrator of George Harsfort,
sworn 26 March 1688. Securities:
Richard Speare, Michael Miller.

Willemott Hill widow of Richard Hill
(SO) exhibited accounts, via her son.
She is very sick & very old. Mentions:
no debts.

Maj. Thomas Long (sheriff, BA)
exhibited summons to Mark Richardson &
his wife Susanna to answer libel of
Andrew Drew.

Sheriff (CV) exhibited summons to Jonah
Winfield & his wife Ellione & to Sarah
Hooper to answer libel of William
Chaplin.

Sheriff (AA) exhibited summons to Ursula
Burges to render accounts, per Nicholas
Painter.

14:61   Sheriff (SO) exhibited summons to
William Elgate to answer libel of John
Mahenny.

William Chaplin vs. (N) Winfield. Libel exhibited.

(N) Mahenney vs. (N) Elgate. Libel exhibited.

Maj. Thomas Long exhibited oath of Abigail Scudamore administratrix of Thomas Scudamore (BA). Security: Thomas Long. Also exhibited oath of John Boring & Francis Watkins, appraisers.

John Griggs exhibited oath of Thomas Spencer & William Brown (witnesses to will of Elisabeth Mackdowell (CV)).

Abigail Scudamore administratrix of Thomas Scudamore (BA) exhibited accounts.

4 April. Exhibited inventory of Nathaniell Ascomb (CV), by appraisers Samuell Bourne & John Evans. Exhibited inventory of Samuell Ascom (CV), by appraisers Samuell Bourne & John Evans. Richard Ladd exhibited oath of Mary Ascom administratrix of Nathaniell Ashcom & administratrix of Samuell Ashcom. Also exhibited oath of Samuell Bourne & John Evans, appraisers.

Dr. John Brooke (DO) exhibited verbal will of William Tike (DO), proved.

George Bussy administrator of John King (CV) exhibited accounts.

14:62 John Hinson (KE) exhibited oath of Josias Lanham administrator of John Salsbury (KE). Securities: William Perkett, William Kemp. Also exhibited oath of William Hodges & Morgan Jones, appraisers. Also exhibited inventory.

James Thompson administrator of Andrew Clarke exhibited that they were partners, as per friends in Scotland. Date: 27 March 1688. Witness: John Wheeler. John Wheeler exhibited oath of said Thompson. Also exhibited oath of William Hutchison & Robert Middleton. Securities: Robert Middleton, William

Court Session: 1688

Keemp.

Alice Smith executrix of Thomas Smith
(CV) exhibited receipt from her sons &
daughters on estate of said Thomas.
Date: 2 April 1688. Signed: Thomas
Smith, Nathan Smith, Joseph Smith,
Margret Smith, Sarah Smith.

5 April. Samuell Chamberlin
administrator of Thomas Wright (SM)
exhibited additional accounts.

14:63   Exhibited inventory of Hugh Marshall
(CH), by appraisers Anthony Neale &
William Hawton.

Exhibited inventory of Seaborne Battee
(AA), by appraisers John Gresham & James
Saunders.

David Blaney administrator of Symon
Harris (TA) exhibited accounts.

Cornelius Comegys administrator of
Sibilla Broadribb (KE) exhibited
accounts.

Exhibited inventory of William Young
(KE), by appraisers Edward Beck & John
Willis.

Henry Hanslap (AA) exhibited oath of
Thomas Knighton, Henry Ridgely, & Marin
Duall, appraisers of Col. William
Burges.

Thomas Smithson (TA) exhibited oath of
James Scott appraiser of Francis Brooke.

Edward Dorsey (AA) exhibited oath of
Theophilus Kitton administrator of John
Buck (AA). Securities: Robert Procter,
Richard Owing. Also exhibited oath of
John Gaither & Philip Howard,
appraisers. Also exhibited inventory.

Exhibited inventory of Richard Bennisson
(AA), by appraisers James Orruck &
Robert Eagle.

14:64   Susanna relict of William Melton (CV) was granted administration on his estate. Appraisers: John Turner, Daniell Phillips. John Griggs to administer oath.

6 April. Exhibited will of Thomas Abbot (DO), constituting his relict Mary executrix. Said Mary was granted administration. Appraisers: John Hodson, William Mishew. John Woodward to administer oath.

John Wyait & his wife Sarah administrators of Thomas Jones (KE) exhibited accounts.

Edward Burges exhibited oath of Walter Phelps administrator of George Benson (AA). Securities: John Edwards, John Gray. Also exhibited oath of John Edwards & John Gray, appraisers. Also exhibited inventory, by appraisers John Edwards & Joseph Gray.

Edward Burges exhibited oath of John Fairebowrough & his wife Jane executrix of William Mitchell (AA). Also exhibited oath of James Orick & William Ferguson, appraisers. Also exhibited inventory.

Exhibited inventory of Patrick Dunkin (AA), by appraisers Henry Ridgely & Lancelott Todd.

William Elgate son & heir of William Elgate (SO) exhibited his answer to libel by Jane Mackenny, John Gladstone, & Thomas Gorden.

7 April. Ruth relict of John Boucher (KE) was granted administration on his estate. Appraisers: Allen Smith, Thomas Osborne. Christopher Goodhand to administer oath.

14:65   Elisabeth relict of Ephraim Herman (CE) was granted administration on his estate. Appraisers: William Dare, Edward Jones. Nicholas Allom to administer oath.

Court Session: 1688

Michaell Miller was granted administration on estate of Henry Kennett (KE), as greatest creditor. Appraisers: William Breerton, William Pigett. William Frisby to administer oath.

Mary relict of James Derumple (TA) was granted administration on his estate. Appraisers: William Winter, John Price. Edward Man to administer oath.

Christopher Green who married relict of Edward Jones (AA) was granted administration on his estate. Appraisers: Humphry Boone, Robert Eagle. Capt. Nicholas Greenbury to administer oath.

David Browne administrator of Alexander Innes (SO) exhibited accounts.

Thomas Deakins administrator of Daniell Hamon (SM) exhibited accounts.

Exhibited inventory of Joseph Everett (KE), by appraisers Thomas Pinner, William True, & Daniel Norris.

Exhibited inventory of Alexander Nash (KE), by appraisers Michaell Miller & Allen Smith.

Exhibited inventory of Andrew Clementson (CE), by appraisers Henry Rigg & Gesburde Cocke.

Exhibited bond of Michael Miller administrator of Henry Kennit (KE). Securities: Andrew Abington, Samuell Wheeler.

Exhibited bond of Mary Ashcom administratrix of Nathaniell Ashcom (CV). Securities: Thomas Fisher, Richard Keene. Also exhibited bond of Mary Ashcom administratrix of Samuell Ashcom (CV). Securities: Thomas Fisher, Richard Keene.

14:66   George Stevens (CE) exhibited will of Andrew Clementson (CE), proved by Henry

Rigg, Gisbarde Cocke, & Hewe Risse (witnesses). Also exhibited oath of Henry Rigg & Gibart Cock, appraisers.

9 April. John Hall administrator of John Collier (BA) exhibited accounts.

John Kirk administrator of Edward Furlong (SO) exhibited accounts.

Thomas Dant administrator of Peter Miles (SM) exhibited additional accounts.

Florence Tucker administrator of Edward Stevens exhibited accounts.

Exhibited oath of Michaell Miller administrator of Henry Kennit (KE).

10 April. Thomas Braine administrator of Arthur Ludford (CV) exhibited accounts.

Exhibited will of Nathaniell Garrett (CE), constituting Mary Stook daughter of John Stook executrix, & John Stook & John Tompson guardians of said Mary. Said John Stook & John Tompson were granted administration. Appraisers: Henry Pennington, Sr., Isaak Caske. Nicholas Allom to administer oath.

Exhibited will of Thomas Madox (AA), constituting his relict Rachell executrix. Said Rachell was granted administration. Appraisers: Leonard Wayman, Robert Hopper. Capt. Hanslap to administer oath.

Madam Ursula Burges was granted continuance.

11 April. Anthony Underwood to administer oath of Garrett Vansweringen & Thomas Baile, appraisers of George Reed (SM).

14:67 Sarah Kennard relict & executrix of Capt. Joseph Hopkins (CE) exhibited accounts.

Court Session: 1688

Alexander Mackforland & his wife
Elisabeth Selley executrix of Mathew
Selley (AA) exhibited accounts.

Exhibited inventory of Thomas Scudamore
(BA), by appraisers John Boring &
Francis Watkins.

12 April. James Philips administrator
of Richard Sims (BA) appeared. No
accounts to be filed.

James Philips administrator of William
White (BA) appeared. No accounts to be
filed.

James Philips summoned to exhibit
inventory of (N). Button.

Capt. Henry Hanslap to prove will of
Edward Mariate (AA).

18 April. Exhibited will of Henry
Hollis (CV), constituting Mary Daw, Jr.
executrix. Capt. Richard Ladd to prove
said will. Said Daw was granted
administration. Appraisers: Fran. Hyam,
Thomas Howe. Said Ladd to administer
oath.

William Frisby (KE) exhibited will of
Henry Kennett (KE), proved by Benjamin
Ricaud, John Stokes, & Thomas Ricaud
(witnesses).

20 April. Henry Johnson (BA) vs. estate
of Robert Langly & vs. estate of John
Langly. Caveat exhibited. Said John is
the son of said Robert. Both are dec'd.
14:68   Said Robert was sheriff (BA).

Clement Hill petitioned for Frances Toat
widow of Robert Toate (SM). Appraisers:
Capt. Justinian Gerrard, Thomas
Attaway. Date: 19 April 1688.

23 April. Elisabeth Rasin widow of
Thomas Rasin (SM) exhibited his will,
constituting her, Philip, Thomas, John,
Mary, & Elisabeth Rasin executors. Said
Thomas, John, and Elisabeth are not of
age. Petition for LoA to her & her

children Philip & Mary. They were
granted administration.

25 April. Robert King (SO) exhibited
will of Col. William Stevens (SO),
proved by Philip Hamon, Thomas Purnall,
& Henry Scafield (witnesses). Also
exhibited oath of Elisabeth Stevens
executrix. Also exhibited oath of
Thomas Johns & William Planner,
appraisers.

2 May. Col. Thomas Taylor (AA)
exhibited will of John Sinicke (AA),
proved by Thomas Knighton, John Spencer,
Herman Churchyard, & John Christian
(witnesses). Also exhibited oath of
Susanna Sinicke executrix.

14:69   Robert Carvile for Madam Burges vs.
estate of George Parker (CV). Caveat
exhibited.

Robert Carvile for Robert Bridgeforth
vs. estate of George Parker (CV).
Caveat exhibited.

4 May. Anthony Underwood procurator for
Anthony Drew & his wife Mary Ann
(daughter of George Uty (BA, dec'd)) vs.
Mark Richardson & his wife Susanna
executrix of said Uty. Petition for
attachment.

Richard Bishop, Sr. brother & heir of
William Bishop (TA) was granted
administration dbn on his estate. Col.
Lowe to administer oath.

Exhibited inventory of Richard Goold
(TA), by appraisers Robert Smith & John
Whittington.

Exhibited inventory of Samuell Rhamsey
(CV), by appraisers Michael Swift & John
Stone.

Exhibited inventory of Henry Staples
(KE), by appraisers William Thomas &
Daniell Norris.

Court Session: 1688

5 May. Robert Burman & his wife Ann administratrix of Henry Staples exhibited accounts. Symon Wilmer to examine additional accounts.

Thomas Price administrator of Samuell Rhamsey (CV) exhibited accounts.

14:70 Randall Revell (SO) was granted administration on estate of Katharine Revell (SO). Appraisers: Robert King, John King. Stephen Luffe (SO) to administer oath.

7 May. Richard Marsham (CV) exhibited will of John Golaishe (CV), proved by Robert Dove (witness). Other witnesses are dead or runaway. Also exhibited bond of Margarett Golaish administratrix. Securities: Joseph Fry, James Spendergrass.

Exhibited additional inventory of John Edwards (SM), by appraisers Richard Tull & John Powell.

9 May. James Heath, Register of Court, is bound for ENG. John Blomfield is appointed in his stead.

28 April. Exhibited will of Roger Wedell (TA), proved before Henry Coursey, Jr. (g). Also exhibited oath of Mary Wedell executrix, sworn 31 March. Also exhibited oath of John Chaffe & John Swaine, appraisers sworn same day.

11 May. Exhibited bond on estate of Robert Toate (SM). Security: John Courts.

14 May. Exhibited inventory of John Miller (tinker, SM).

17 May. Exhibited inventory of Edward Inman (TA).

Exhibited bond of Henrietta Maria Loyd administratrix. Security: Charles Smith.

Court Session: 1688

Sarah Meeke petitioned for LoA on estate of her husband, as executrix. Appraisers: John Gibbs, Giles Porter. Mr. Richard Pullen to administer oath. Date: 27 March 1688. Said Sarah was granted administration. James Wroth (g) to administer oath. (Said Pullen is dec'd.) Date: 20 April 1688.

14:71 21 May. Col. Vincent Lowe to examine accounts of Henrietta Maria Lloyd administratrix of Col. Philemon Lloyd.

George Robotham (g) to examine accounts of Edward Tomlins administrator of Nathaniel Read (TA).

22 May. Elisabeth Turner widow of John Turner (d. 19 January) was granted administration on his estate. Appraisers: Timothy Gunter, Newman Barbier. John Craycroft (g) to administer oath.

James Bery (CV) vs. Henry Cox (CV). Said Bery had guardianship of orphan of (N) Melson & said Cox has taken him away. Ruling: said Cox to return the boy to his father-in-law (Bery).

Ann Weaver widow of Richard Weaver petitioned for LoA on his estate. Date: 8 May 1688. Said Ann was granted administration. Mr. Francis Collier to administer oath.

Exhibited will of John Evans (St. George's Hundred, SM). William Hatton (g) to prove said will. Edward Morgan executor was granted administration. Appraisers: Maj. John Cambell, William Husband. Said Hatton to administer oath.

John Holloway & his wife Martha Vines executrix of Samuel Vines (CV) were granted administration on his estate. Appraisers: James Veitch, James Whinfell. Capt. Richard Ladd to administer oath.

Page 82

Court Session: 1688

Ann Pullen (CE) relict of Richard Pullen
(g) was granted administration on his
estate. Appraisers: William Elmes,
Josias Crouch. James Wroth (g) to
administer oath.

Exhibited will of Samuel Rhamsey (CV),
proved before Col. Henry Jowles by
Thomas Price. Other witnesses are
dec'd. Also exhibited oath of Thomas
Price administrator. Securities: Thomas
Lawson, John Stone. Also exhibited oath
of Michael Smith & John Stone,
appraisers.

14:72 Exhibited inventory of James Wheeler
(CH), by appraisers John Clarke & John
Godshall.

23 May. Thomas Parker administrator of
James Parker (KE) exhibited accounts,
proved before Simon Wilmer (g). Said
Thomas was granted administration, as
greatest creditor. Appraisers: Thomas
Keare, Rice Jones. Daniel Norris (g) to
administer oath.

Robert Burger (CE) who married relict of
Nicholas Shaw (CE) was granted
administration on his estate.
Appraisers: Charles James, John Willis.
James Wroth (g) to administer oath.

William Carr who married Mary relict of
John Diamont (BA) was granted
administration on his estate.
Appraisers: John Hubart, Richard
Sampson. Francis Watkins (g) to
administer oath.

Simon Jackson (BA) who married Elisabeth
Chadwill eldest daughter of John
Chadwill (BA) was granted administration
on his estate, in right of the orphans.
Appraisers: Thomas James, John Birens.
Francis Watkins (g) to administer oath.

Thomas Morris (SO) was granted
administration on estate of John Murfue
(SO), for use of orphans. Samuel
Hopkins (g) to administer oath.

Court Session: 1688

Mary relict & executrix of Ambrose Dixon (SO) was granted administration on his estate. David Browne (g) to administer oath.

Elisabeth relict & executrix of Thomas Osbourne (SO) was granted administration on his estate. Samuel Hopkins (g) to administer oath.

Samuel Hopkins (g) to examine accounts of James Round administrator of John Clarke (SO).

William Burton (TA) was granted administration on estate of Thomas Young (TA). George Robotham (g) to administer oath.

Thomas Boswick son & executor of Thomas Boswick was granted administration on his estate. James Wroth (g) to administer oath.

Martha Gibson relict & executrix of William Odary (CE) was granted administration on his estate. Appraisers: John Willis, Ezehiel Jackson. James Wroth (g) to administer oath.

Philip Hoskins exhibited will of John Lemaire (CH), constituting his widow Margaret executrix. Said Margaret died prior to administration, leaving one sister Elisabeth Hoskins as next of blood. Mr. John Stone to prove said will. Said Philip & Elisabeth were granted administration on estate of said Margaret. Appraisers: Maj. John Wheeler, John Godshall. Said Stone to administer oath.

Mary relict & executrix of Nathaniel Howell (CE) was granted administration on his estate. Appraisers: William Elmes, Edward Beck. James Wroth (g) to administer oath.

Petition of William Harris (g, KE) for LoA to Michael Miller administrator of Henry Kennit (KE), as greatest creditor,

14:73

Page 84

to be revoked. Said Harris & John Hinson (KE) were granted administration. Appraisers: William Deane, William Pickett. William Frisby (g) to administer oath.

24 May. Exhibited inventory of George Hasfurt (KE), by appraisers Michael Miller Richard Speare.

William Harris exhibited oath of Anthony Alexander administrator of George Browne (KE). Securities: William Deane, Benjamin Ricaud. Also exhibited oath of William Deane & Benjamin Ricaud, appraisers.

25 May. Cornelius Ward (SO) was granted administration on estate of his son-in-law Nathaniel Doughestie, in right of orphans. Said Doughestie's widow & several small children are also dec'd. Col. William Colebourne to administer oath.

Donagh Denis (SO) executor of Roger O'Cane (SO) was granted administration on his estate. Thomas Newboll (g) to administer oath.

Henry Jowles exhibited his renunciation as executor of Mr. George Parker. Mrs. Katharine Parker widow is co-executrix. Date: 14 May 1688. Witness: E. Humpheryes.

14:74 Col. Henry Jowles executor of George Parker exhibited his renunciation. Date: 25 May 1688. Mentions: Ellis Humphereys. Mrs. Katherine Parker one of executors was granted administration. Appraisers: MM John Craycroft, Edward Isaac. Mr. Francis Hutchins to administer oath.

Thomas Knighton (g, AA) exhibited oath of Samuel Garland & Robert Lockwood, appraisers of Robert French. Also exhibited was administration bond. Securities: John Garland, William Harris. Also exhibited was inventory.

Court Session: 1688

26 May. Exhibited was bond on estate of
Benjamin Lawrence (AA). Securities:
Daniel Longman, John Lynam. Also
exhibited inventory, by appraisers
Daniel Longman & John Watkins.

28 May. Exhibited will of Joshua Dorsey
(AA). Edward Dorsey & John Dorsey
executors were granted administration.
Appraisers: Capt. Richard Hill, John
Hamond. Col. Thomas Taillor to
administer oath.

Henry Coursey, Jr. (TA) exhibited:
* oath of Margaret Peterson executrix
of Mathias Peterson, sworn 25 July
1686. Also oath of Robert Smith &
Thomas Britt, appraisers, sworn same
day.
* oath of John Hawkins & William
Coursey, appraisers of William
Carpenter. Date: 23 November 1686.
Also oath of Ann & Mary Carpenter,
administratrices, sworn 26 November
1686.
* oath of Priscilla Thompson executrix
of Zachary Thompson, sworn 20
February 1686. Also oath of Solomon
Wright & Daniel Glover, appraisers,
sworn same day.
* oath of Frances Young executrix of
William Young, sworn 1 June 1687.
Also oath of John Sergeant & Andrew
Price, appraisers, sworn same day.
* oath of Ann Bonham administratrix of
William Bonam, sworn 31 October.
Also oath of John Chairs & Richard
Jones, appraisers of William Bonham,
sworn same day.
* oath of Margaret Walker executrix of
John Walker, sworn 13 February.

14:75 ...

Also oath of Henry Price & Thomas
Bruff, appraisers, sworn 10 March
1667 [sic].
* oath of Mary Weddill executrix of
Roger Weddill, sworn 31 March. Also
oath of John Chafe & John Swaine,
appraisers.

David Browne exhibited oath of Mr.
Stephen Luffe administrator of Edward

Court Session: 1688

Watkins, sworn 24 May 1688. Also oath of Arnold Elzey & William Waller, appraisers, sworn same day.

Stephen Luffe (SO) exhibited oath of Robert King & John King, appraisers of Katherine Revell, sworn 23 May 1688. Also oath of Randall Revell administrator, sworn same day.

Edward Tomlins administrator of Nathaniel Read (TA) exhibited accounts, proved before Henry Coursey, Jr. (g).

Exhibited bond on estate of John Walker (TA). Securities: Thomas Simmons, Hugh Paxton. Also exhibited inventory, by appraisers Thomas Bruff & Henry Price.

29 May. Exhibited will of John Acton (AA), constituting John Marriott executor. Said Marriott was granted administration. Capt. Richard Hill to prove said will & administer oath.

30 May. Exhibited will of Thomas Rasin (SM), proved. Also exhibited oath of Elisabeth Rasin, Philip Rasin, & Mary Rasin executors.

Exhibited will of John Evans (St. George's Hundred), proved. Also exhibited oath of Edward Morgan administrator. Also exhibited oath of John Cambell & William Husband, appraisers.

12 April. Capt. Henry Hanslapp to summon witnesses to verbal will of John Wheeler (AA) & to administer oath to Christian Wheeler administratrix.

4 April. Nathaniel Garret (g, CE) to administer oath to Philip Holleadger administrator of Bartholomew Henderson. Also oath to Samuel Wheeler & Thomas Linsey, appraisers.

14:76 5 June. William Richardson had exhibited will of Mathew Sely (AA), constituting his daughter executrix. Maj. Welsh to prove said will.

Court Session: 1688

Alexander Mackfarland is in possession of said estate.

John Waters was granted administration on estate of Michael Williams (AA), as greatest creditor. Col. Taylor to administer oath.

6 June. Mary widow of Henry Harman (DO) was granted administration on his estate. Inventory was exhibited.

11 June. Anthony Underwood procurator for Alice Cooper (alias Alice Goddard) exhibited answer to libel by Grace Goddard. Edward Man (TA) to administer oath.

12 June. William Boarman, Jr. (g) exhibited will of Denis Husculoe (SM), proved by Maj. William Boarman, Richard Edelin, & Thomas Hager. Also exhibited oath of James Bowling & Thomas Mudd (g), administrators, sworn 27 April 1688. Securities: Marmaduke Semme, Richard Edelin.

14:77   13 June. George Plowden (CV) was granted administration on estate of Robert Thompson (CV), as greatest creditor. Appraisers: Thomas Gant, Walter Smith. Richard Marsham to administer oath.

14 June. Exhibited inventory of Andrew Clarke (CH).

Exhibited will of Bryan Crowley (SM), proved before Mr. John Dent. Also exhibited oath of Ann Crowley executrix, sworn 21 April 1688. Also exhibited oath of Giles Wilson & Henry Norris, appraisers.

22 June. Exhibited will of John Edwards (DO), constituting his wife Susanna executrix. Jacob Lookerman (g) to prove said will. Said Susanna was granted administration. Appraisers: Peter Stoakes, Anthony Taylor.

Page 88

Court Session: 1688

23 June. Exhibited will of George
Parker (CV), proved before Mr. Francis
Hutchins. Also exhibited oath of John
Craycroft & Edward Isaac, appraisers
sworn 2 June.

Exhibited will of Henry Simonds (CV),
proved before George Lingan (g). Also
exhibited oath of John Sollers & John
Sunderland, appraisers.

James Sedgwick (TA) was granted
administration on estate of Thomas
Collins (TA), as executor of Capt.
Francis Strong, greatest creditor to
said Collins. Appraisers: William
Scott, William Gray. James Murphey (g)
to administer oath.

Elisabeth Carman widow of Thomas Carman
(TA) was granted administration on his
estate. Appraisers: John Hollinsworth,
John Whittell. George Robotham (g) to
administer oath.

25 June. Exhibited will of Peter
Ollison (CE). Also exhibited
renunciation of Ellinor Ollison widow,
recommending Olley Ollison
administrator. Date: 20 June 1688.
Witnesses: Andrew Poulson, Richard
Tutstone.
14:78 William Dare (g) to prove said will.
Said Olley was granted administration.
Appraisers: Richard Tutstone, Thomas
Casey.

Mark Richardson (g, BA) to examine
additional accounts of Miles Gibson
administrator of John Yeo.

Miles Gibson (g) to examine additional
accounts of John Hall & his wife Sarah
administratrix of John Collier.

Miles Gibson to examine accounts of
Sarah Hooper administratrix of George
Hooper.

Miles Gibson to examine accounts of
Sarah Holman administratrix of Abraham
Holman.

Page 89

27 June. Exhibited verbal will of John
Wheeler (AA), proved by Capt. Henry
Hanslap. Also exhibited oath of
Christian Wheeler administratrix, sworn
15 June. Also exhibited oath of John
Gray & Walter Phelps, appraisers, sworn
same day. Also exhibited bond of
William Bateman & his wife Christian
administratrix. Securities: Walter
Phelps, John Gray.

Exhibited will of Humphry Emerton (AA),
proved before Capt. Henry Hanslap, by
oath of one of witnesses; other witness
is dec'd. Petition of Jane Emerton
executrix was refused. Also exhibited
oath of Richard Wells & John Chappell,
appraisers.

Capt. Henry Hanslap exhibited that
William Ferguson who married Jane
administratrix of Patrick Dunkin, is
since dec'd & did not make accounts on
said estate. Said Hanslap to examine
accounts of said Jane.

Exhibited will of Richard Cheyney, Sr.
(AA). Witnesses Col. William Burges &
William Cocks are both dec'd. Ellinor
widow was granted administration. Capt.
Henry Hanslap to administer oath.

1 July. Exhibited inventory of William
Walton (SO), by appraisers John Townsend
& Mathew Scarborough.

Exhibited inventory of Edward Smith
(SO), by appraisers John Smock & William
Richardson.

Exhibited inventory of Henry Bishop, Jr.
(SO), by appraisers John Smock & William
Richardson.

3 July. Exhibited inventory of
Katherine Revell (SO), by appraisers
Robert King & John King.

14:79   William Frisby (g) exhibited bond of
William Harris & John Hynson
administrators of Henry Kennit (KE).
Securities: Edward Sweatnam, Charles

Hynson. Said administrators &
appraisers were sworn 4 May.

Exhibited will of John Murfue (SO),
proved before Samuel Hopkins (g). Also
exhibited oath of Thomas Morris
executor, sworn 9 June. Also exhibited
oath of John Smock & John Miller,
appraisers.

Exhibited will of Thomas Osborne (SO),
proved before Samuel Hopkins (g). Also
exhibited oath of Elisabeth executrix,
sworn 9 June. Also exhibited oath of
John Smock & John Miller, appraisers,
sworn same day.

Exhibited inventory of Thomas Profitt
(SO), by appraisers Samuel Hopkins &
John Smock.

4 July. Francis Green & Thomas Clarke
exhibited will of Leonard Greene (g,
SM). John Luellin (g) to prove said
will. Said Francis & Clarke were
granted administration. Appraisers:
John Watson, Henry Lawrence. Said
Luellin to administer oath.

5 July. Exhibited bond of John Stanley
administrator of Miles Thornton (TA).
Securities: Thomas Anderson, Edward
Pollard. Also exhibited inventory, by
appraisers Robert Bryan & James Bishopp.

Exhibited will of Daniel Carnoll (TA),
proved before Edward Man (g). Exhibited
oath of Deborah Carnoll executrix, sworn
21 June. Also exhibited oath of Thomas
Robins & John Stanley, appraisers, sworn
same day. Also exhibited inventory.

Francis Harrison (TA) was granted
administration on estate of Benony
Porter (TA). Appraisers: Richard Moore,
Robert Clarke. William Combes (g) to
administer oath.

6 July. Exhibited inventory of Seth
Sergeant (SM), by appraisers James
Mockawin & Thomas Grunwin.

Court Session: 1688

Exhibited inventory of Robert Toate (SM), by appraisers Justinian Gerard & Thomas Attoway.

Exhibited inventory of John Golaish (CV), by appraisers Robert Dove & Joseph Fry.

14:80 Thomas Piles (SO) who married widow of John Storey (SO) was granted administration on his estate. Mentions: Mr. Samuel Hopkins. Joseph Hopkins (g) to administer oath.

7 July. Bryan FitzPatrick (DO) exhibited letter from Thomas Taylor regarding estate of John Stuart (DO). Date: 12 May 1688. Said FitzPatrick exhibited verbal will of said Stuart. Maj. Thomas to prove said will. Said FitzPatrick was granted administration. Appraisers: Richard Owen, John Haslewood.

Mary widow of John Giles (AA) was granted administration on his estate. Appraisers: Robert Lockwood, John Waters. Col. Thomas Taillor to administer oath.

Sheriff (KE) to summon Cornelius Comegys administrator of Isabell Broadrib (KE), granted 4 December 1685, to show cause why administration should not be revoked & granted to next of blood. (N) Underwood is procurator.

Samuel Hopkins (g, SO) to summon Sarah Paramore (Mattapany Hundred, SO) & demand will of her late husband.

14:81 Sheriff (SM) to summon Lewis Jones & his wife Katherine widow of William Ferguson (SM) to show cause why said estate should not be taken out of their hands. Cites that they embezzle & waste said estate, at expense of orphans.

9 July. Sheriff (TA) to summon Richard Mirax & Thomas Thompson executors of Richard Jackson (TA) to render accounts.

Court Session: 1688

Robert Carvile attorney for James Dryden
(merchant, London) vs. estate of John
Kirke (merchant). Caveat exhibited.

Col. William Coleborne (SO) to prove
will of Samuel Cooper (SO), constituting
his widow Sarah (now dec'd) executrix.

Sheriff (SM) to summon Lewis Jones & his
wife Katherine widow of William Ferguson
to show cause why estate should not be
taken from them.

Mary Parsons relict & executrix of John
Parsons (SM) exhibited his will, proved
before Robert Carvile (g). Said Mary
was granted administration. Appraisers:
Abraham Rhoads, William Aisquith.

John Griggs (CV) to examine accounts of
John Hambleton executor of Elisabeth
Mackdowell, to answer libel of John
Mackdowell sole brother of Henry
Mackdowell.

10 July. Capt. Nicholas Greenbury
exhibited oath of Christopher Green
administrator of Edward Jones (AA).
Securities: Henry Meredith, Jonathon
Neale. Also exhibited oath of Humphry
Boone & Robert Eagle, appraisers. Also
exhibited inventory.

Exhibited inventory of Henry Hollis
(CV), by appraisers Francis Higham &
Thomas How.

Mary widow of THomas Cottingham (SO) was
granted administration on his estate.
Appraisers: John West, Samuel Horsey.
Col. William Coleborne to administer
oath.

12 July. William Richardson, Samuel
Thomas, & Edward Talbott petitioned that
Daniel Longman administrator of Richard
Arnold never tendered 2/3rds of estate
to petitioners, as trustees for orphans
of dec'd. Date: 5 July 1688.
14:82   Ruling: proceed as per law for
Preservations of Orphan's Estate.

Grace Goddard vs. Ann Cooper (alias Ann Goddard) James Murphy, John Whittington, & Samuel Creyker to testify for plaintiff. Continuance was granted.

Exhibited will of John Viner (TA), proved before James Murphey (G). Also exhibited oath of Richard Halstine & Nicholas Bishopp, appraisers.

James Murphey (g) exhibited oath of John Mountfort administrator of Thomas Mountfort (TA), sworn 20 January last. Securities: Vincent Lowe, Esq., Mary Turbutt. Also exhibited oath of John Stanley & William Eastgate, sworn same day. Also exhibited inventory.

Mary Bucknold (AA) (alias Mary Eager) administratrix & widow of Thomas Eager petitioned that Capt. Richard Hill examine her accounts on his estate.

13 July. Exhibited inventory of Humphry Emerton (AA), by appraisers John Chappell & Richard West.

M. George Stephens (CE) to examine accounts of Jacob Divellard executor of Humphry Nichols.

16 July. John Griggs (g, CV) exhibited oath of Susanna administratrix of William Melton (CV), sworn 14 May last. Securities: John Kent, John Griggs. Also exhibited oath of John Tarner & Daniel Philipps, appraisers, sworn same day. Also exhibited inventory.

John Griggs (g, CV) exhibited oath of Margaret administratrix of William King (CV), sworn 22 May last. Securities: Richard Keene, John Nutthall. Also exhibited oath of John Evans & Hugh Hopewell, appraisers, sworn same day. Also exhibited inventory.

17 July. John Hynson (g, KE) exhibited will of Thomas Seaward (KE), proved. Also exhibited oath of John Lanham & Thomas Smith, appraisers. Also exhibited inventory. Also exhibited

oath of Griffith Jones & his wife Lucy
executrix.

14:83   At request of John Howard (AA), John
Hamond (g) to examine accounts of said
John Howard & his wife Ellinor executrix
of John Maccubin (AA).

18 July. Exhibited will of Robert
Wilson (SO), constituting his widow
Elisabeth executrix. James Dasheile (g)
to prove said will. Said Elisabeth was
granted administration. Appraisers:
Peter Doughty, Stephen Cannon. Said
Dasheile to administer oath.

19 July. John Gardner who married
Constant relict of Thomas Riggs (CH) was
granted administration on his estate.
Appraisers: Francis Adams, John Clement.
Maj. John Wheeler to administer oath.

William Nowell (clerk, CE) petitioned
for copy of inventory & accounts
relative to Sarah Vanheck orphan &
heiress of John Vanheck (CE). Date: 19
June 1688. Mentions: Mr. Stiles, Mr.
Inglish. Balance:
14:84   #42618.

21 July. John Holloway (CV) exhibited
that Jonas Whinfell, one of appraisers
of Samuel Vines (CV), is dec'd. New
appraisers: James Veitch, John Guyat.
Capt. Richard Ladd to administer oath.

Edmond Howard (G) exhibited will of John
Roberts (SO). Samuel Hopkins (g) to
prove said will. Widow of said Roberts
was granted administration. Appraisers:
Mathew Scarbrough, William Cord. Said
Hopkins to administer oath.

Francis Watkins (g, BA) to examine
addition accounts of Robert Benjar & his
wife Katherine administratrix of John
Shadwell.

25 July. Exhibited will of Richard Hall
(CV), constituting his widow Elisabeth
executrix. Col. Thomas Taillor to
prove said will, by witnesses: George

Court Session: 1688

Lingan, Edward Boteler, John Baty,
George Cole, Ann Tanehill.

Exhibited inventory of Roger Baker (CV),
by appraisers Thomas Clegatt & John
Turner.

At the request of Hugh Ellis who married
relict of Mordecay Hunton one of
administrators of Thomas Cosden, sheriff
(CV) to summon Katherine Parker
executrix of George Parker, surviving
administrator of said Cosden, to render
accounts on estate of said Cosden.

26 July. Richard Smith for Sarah widow
of Jonah Whinfeild (CV) was granted
administration on his estate.
Appraisers: Robert Day, John Holloway.
Capt. Richard Ladd to administer oath.

John Ford (DO) brother-in-law to Edward
Creik (DO) was granted administration on
his estate. Appraisers: William Dorsey,
William Mishew. John Woodward (g) to
administer oath.

27 July. Exhibited inventory of Thomas
Rasin (SM), by appraisers Kenelm
Cheseldyn & Peter Watts.

Exhibited will of Lyonell Oakely (SM),
constituting John Bullock executor,
proved by Henry Poulter, John Skipper, &
Benjamin Reader. Said Bullock was
granted administration. Appraisers:
Henry Poulter, John Skipper.

14:85   William Combes (g, TA) exhibited oath of
Richard Moore & Robert Clarke,
appraisers of Benny Porter. Also
exhibited inventory. Also exhibited
bond of Francis Harrison administrator.
Securities: said Moore, said Clarke.

Thomas Wall (DO) who married Jone relict
of John Walker (DO) was granted
administration on his estate.
Appraisers: Peter Stoakes, Thomas
Skinner. John Woodward (g) to
administer oath.

Court Session: 1688

28 July. Exhibited will of Nathaniel
Garrett (g, CE), proved before Nicholas
Allome (g). Also exhibited oath of John
Thompson & John Stoop, administrators.
Securities: Lawrence Christian, Henry
Pennington, Sr. Also exhibited oath of
Henry Pennington, Sr., Isaac Caske.
Also exhibited inventory.

Ruth widow of John Boucher (KE) was
granted administration on his estate on
7 April last. She is now married to
Samuel Wheeler, & one of appraisers is
dec'd. Samuel Wheeler was granted
administration. New appraisers: Anthony
Workman, Thomas Osborne. Christopher
Goodhand (g) to administer oath.

James Wroth (CE) exhibited will of
Richard Pullen (CE), proved. Also
exhibited oath of Josias Crouch &
William Elmes, appraisers, sworn 29
June. Ann Pullen administratrix refused
to give bond; she has the oath. Also
exhibited inventory.

James Wroth (g) exhibited will of
William Odery (CE), proved. Also
exhibited oath of Martha Gibson
executrix. Also exhibited oath of John
Willis & Ezekiel Jackson, appraisers.
Also exhibited inventory.

James Wroth (g) exhibited will of
Nathaniell Howell (g, CE), proved. Also
exhibited oath of Mary Howell executrix.
Also exhibited oath of William Elmes &
Edward Beck, appraisers.

James Wroth (g) exhibited oath of Robert
Benjar administrator of Nicholas Shaw
(CE). Securities: John Willis, Robert
Gibson. Also exhibited oath of Charles
James & John Willis, appraisers.

30 July. William Holland procurator for
John Miles & Jacob Duhattaway (AA) vs.
Lydia Conant administratrix of Robert
Conant (AA). Summons to render
accounts.

Court Session: 1688

14:86 31 July. Renunciation of Samuel Cluely & his wife Elisabeth relict of William Marshall (CV). Date: 6 May 1687. Witnesses: John Sunderland, Thomas Nelson. Thomas Tench (AA) was granted administration, as principle creditor. Appraisers: John Sunderland, George Cole. George Lingan (CV) to administer oath.

William Holland (g) returned LoA of Elisabeth widow of John Turner (CV), as unexecuted.

Exhibited inventory of Mr. George Parker (CV), by appraisers John Craycroft & Edward Isacke.

2 August. Capt. Richard Hill exhibited will of John Acton (AA), proved. Also exhibited oath of John Marriott executor, sworn 25 July. Also exhibited oath of Lancelott Todd & Thomas Baker, sworn same day. Also exhibited inventory.

13 August. Exhibited inventory of John Wheeler (AA), by appraisers Walter Phelps & John Gray.

Edward Burges (g, AA) exhibited oath of James Orrick & William Ferguson, appraisers of William Mitchell (AA), sworn on 23 April 1687. Also exhibited inventory.

Jane relict & administratrix exhibited additional inventory of Patrick Dunkin (AA).
14:87 Also exhibited were accounts, proved before Capt. Henry Hanslap.

Capt. Henry Hanslap to examine accounts of John Fairbrother & his wife Jane executrix of William Mitchell (AA).

John Pettibone (AA) was granted administration on estate of his brother Thomas Pettibone (who died 2 years ago). Capt. Richard Hill to administer oath.

Court Session: 1688

Jane widow of William Ferguson (AA) was granted administration on his estate. Capt. Henry Hanslap to administer oath.

7 August. On 28 November 1684, Judith widow of William Nyfinger (SM) was granted administration on his estate. Now, James Swan has married said Judith. Said James was granted administration. Appraisers: Philip Brisco, John Vaudry. Capt. Joseph Pile to administer oath.

13 August. Philip Lynes (SM) administrator of Robert Langly (BA) petitioned that appraiser Richard Edmunds is dec'd. New appraisers: John Goldsmith, Richard Ascue. Col. George Wells to administer oath.

Exhibited inventory of Samuel Vines (CV), by appraisers James Veitch & John Guyat.

16 August. Exhibited inventory of John Roult (KE), by appraiser Benjamin Ricaud. Other appraiser is dec'd. Date: 29 June 1688. Signed: William Harris.

Exhibited inventory of Henry Kennitt (KE), by appraisers William Deane & William Perkett. Continuance was granted.

Exhibited will of William Inglish (CE), constituting Catherine Plaine (alias Catherine Inglish) relict executrix. 14:88 Appraisers: Anthony Alexander, Walter Talley. William Harris (g, KE) to administer oath.

Exhibited inventory of Col. William Stevens, Esq. (SO), by appraisers Thomas Jones & William Planner.

21 August. William Hatton (g) exhibited oath of Kenelm Cheseldyn & Peter Watts, appraisers of Thomas Rasin (SM).

William Hatton (g) exhibited oath of John Watson & Henry Lawrence, appraisers of Lawrence Greene (SM).

22 August. Catherine Plaine was granted
administration on estate of Edward
Inglish (CE). Appraisers: Anthony
Alexander, Walter Talley. William
Harris (g, KE) to administer oath.

23 August. William Brereton (g, SO) to
examine accounts of Ellinor Hayman
administratrix of Henry Hayman (SO).

25 August. Edward Morgan executor of
John Evans (St. George's Hundred)
exhibited inventory, by appraisers John
Cambell & William Husband.

Mary Eager (alias Mary Bucknold)
executrix of Thomas Bucknold (AA)
exhibited additional accounts. Also
exhibited letter from Capt. Richard
Hill, citing error in appraisal of
chattel belonging to Peter Hide.
Signed: William Hopkins, Nicholas
Greenbury. Date: 3 August 1688.

Exhibited inventory of Joshua Dorsey
(AA), by appraisers Capt. Richard Hill
& John Hammond.

John Hammond (g) exhibited oath of John
Howard & his wife Ellinor that they
returned an inventory on estate of John
Maccubin. Date: 3 August 1688.

Exhibited will of Thomas Maddox (AA),
proved before Capt. Henry Hanslap by
oath of 3 of witnesses. Also exhibited
oath of Rachaell executrix, sworn 21
July last. Also exhibited oath of
Leonard Wayman & Robert Hopper,
appraisers. Also exhibited bond of
Anthony Arnold & his wife Rachael
administratrix. Securities: John Purdy,
Thomas Feild.

14:89

27 August. Exhibited will of Robert
Wilson (SO), proved before James
Dasheile by oaths of Samuel Hayden,
Benjamin Larrence, Sr., & Benjamin
Laurence, Jr. (witnesses). Also
exhibited oath of Elisabeth relict &
executrix. Also exhibited oath of
Stephen Cannon & Peter Doughty, sworn 6

August instant. Also exhibited
inventory.

28 August. James Dasheill for William
Wheatley (SO) son-in-law to Jenkin
Morris was granted administration on his
estate. Said Wheatley's wife is dec'd,
& he takes 2 of the children in keeping.
Appraisers: James Wetherly, Christopher
Nutter. Said Dasheill to administer
oath.

Exhibited will of Joshua Dorsey (AA),
proved before Col. Thomas Taillor.
Also exhibited oath of Edward Dorsey &
John Dorsey executors. Also exhibited
oath of Capt. Richard Hill & John
Hammond, appraisers.

Exhibited bond of John Gardner
administrator of Thomas Riggs (CH).
Securities: Francis Adams, John Clement.

1 September. Exhibited will of Thomas
Lampin (SO), but no executor was named.
James Round (g) to prove said will.
Elisabeth relict was granted
administration. Appraisers: William
Fasit, Richard Harris. Said Round to
administer oath.

William West (CH) administrator of
Robert Castleton (CH) exhibited
accounts. Mr. John Stone to examine.

4 September. Capt. Richard Hill (AA)
to examine accounts of Henry Constable
(g) administrator of Rowland Nance (BA).

Said Hill to examine accounts of said
Constable administrator of said Nance
administrator of James Wells (BA).

Said Hill to examine additional accounts
of said Constable & his wife Catherine
executrix of James Rigbie (AA).

Said Hill to examine additional accounts
of said Constable administrator of
Richard Bennett (AA).

14:90 5 September. Exhibited will of John Tonge (St. Clement's Hundred, SM), proved before Clement Hill, Esq. Penelope Hayden, daughter of Francis Hayden, executrix was granted administration.

Exhibited inventory of Robert Wright (CH), by appraisers John Standbury & John Ratcliff.

6 September. Edward Cox (KE) petitioned for:
- Christopher Goodhand (g, KI) to prove will of (N) Stuarts.
- Appraisers: Henry Carter, Lewis Meredith.
- LoA to said Cox & Tabitha Williams wife of George Williams (KI). It is said that her husband refuses administration. If so, Anthony Workman is to be granted administration.

Signed: Ro. Carvile. Said Edward Cox & Tabitha Williams executors of Charles Stuart were granted administration. Said Goodhand to prove said will & administer oath.

10 September. Exhibited bond of Richard Haseldyne administrator of Francis Brooke (TA). Securities: Daniel Walker, Henry Pride.

Vincent Lowe petitioned that Richard Headger (TA) died indebted to Charles Hemsley. The small estate is in hands of his widow, who desires said Hemsley to administer. Date: 22 August 1688. Mary Headger widow of said Richard gave PoA to Thomas Collins (TA) to administer as attorney for Thomas Hinds (IRE). Date: 24 August 1688. Witnesses: John Bregran, Anthony Fanning. Thomas Collins attorney for Thomas Hinds (IRE) assigned his right to Charles Hemsley. Date: 27 August 1688. Witnesses: Flo. Sullivane, Nich. Tenant. Said Hemsley was granted administration, as greatest creditor. William Finey (TA) to administer oath.

Exhibited will of John Kennimont (TA), constituting his widow Frances executrix.

14:91 James Murphy to prove said will. Said Frances was granted administration. Said Murphy to administer oath.

Exhibited will of John Michell (TA), constituting his widow Ann executrix. James Murphy (g) to prove said will. Said Ann was granted administration. Said Murphy to administer oath.

14 September. Exhibited will of Henry Hollis (CV), proved before Capt. Richard Ladd. Also exhibited oath of Mary Daw executrix. Also exhibited oath of Francis Hyam & Thomas How, appraisers.

Exhibited will of Samuel Vines (CV), proved before Capt. Richard Ladd. Also exhibited oath of Martha Vines (alias Martha Holloway) executrix. Also exhibited oath of James Veitch & John Guyat, appraisers.

Anthony Underwood procurator for Anthony Drew & his wife vs. Mark Richardson & his wife executrix of George Utie. Libel exhibited.

15 September. Exhibited will of Richard Hull (CV), proved before Col. Thomas Taillor.

Exhibited inventory of John Sirick, by appraisers James Murray & John Trundell.

17 September. Exhibited will of Edward Selby, Sr. (AA), constituting Edward Selby, John Cross, & James Hackett executors. Witnesses (will): John Greene, James Saunders, Abell Browne, Christian Blake. Maj. Nicholas Gassaway to prove said will.

Exhibited will of Thomas Willen (SO), constituting his widow Alice executrix. William Brereton to prove said will. Said Alice was granted administration. Appraisers: James Dasheile, Daniel Hast.

Court Session: 1688

Said Brereton to administer oath.

Exhibited will of Samuel Jackson (SO).
There are only 2 witnesses to said will.
William Brereton (g) to prove said will.
John Davis who married Ann relict was
granted administration. Appraisers:
Simon Perkins, James Wetherly. Said
Brereton to administer oath.

Exhibited will of Alexander Addison
(SO), but no executor was named. Maj.
William Brereton to prove said will.
Ann relict was granted administration.
Appraisers: Philip Ascue, Thomas
Horsman. Said Brereton to administer
oath.

Ellinor Hayman administratrix of Henry
Hayman exhibited accounts, proved before
Maj. William Brereton.

SO County Court, 15 August 1688.
Commissioners present: Col. William
Coleborne, Capt. David Browne, Mr.
William Brereton, Mr. Robert King, Mr.
Stephen Woolford Mr. Stephen Luff.
Thomas Gordon (SO) exhibited that
14:92   Thomas Gordon, Marmaduke Mister, William
Wheatley, & Ann Connaway for orphans of
Jenkin Morris (dec'd) & his wife (dec'd)
petitioned for administration on estate
of said Morris. All were denied except
said Gordon. Signed: William Aylward
(clerk, SO). Said Gordon was granted
administration, on behalf of orphans.
LoA originally granted to said Wheatley
was annulled. Appraisers: Capt. John
Winder, James Wetherly. Maj. William
Brereton to administer oath.

17 September. Dr. John Vigorous (SO)
exhibited will of Ann Smith, but no
executor was named. Samuel Innis,
Richard Hill, & Elisabeth Smith
petitioned for said Vigorous to have
administration. Date: 8 September 1688.
Samuel Hopkins (g) to prove said will.
Said Vigorous was granted
administration. Appraisers: John Smock,
William Richardson. Said Hopkins to
administer oath.

Court Session: 1688

Maj. William Brereton to examine
accounts of Mary Evans executrix of John
Evans (SO).

19 September. Samuel Heyden
administrator of Summer Adams (SO)
exhibited accounts. Capt. David Browne
to examine.

20 September. Exhibited will of Charles
Stuart (KE), proved before Mr.
Christopher Goodhand. Also exhibited
oath of Lewis Meredith & Henry Carter,
appraisers. Also exhibited oath of
Edward Cox & Tabitha Williams executors.

Exhibited bond of Samuel Wheeler
administrator of John Boucher (KE).
Securities: Thomas Osborne, Anthony
Workman. Christopher Goodhand (g)
exhibited oath of appraisers &
administrator. Also exhibited
inventory.

Exhibited will of John Meconikin (KE),
proved before Christopher Goodhand (g).
Also exhibited oath of John Meconikin
executor. Also exhibited oath of
Alexander Walters & Lewis Meredith,
appraisers. Also exhibited inventory.

Exhibited will of William Inglish (CE),
proved before William Harris (g, KE).

Exhibited inventory of Leonard Green
(SM), by appraisers John Watson & Henry
Lawrence.

21 September. Mr. Robert Carvile
petitioned that Charles Turner (KE) died
in May or June 1686. With the consent
of said Turner's widow, Maj. Joseph
Weickes was granted administration.
Said Weikes let the administration fall.
Henry Staples who married widow of said
Turner was granted administration. Said
Staples is now dec'd. Mr. Robert
Burman who married relict of
14:93   said Staples & refuses to administer
estate. Petition for Mr. Daniel Norris
to administer oath. Appraisers: MM
Simon Wilmore, Elias King. Signed:

Court Session: 1688

William Harris. Date: 14 September 1688
at KE. At Court at Towne of New
Yarmouth for KE on 23 November 1686.
Present: MM John Hynson, William Frisby,
Charles Tilden, Christopher Goodhand,
Hans Hanson, Daniel Norris, William
Harris, Simon Wilmer.
- John Lean vs. Joseph Wicks
  administrator of Charles Turner.
  Ruling: plaintiff.
- Robert Hearn administrator of John
  Lawrence vs. Joseph Wickes
  administrator of Charles Turner.
  Ruling: plaintiff.
Said William Harris attorney for John
Lean & Robert Hearn administrator of
John Lawrence were granted
administration on said Turner's estate,
as greatest creditors. Appraisers:
Simon Wilmer, Elias King. Daniel Norris
(g) to administer oath.

24 September. Katherine OBryan relict
of Bryan OBryan (SM) was granted
administration on his estate.
Appraisers: Derick Browne, William Fout.
William Langworth (g) to administer
oath.

25 September. Thomas Mason who married
Margaret relict of Robert Wild (TA) was
granted administration on his estate.
Appraisers: Hugh Sherwood, James
Sedgwick. James Murphy (g) to
administer oath.

14:94 Exhibited will of Capt. William Leeds
(TA), constituting Col. Philemon Loyd
executor who is now dec'd. James Murphy
(g) to prove said will. Michael Leeds
(2nd son) was granted administration.
William Leeds (eldest son) is bedridden.
Appraisers: Hugh Sherwood, James
Sedgwick. Said Murphy to administer
oath.

26 September. George Lingan (g, CV)
exhibited oath of Thomas Tench (AA)
administrator of William Marshall, sworn
15 September last. Securities: Timothy
Sewall, William Johnson. Also exhibited
oath of John Sunderland & George Cole,

appraisers, sworn same day.

Capt. Joseph Pile to examine accounts of John Rose who married Mary relict & executrix of John Johnson (SM).

27 September. Exhibited bond of Mr. Robert Carvile administrator of Dr. James Bourne (SM).

Robert Carvile (g) procurator for Mark Richardson & his wife executrix of George Utye entered his appearance to libel of Anthony Drew & his wife.

(N) Mohany & his wife vs. Robert Carvile attorney for William Elgate. Said Carvile petitioned.

Nicholas Nicholson attorney for Capt. Edward Burford (mariner, London) was granted administration on estate of John Baker (AA), as greatest creditor. Appraisers: Walter Phelps, Leonard Wayman. Maj. Nicholas Gassaway to administer oath.

29 September. Joseph Edloe (CV) was granted administration on estate of Peter Phipphurd (mariner, Poole), as greatest creditor. Securities: William Haines, Thomas Hopkins. Appraisers: John Wiseman, William Kirby. Maj. Nicholas Sewall to administer oath.

Francis Collier (g, CV) exhibited oath of Ann Weaver administratrix of Richard Weaver. Security: James Moire. Also exhibited oath of Ninian Beale & Thomas Ellis, appraisers. Also exhibited inventory.

Clement Hill, Esq. exhibited oath of John Burch & Benjamin Reeder administrators of John Tonge.

Mr. William Langworth exhibited oath of Katherine OBryan administratrix of Bryan OBryan (SM). Securities: Derick Browne, William Farding. Also exhibited oath of Derick Browne & Robert Ford, appraisers.

Court Session: 1688

1 October. Exhibited will of William
Hathley (SO), but no executor was named.
Katherine relict was granted
administration. Appraisers: Daniel
Hast, Christopher Nutter. James
Dasheill (g) to administer oath.

14:95 Exhibited inventory of Robert Potts
(CH), by appraisers Edward Potter &
William Sundley.

Exhibited will of Edward Selby (AA),
proved before Maj. Nicholas Gassaway.

Capt. Richard Hill (AA) exhibited oath
of John Pettibone administrator of
Thomas Pettibone. Securities: Humphry
Boone, Robert Eagle. Also exhibited
oath of Humphry Boone & Robert Eagle,
appraisers. Also exhibited inventory.

Exhibited inventory of Thomas Maddox
(AA), by appraisers Leonard Wayman &
Robert Hopper.

Capt. Henry Hanslap exhibited oath of
Jane Ferguson (AA) administratrix &
widow of William Ferguson. Securities:
John Fairbrother, Henry Peirpoint. Also
exhibited oath of Henry Peirpoint & John
Fairbrother, appraisers. Also exhibited
inventory.

Capt. Henry Hanslap exhibited oath of
Ellinor Cheyney administratrix of
Richard Cheyney (AA). Securities: John
Gray, Walter Phelps. Also exhibited
oath of Robert Hopper & Walter Phelps,
appraisers. Also exhibited inventory.

Exhibited accounts of John Fairbrother &
his wife executrix of William Mitchell,
examined by Capt. Henry Hanslap.

Capt. Henry Hanslap administrator of
John Wheeler (AA) exhibited additional
accounts, examined by Col. Henry
Darnall.

Anthony Underwood procurator for John
Mackdowell vs. John Hambleton executor
of Elisabeth Macdowell. Attachment

Court Session: 1688

granted.

Robert Carvile procurator for Cornelius
Comegys administrator of Isabella
Broadrib appeared, regarding why LoA
should not be rescinded & granted to
next of blood. Court date set.

Capt. Henry Hanslap exhibited will of
Edward Marriote, proved before him.
Also exhibited oath of Richard Tydings &
John Gray, appraisers, sworn 4 June
last.

William Harris (CV) administrator of
Henry Harris & his wife exhibited
accounts.

14:96   Joseph Connaway administrator of Joseph
Freene (AA) exhibited accounts.
Continuance was granted.

John Smart who married Susan
administratrix of Richard Bennison (AA)
exhibited accounts. Continuance was
granted.

Thomas Lindsey (CH) who married Jane
relict & executrix of Robert Potts
exhibited accounts. Continuance was
granted.

Said Lindsey & his wife Jane relict of
Robert Potts executor of Richard Jones
exhibited accounts on estate of said
Jones.

James Wroth (g, CE) exhibited that Mrs.
Ann Pullen refused to give bond. The
will of William Meekes was proved by
only one witness; the other has gone for
ENG. Date: 28 September 1688. Said
Pullen summoned to render accounts on
her husband's estate.

Exhibited will of Humphry Emerton (AA),
constituting his widow Jane executrix.
Capt. Henry Hanslap to prove said will.
Said Hanslap exhibited that said Jane
refused to take oath. Date: 4 June
1688. Said LoA declared void.

Page 109

14:97   Exhibited will of Robert Lambden (TA),
        proved before George Robotham (g), which
        seem to the judges not sufficiently
        proved. William Lamden (son of dec'd,
        of full age) chose Ralph Fishbourne as
        guardian. Robert Lambden made will on
        10 September 1680. James Wilson (one of
        witnesses) swore to its validity. John
        Pitt attested to its validity, but would
        not swear for conscience sake. William
        Godling is out of the country. William
        Thomas who married relict &
        administratrix exhibited inventory.

        John Fairbrother & his wife Jane
        executrix of William Mitchell (AA)
        exhibited accounts, proved before Capt.
        Henry Hanslap.

        Exhibited bond of Sarah Bishop
        administratrix of Henry Bishop (SO).
        Securities: John Bishop, William Innis.

        Charles Ratcliff & Thomas Pointer
        executors of Alexander Williams (SO)
        exhibited that they have nothing to
        account, as estate is in the hands of
        the heir.

        Edward Wale & Nathaniel Innis executors
        of Edward Smith (SO) exhibited that they
        have nothing to account, as estate is in
        the hands of the heir.

        Willmott Hill executrix of Richard Hill
        (SO) exhibited that she has nothing to
        account. Continuance was granted.

14:98   2 October. Petition of Richard
        Haseldyne (TA) administrator of Francis
        Brookes (TA) that he was unable to come
        due to indisposition of the body. Mr.
        Thomas Smithson ("my near neighbor") to
        examine accounts.

        James Warren administrator of Robert
        French (AA) exhibited that he has
        received no debts nor paid anything.
        Date: 28 September 1688. Continuance
        was granted.

Court Session: 1688

Thomas Anderson administrator of George
Allumby exhibited additional accounts.
Continuance was granted.

Francis Hamersley administrator of
Nathan Barton (CH) exhibited accounts.

Elisabeth Mattox (alias Elisabeth
Mitchell) administratrix of John
Mitchell (SM) exhibited accounts.

3 October. Exhibited inventory of
Thomas Bostick (CE), by appraisers Henry
Pennington, Sr. & Thomas Pennington.

Exhibited inventory of Walter Meekes, by
appraisers John Gibbs & Giles Porter.

Exhibited inventory of Thomas Young, by
appraisers Thomas Himes & John Whittell.

Exhibited inventory of Roger Weedill, by
appraisers John Chafe & John Swaine.

Exhibited inventory of Zachary Thompson,
by appraisers Daniel Glover & Thomas
Begley.

14:99   Exhibited inventory of William Bonham,
by appraisers John Chairs & Richard
Jones.

Exhibited will of John Edwards, proved
before Mr. Jacob Lockermaine. Also
exhibited oath of Peter Stoakes &
Anthony Taylor, appraisers.

Edward Day administrator of William
Stevens (SO) exhibited accounts.

John Pursell, Jr. administrator of Simon
Stephens (TA) exhibited additional
accounts.

4 October. William Finey (g, TA) to
examine accounts of Elisabeth Carman
administratrix of Thomas Carman.

Thomas Thomas eldest brother of
Christopher Thomas (TA) was granted
administration on his estate.
Appraisers: Nicholas Broadaway, John

Glandining. William Finey (g) to administer oath.

Margaret relict of William Dundedale (TA) was granted administration on his estate. Appraisers: John Glandining, Edward Tomlins. William Finey (g) to administer oath.

Exhibited will of Walter Meekes, proved before James Wroth (g). Also exhibited oath of Henry Pennington, Sr. & Thomas Pennington, appraisers.

William Cole who married Ann relict of David Adams (BA) was granted administration on his estate. Appraisers: John (N), Edward Mountford.

5 October. Exhibited additional inventory of Lawrence Hoskins (CH), by appraisers Joseph Cornell & Ralph Smith.

Exhibited additional inventory of Robert Conant (AA), by appraisers John Sollars & Robert Gover.

Exhibited inventory of Margarett Lemaire (CH), by appraisers John Wheeler & John Godshall.

Michael Tawney & his wife Margaret vs. Ann Dennis (alias Ann Bankes) executrix of Thomas Bankes. Capt. Thomas Clegate (g, CV) to summon said Ann Dennis to answer complaint.

14:100 Elisabeth Vasseen relict of Francis Vasseen (AA) was granted administration on his estate. Appraisers: John Davis, William Meares. Thomas Tench (g) to administer oath.

Robert Yates who married Rebecca relict of James Tyer executor of Laurence Hoskins (CH) exhibited accounts on estate of said Hoskins.

Robert Yates who married Rebecca Tyre executrix of James Tyre administrator of Nathaniel Verin exhibited additional accounts on estate of said Verin.

Court Session: 1688

Mary Huggins executrix of Michael Huggins exhibited accounts.

Lydia Conant administratrix of Robert Conant (AA) exhibited accounts.

William Legg administrator of John Dobbs (KE) exhibited additional accounts.

Abraham Clarke administrator of Henry Bennet (AA) exhibited accounts.

6 October. Exhibited bond of Randall Revell administrator of Katherine Revell (SO). Securities: Stephen Horsey, John Roach.

Miles Gibson administrator of John Yeo exhibited additional accounts, proved before Mark Richardson (g). Discharge was granted.

Receipts exhibited:
- Henry Mackdowell received from estate of his father William Mackdowell all moveables received of David Evans. Date: 8 January 1685. Witnesses: James Scott, Joseph Whittly.
- John Mackdowell received for self & his brother James (dec'd) the full portion of the estate of their father William Mackdowell. Date: 3 October 1688. Witnesses: Robert Holdsworth, Margaret Mitchell.

Exhibited additional inventory of Richard Garforth, by appraisers Francis Harrison & John Davis.

Walter Phelps administrator of George Benson (AA) petitioned for Capt. Henry Hanslap to examine accounts.

Susanna Sirick executrix of John Sirick (AA) petitioned for Capt. Henry Hanslap to examine accounts.

14:101 Cornelius Comegys & wife administratrix of John Cambell petitioned for Daniel Norris (g) to examine accounts.

Court Session: 1688

Jacob Devilliard executor of Humphry
Nicholson (CE) exhibited accounts,
proved before George Stevens (g).

Robert Benjar & wife administratrix of
John Chadwell (BA) exhibited additional
accounts, proved before Francis Watkins
(g).

Edward Larrimore administrator of his
father Roger Larrimore (CE) exhibited
that there is no estate to be
administered.

John Stone (g, CH) to examine accounts
of John Godshall administrator of Mary
Wayman.

Said Stone to examine accounts of Philip
Hoskins administrator of Richard
Gaforth.

Capt. Richard Ladd exhibited oath of
Sarah Whinsell administratrix of Jonah
Whinsell. Securities: Elisha Hall, John
Holloway. Also exhibited oath of Robert
Day & John Holloway, appraisers.

Richard Southerne one of executors of
Mary Truman exhibited accounts.
Continuance was granted.

James Keetch administrator of
Christopher Pinkney (CV) exhibited
accounts.

John Hall & his wife Sarah
administratrix of John Collier (BA)
exhibited additional accounts, proved
before Miles Gibson (g).

Mark Richardson & his wife Susanna
executrix of George Utye (BA) exhibited
additional accounts. Continuance was
granted.

Sarah Hooper administratrix of George
Hooper (BA) exhibited accounts, proved
by John Hall & his wife Sarah
administratrix of dec'd, proved before
Miles Gibson (g).

Court Session: 1688

Sarah Hall (alias Sarah Holman)
executrix of Abraham Holman (BA)
exhibited accounts, proved by oath of
John Hall & his wife Sarah executrix,
proved before Miles Gibson (g).

5 October!. Ellinor Sprigg on behalf of
orphans of James Nuthall (CV) vs. James
Bigger. Michael Taney (sheriff, CV) to
summon said Bigger, to produce accounts
from William Hiccocks (London) & to
compile accounts of the estate.
14:102 Date: 22 October 1688. On 6 November,
said Bigger exhibited additional
accounts. Mrs. Ellinor Sprigg (sister
to James Nuthall) petitioned for
examination of estate of the orphans.
Mentions: James Bigger married
executrix.

Exhibited inventory of Thomas Carman
(TA), by appraisers John Hollinsworth &
John Whittell.

8 October. Samuel Hickman & his wife
Elisabeth relict of Thomas Brayne (CV) &
administrator of Arthur Ludford
exhibited renunciation, recommending
Richard Clarke & Joseph Fry as
administrators of Thomas Brayne. Date:
18 September 1688. Witness: Thomas
Davis. Said Clarke & Fry were granted
administration. Appraisers: Thomas
Peirson, Thomas Davis. Col. Henry
Jowles to administer oath.

9 October. Thomas Bruff & his wife
Rhoda executrix of James Earle (TA)
petitioned for William Finey (g) to
examine accounts.

Exhibited inventory of William Latrupp
(KE), by appraisers Thomas Piner &
Edward Fry.

14:103 Richard Mirax & Thomas Thompson
executors of Richard Jackson (TA)
petitioned for William Finey (g) to
examine accounts.

Frances Young executrix of William Young
(TA) petitioned for William Finey (g) to

Court Session: 1688

examine accounts.

Johanna Longman relict of John Longman
(AA) was granted administration on his
estate. Capt. Henry Hanslap to
administer oath.

James Wilson who married Mary relict of
William Jones (CE) was granted
administration on his estate.
Appraisers: Henry Pennington, Sr.,
Nathaniel Pearce. Gideon Gundry (g) to
administer oath.

Thomas Webb who married Elisabeth relict
of Nicholas Jones (CE) was granted
administration on his estate.
Appraisers: Giles Porter, Humphry
Tilton. Gideon Gundry (g) to administer
oath.

Capt. Henry Hanslap to examine accounts
of Alexander Mackfarland & his wife
Elisabeth executrix of Mathew Sely (AA).

Ann Smith (alias Ann Bonham)
administratrix of William Bonham (TA)
petitioned for William Finey (g) to
examine accounts.

John Bearecroft (SM) administrator of
Kazia White exhibited joynture to
inventory.

10 October. Elisabeth Murphy
administratrix of Nicholas Murphy (TA)
exhibited her renunciation. She is a
poor indigent needy widow.

Daniel Walker executor of Henry Parker
(TA) exhibited accounts.

John Kirke administrator of John Kirke
(DO) exhibited accounts.

14:104 Mathias Vanderheydon who married
Margaret relict & administratrix of
Henry Ward (CE) exhibited accounts &
additional accounts.

John Walters one of executors of Thomas
Pratt (AA) exhibited accounts.

Court Session: 1688

12 October. George Parker & Mordecai
Hunton (dec'd) were former
administrators of Thomas Cosden. Hugh
Ellis who married Elisabeth executrix of
said Hunton was granted administration
dbn on said Cosden's estate.
Appraisers: Henry Fernley, Henry Truman.
Roger Brooke (g) to administer oath.

Edmond O'Dwyer was granted
administration on estate of John Steward
(TA), as principle creditor.
Appraisers: William Gary, William Scott.
James Murphy (g) to administer oath.

Exhibited will of John Younger (TA),
constituting William Wealch executor.
Edward Man (g) to prove said will. Said
Wealch was granted administration.
Appraisers: Thomas Martin, Henry
Alexander. Said Man to administer oath.

Sarah Hall executrix of James Hall (TA)
exhibited accounts, proved before Thomas
Smithson (g).

13 October. Philip Kenard was granted
administration on estate of Thomas
Williams (CE), as principle creditor.
Appraisers: Ezekiel Jackson, Edward
Beck. Gideon Gundry (g) to administer
oath.

Exhibited will of Richard Edmonds (BA),
constituting his widow Elisabeth
executrix. Col. George Wells to prove
said will. Said Elisabeth was granted
administration. Appraisers: Henry
Johnson, Edward Beedle. Said Wells to
administer oath.

John Meconikin executor of John
Meconikin (KE) exhibited accounts.

Exhibited will of Ambrose Dixon (SO),
proved before Capt. David Browne. Also
exhibited inventory, by appraisers
William Colebourne & John West.

Exhibited bond of Stephen Luffe
administrator of Edward Watkins (SO).
Securities: Arnold Elzey, William

Page 117

Waller. Also exhibited inventory, by
appraisers Arnold Elzey & William
Waller.

Exhibited inventory of Bryan Crawley
(SM), by appraisers Giles Wilson & Henry
Norris.

James Round administrator of John Clarke
(SO) exhibited accounts, proved before
Samuel Hopkins (g).

14:105 Exhibited inventory of Thomas Osborne
(SO), by appraisers John Smock & John
Miller.

Exhibited bond of Thomas Morris
administrator of John Murphy (SO).
Securities: James Round, Samuel Hopkins.
Also exhibited inventory, by appraisers
John Miller & John Smock.

Exhibited bond of Thomas Piles
administrator of John Stery (SO).
Securities: Samuel Hopkins, William
Ainsworth. Also exhibited inventory, by
appraisers John Smock & John Miller.

Robert Kent executor of Mathew Read (TA)
exhibited additional accounts, proved
before George Robotham (g).

Exhibited will of Thomas Lewis (TA),
proved before George Robotham (g).

Exhibited bond of Richard Sweatnam
administrator of John Stephens (TA).
Security: Griffith Jones.

Exhibited will of Thomas Young (TA),
proved before George Robotham (g) by 2
witnesses; 3rd has gone to ENG. Also
exhibited bond of William Burton
administrator. Security: Thomas
Collins.

James Saywell executor of Thomas Davis
(TA) exhibited accounts.

Josias Lanham administrator of John
Salisbury (KE) exhibited accounts.

Court Session: 1688

15 October. Exhibited will of
Bartholomew Ennalls (DO), constituting
his widow Mary, son Thomas, son William,
& son Joseph executors. John Brookes
(g) to prove said will. Said executors
were granted administration.
Appraisers: John Woodward, Charles
Hutchins. Said Brookes to administer
oath.

Capt. James Murphy exhibited oath of
Frances Kennimont executrix of John
Kennimont (TA). Also exhibited oath of
John Stanley & William Scott,
appraisers. Also exhibited inventory.

Thomas Nubald (g, SO) exhibited will of
Roger Ocaine (SO), proved. Also
exhibited oath of Donagh Dennis
executor. Also exhibited oath of Walter
Lane & Hope Taylor, appraisers.

Alexander Thomas who married Mary Evans
executrix of John Evans (SO) exhibited
accounts, proved before Maj. William
Brereton.

Nicholas Allome (g, CE) exhibited will
of Humphry Nichols (CE), proved. Also
exhibited oath of Jacob Devillyard
executor. Also exhibited oath of Henry
Riggs & Andrew Clements, appraisers.

14:106 John Strawbridge & his wife Honora
administratrix of William Furnace (SO)
exhibited accounts, proved before Edmond
Howard (g).

Capt. Joseph Pile exhibited oath of
James Swann administrator of William
Nyfinger. Securities: Philip Brisco,
John Long. Also exhibited oath of
Philip Bisco & John Vadery, appraisers.

Exhibited inventory of Thomas Collings
(TA), by appraisers William Garey &
William Scott. Exhibited bond of James
Sedgwick executor of James Strong
administrator of said Collings.
Securities: James Scott, William Webb.

Court Session: 1688

Exhibited will of Thomas Impey (TA),
proved before James Murphy (g). Also
exhibited oath of John Newman & James
Sedgwick, appraisers.

Exhibited will of Johanna Goldsmith
(BA), proved before Edward Beedle (g).
Also exhibited oath of Susanna
Richardson executrix. Also exhibited
oath of James Philipps & George
Goldsmith, appraisers. Also exhibited
inventory.

Maj. Thomas Taylor exhibited will of
John Steward (DO), proved. Also
exhibited bond of Bryan FitzPatrick.
Securities: Henry Wilmott, Thomas
Kilman. Also exhibited oath of John
Haslewood & Richard Owen, appraisers.
Also exhibited inventory.

Edward Beedle exhibited oath of James
Phillips administrator of John Mould
(BA). Securities: Edward Dowce,
Nicholas Rogier. Also exhibited oath of
John Walston & George Goldsmith,
appraisers. Also exhibited inventory.

Exhibited bond of Mary Cottingham relict
& administratrix of Thomas Cottingham
(SO). Securities: Thomas Dixon, Robert
Dakes. Also exhibited inventory, by
appraisers John West & Samuel Horsey.

Col. William Colebourne exhibited will
of Samuel Cooper (SO), proved.

Exhibited bond of Cornelius Ward
administrator of Nathaniel Doughterty
(SO). Securities: John Roach, Thomas
Dixon. Also exhibited inventory, by
appraisers Thomas Jones & Benjamin
Summers.

Exhibited inventory of William English
(CE), by appraisers Walter Talley &
Anthony Alexander.

Exhibited inventory of Edward English
(CE), by appraisers Walter Talley &
Anthony Alexander.
14:107 William Harris (g) exhibited oath of

Court Session: 1688

Catherine Plaine (alias Catherine
Inglish) administratrix of Edward
Inglish (CE). Securities: Gerardus
Wessells, Anthony Alexander.

<u>17 October</u>. Mr. Charles Tilden
exhibited renunciation of James Sanders
one of executors of Samuell Pilliworth.
Said Sanders "shall not come to MD this
year". Date: 18 October 1686. Said
Tilden exhibited additional accounts on
estate of said Samuel Pillisworth. Said
Tilden petitioned:
- John Hynson & Charles Tilden were
  administrators of Morgan Williams &
  charged with debt from John
  Salisbury (dec'd). The suit against
  Josias Lanham administrator of said
  Salisbury was found for plaintiffs.
  Said Lanham pleads no assets.
  Petition for allowance to
  petitioners from estate of said
  Williams. Date: 17 October 1688.
Ruling: petition granted.

Edward Sweatnam (KE) was granted
administration on estate of John
Abrahams (KE), as greatest creditor.
Appraisers: William Hedger, Morgan
Jones. John Hynson (g) to administer
oath.

14:108 Samuell Preston exhibited:
- will of Nathaniel Cleave (TA),
  constituting John Aseldale & James
  Wilson executors. George Robotham
  (g, Choptank) to prove said will.
- will of Sarah Marsh (TA),
  constituting her friend John Wotton
  & uncle John Pitt executors. George
  Robotham (g, Choptank) to prove said
  will.
Charges to be made to William Berry
(Great Choptank). Date: 29 September
1688.

William Howes was granted administration
on estate of William Edmonds (CV), as
greatest creditor. Appraisers: John
Wilmott, James Wilmott. John Craycroft
(g) to administer oath.

Exhibited inventory of Lionell Oakely
(SM), by appraisers Henry Poulter & John
Skipper.

Mary Poteet relict of Francis Poteet
(BA) was granted administration on his
estate. Appraisers: Anthony Demundeder,
John Thomas. John Boring (g) to
administer oath.

William Jenkinson was granted
administration on estate of Amos Cooke
(SO), as greatest creditor. Appraisers:
Cornelius Ward, William Planner. Col.
William Colebourne to administer oath.

Exhibited LoA of George Elwes (merchant,
London) administrator of Thomas Elwes
(merchant, CH), by Rev. William
Archbishop of Canterbury. Date: 27
March 1688. Exhibited PoA from James
Dryden (merchant, London) & said George
to Robert Thompson, Jr. (Wiccocomoco,
MD), in case of his death to Henry Lowe
(merchant),

14:109   to recover all goods, etc., belonging to
said Thomas. Witnesses (for Dryden):
John Barons, Henry Ashwell, John Thomas.
Witnesses (for Elwes): John Thomas,
Henry Ashwell. Before: Nicholas Hayward
(notary). Said Thompson was granted
administration, as attorney for George
Elwes. John Stone (g, CH) to administer
oath.

John Bayne who married Ann relict &
executrix of Thomas Gerard (SM)
exhibited accounts.

14:110   Continuance was granted.

John Bayne who married Ann relict &
executrix of Thomas Gerard administrator
of Timothy Richardson (SM) exhibited
accounts on estate of said Richardson.

Richard Jones & his wife Elisabeth
administratrix of William Vaughan (KE)
exhibited accounts.

Richard Jones administrator of Thomas
Cooper (KE) exhibited accounts.

Court Session: 1688

19 October. Capt. Humphry Warren to
examine accounts of Ann Burford
executrix of Thomas Burford (CH).

21 October. Col. Edward Pye exhibited
oath of Samuel Jefferson & John Hinson,
appraisers of Giles Blizard, sworn 16
May last. Also exhibited will.

Col. Edward Pye exhibited oath of Mrs.
Ann Burford executrix of Thomas Burford.
Also exhibited oath of William Dent &
Capt. Humphry Warren, appraisers.

22 October. Elisabeth Brewer widow of
James Brewer (SM) was granted
administration on his estate.
Appraisers: John Hilton, Thomas Reeves.
William Langworth (g) to administer
oath.

23 October. Michael Taney & his wife
Margaret vs. Ann Dennis executrix of
Thomas Bankes (CV). Libel exhibited.

29 October. Sheriff (CV) to summon Mary
Ashcom administratrix of Samuel Ashcom
to produce will & show why
administration should not be revoked.
Procurator: (N) Underwood.

Robert Macklin (TA) vs. estate of John
Boyden (TA). Caveat exhibited, as
greatest creditor.

2 November. Jenkin Griffeth
(cordwayner, Philadelphia) exhibited LoA
on estate of Edward Colyer (hatter,
Philadelphia) brother & heir of James
Collyer (MD). Also exhibited PoA from
Christopher Sibthorpe (brazier,
Philadelphia).
14:111   Mentions: said Sibthorpe is executor of
said Edward Collier. Date: 22 October
1688. Witnesses: Thomas Bradford,
Francis Cooke.
14:112   Said Griffeth was granted administration
on estate of James Collier. Appraisers:
Jacob Looton, John Hall. Maj. Thomas
Long to administer oath.

Page 123

Court Session: 1688

3 November. Sarah relict of William
Rought (CV) was granted administration
on his estate. Appraisers: George
Lingam, Andrew Tanehill. Richard
Marsham (g) to administer oath. [See f.
131.]

5 November. Exhibited inventory of
Jonah Whinfell (CV), by appraisers
Robert Day & John Holloway.

Garret Vansweringen (g) exhibited oath
of Henry Denton administrator of John
Edwards. Security: Robert Emerston.
Also exhibited oath of Richard Tull &
John Powell, appraisers.

John Hambleton executor of Elisabeth
Mackdowell (CV) exhibited accounts,
proved before John Griggs, Esq.

James Yore who married Patience relict &
administratrix of Daniel Clocker (SM)
exhibited accounts. Continuance was
granted.

Elisabeth Baker administratrix of John
Baker administrator of Francis Catterson
exhibited an additional inventory &
accounts on estate of said Catterson.

Exhibited inventory of John Baker (SM).

Michael Taney & his wife vs. Ann Dennis
executrix of Thomas Bankes. Mr.
Cheseldyne is procurator for defendant.
Continuance was granted.

Charles Carroll procurator for Charles
Ascom (CV) vs. Mr. Robert Carvile
procurator for Mary Ascom executrix of
Samuel Ascom. Defendant to show cause
why administration should not be
revoked. Said Charles Ascom is sole
brother & heir of said Samuel (g, CV).
Said Samuel
14:113 made his will in presence of Col. Henry
Jowles & James Keetch. When testator
signed the will, plaintiff was in ENG.
Mentions: Mary Ascom relict of Nathaniel
Ascom (brother to testator), her
children by said Nathaniel. On 13

November, said will was exhibited.
Date: 9 September 1686. Legatees:
14:114 brother Nathaniel Ashcomnbe "Squirrel",
friend Col. Henry Jowles, brother
Charles Ashcombe. Executor: said
Charles.
- Col. Henry Jowles relinquished his
  legacy. Said Jowles deposed that
  said Samuel died at "Point
  Patience".
- Capt. Richard Gardner deposed.
  Mentions: Col. Jowles & his lady,
  James Keetch & his wife, deponent &
  his wife.
- Paul Kisby deposed. Mentions:
  Thomas Spencer, Jonathon King, James
  Keetch, Charles Ashcom (PA), Mrs.
  Ashcom.
- Jonathon King deposed. Mentions:
  Nathaniel Ashcom, Thomas Spencer,
  Paul Kisby, Col. Jowles.
14:115 ...
- James Keetch deposed on 12 November.
  Mentions: Col. Jowles, Capt.
  Gardner. Bequests of Samuel Ashcom:
  brother Charles Ashcom, brother
  Nathaniel Ashcom, brother (N)
  Jowles.
- Mr. Thomas Parslow deposed on 10
  November. Mentions: Capt. Bourne.
- Mrs. Ellinor Parslow wife of Thomas
  Parslow deposed on 10 November.
14:116 Ruling: will is valid. Therefore, LoA
to said Mary annulled. Exhibited oath
of Charles Ashcom executor, sworn 14
November. Appraisers: Thomas Parslow,
Capt. Samuel Bourne. John Griggs (g)
to administer oath.

Grace Godard vs. Ann Cooper. Summons
to James Murphy & Samuel Crecker.

Ann Lecset relict of Thomas Cosden (CV)
petitioned. Mentions: Mr. George
Parker & Mr. Mordecay Hunton executors
of nuncupative will of said Cosden,
children, very considerable estate.
After death of said Cosden, petitioner
married John Liesett, who is runaway &
reputed to be dead. Petitioner is
"covert barren" & cannot discharge. Mr.
Hunton is dec'd.

14:117 Anthony Underwood for orphans of said
Cosden. Mentions: executrix of said
Parker.

John Mackdowell vs. John Hambleton
executor of Elisabeth Mackdowell.
Answer exhibited.

Richard Keene vs. Joseph Edloe executor
of Edward Mullins. Ruling: case
dismissed.

John & Jane Makamy, John Gladstone, &
Thomas Gordon vs. Robert Carvile
procurator for William Elgate. Said
Elgate is son of William Elgate (SO,
dec'd). Ruling: defendant.

Ralph Fishbourne executor of Alexander
Nash vs. Samuel Wheeler administrator
of said Nash. Ruling: case dismissed.

Mary, Elisabeth, Ann, & Katherine
Cooksey children of Philip Cooksey vs.
Richard Southern & Richard Brightwell
administrators of Mary Truman.
Continuance was granted.

Orphans of James Nuthall vs. James
Bigger. Ruling: accounts sent to county
court.

14:118 Robert Carvile procurator for Cornelius
Comegys administrator of Isabella
Broadrib. Ruling: administrator to
recover costs for unjust molestation.

Michael Taney (sheriff, CV) to summon
Sarah Whinsell & Ellinor Hooper
daughters & coheirs of Richard Hooper
(dec'd) & Richard Ladd executor of
Francis Swinfen to show cause why
administration bond of estate of William
Chaplin should not be assigned to
William Chaplin. Mentions: Elisha Hall,
Anthony Underwood procurator for
complainant.

Receipt of Giles Thomkins son of Giles
Thomkins (CH, dec'd) for his portion of
his father's estate from Thomas Stone
administrator. Date: 17 January 1687/8.

Court Session: 1688

Witnesses: Antho. Neale, Joan Rattliff.
John Standbury made oath that Giles (the
son) was bound to him for 7 years & said
Giles was now "out of his tyme".
Signed: Hum. Warren, John Courts. Date:
11 August 1688.

17 November. Clement Hill petitioned
that John Breacher have LoA on estate of
Hugh Thomas (CH). Date: 7 November 1688
at Newtowne. Said Breacher was granted
administration. Appraisers: Cleborne
Lomax, John Coates. Capt. William
Barton to administer oath.

Exhibited will of Thomas Carroll, Sr.
(SO), but no executor was named. Mr.
Thomas Nuball to prove said will. Mary
relict was granted administration.
Appraisers: Walter Lane, John Townsend.
Said Nuball to administer oath.

14:119   Exhibited inventory of Patrick Sullivant
(KE), by appraisers Hans Hanson Henry
Hosier (now dec'd).

Exhibited inventory of Nathaniel Howell
(CE), by appraisers Edward Beck &
William Elmes.

6 November!. James Bigger & his wife
Margaret executrix of James Nuthall
exhibited additional accounts.
Continuance was granted.

12 November. John Rose & his wife Mary
executrix of John Johnson (SM) exhibited
accounts, proved before Capt. Joseph
Pile.

Herman Fookes & his wife Elisabeth
administratrix of Samuel Hatton (TA)
were granted continuance.

13 November. Exhibited will of Thomas
Lampin (SO), proved before James Round
(g) by oath of one witness; the other 2
have departed the Province. Also
exhibited oath of Elisabeth relict &
administratrix. Securities: William
Faucit, James Round. Also exhibited
oath of Richard Harris & William Faucit,

appraisers.

<u>19 November</u>. Sarah relict of John Evans (CV) was granted administration on his estate. Appraisers: Richard Fenwick, Charles Ashcom. John Griggs to administer oath.

Exhibited inventory of Nicholas Shaw (CE), by appraisers Charles James & John Willis.

Exhibited inventory of William Jones (CE), by appraisers Henry Pennington, Sr. & Nathaniel Pearce.

<u>22 November</u>. Exhibited will of John Stimson (AA), constituting his widow Rachael executrix. Capt. Edward Burges to prove said will. Said Rachael was granted administration. Said Burges to administer oath.

Exhibited will of Robert Thompson (CH), constituting Capt. humphry Warren executor. John Coates, Jr. to prove said will. Said Warren was granted administration. Appraisers: John Wilder, Thomas Whichaley. Said Warren to administer oath.

<u>23 November</u>. Exhibited will of Phineas Blackwood (DO), constituting his widow Susanna executrix. Jacob Lockermaine (g) to prove said will. Said Susanna was granted administration. Appraisers: John Woodward, Anthony Taylor. Said Lockermaine to administer oath.

Maj. John Wheeler (CH) vs. Moses Jones who married Katherine executrix of James Wheeler (CH). Sheriff to summon said Moses.

14:120 Exhibited inventory of John Tonge (SM), by appraisers John Berch & Benjamin Reader.

Exhibited inventory of John Edwards (DO), by appraisers Anthony Taylor & Peter Stoakes.

Court Session: 1688

24 November. Exhibited will of Michael Bassey (DO), constituting his widow Jone executrix. Mr. John Brooke to prove said will. Said Jone was granted administration. Appraisers: Richard Willhouse, Edward Newton. Said Brooke to administer oath.

Exhibited will of Thomas Yerbery (CE), constituting his widow Elisabeth executrix. Nicholas Allom (g) to prove said will. Said Elisabeth was granted administration. Appraisers: Jacob Archer, James Holloway. Said Allom to administer oath.

William Foreman was granted administration on estate of Thomas Bowles (AA), as principle creditor. Appraisers: Jacob Harness, Charles Whitehead. Capt. Richard Hill to administer oath.

Alice Smith relict & executrix of Thomas Smith (CV) was summoned to appear & was incapacitated by age & indispossessness. Said Alice to provide in writing satisfaction of her sons & daughters (legatees of will), then discharge to be granted.
• Therefore, we sons & daughters of Thomas Smith are satisfied & petition that their mother may be discharged. Signed: Thomas Smith, Margaret Smith, Nathan Smith, Sarah Smith.

26 November. Elisabeth Lampin (SO) executrix of Thomas Lampin exhibited that William Faucit, one of appraisers, is dec'd, & John Smock was appointed in his stead.

James Round (g, SO) to examine accounts of Thomas Bromley & his wife Elisabeth executrix of Thomas Osborne.

14:121 Abraham Rhoades & William Aisquith took oath as appraisers of John Parsons (SM).

27 November. William Harris (g, KE) to examine accounts of Thomas Hicks

administrator of Edward Homan.

28 November. Exhibited will of Ann Smith (DO), proved before Samuel Hopkins (g). Also exhibited oath of John Vigerous administrator. Also exhibited oath of John Smock & William Richardson, appraisers.

Exhibited will of John Roberts (SO), proved before Samuel Hopkins (g). Also exhibited oath of Elisabeth Roberts administratrix. Securities: Thomas Purnall, Daniel Selby. Also exhibited oath of Mathew Scarborough & William Cord, appraisers. Also exhibited inventory.

Col. Thomas Taillor exhibited oath of Mary Giles administratrix of John Giles (AA). Security: John Waters. Also exhibited inventory, by appraisers Robert Lockwood & John Waters.

29 November. Exhibited will of Christopher Goodson (SM), proved, constituting his widow Frances executrix. Appraisers: Thomas Kirtley, William Husband.

30 November. Michael Hastings who married relict of Francis Petite (BA) was granted administration on his estate. Appraisers: John Thomas, Nicholas Corbin. George Ashman (g) to administer oath.

Rebecca relict of Guy Finch (CV) was granted administration on his estate. Appraisers: Michael Ball, Thomas Kinneson. Thomas Brooke (g) to administer oath.

1 December. (N) Price relict of Richard Price executor of Thomas Robinson was summoned to render accounts on estate of said Robinson.

3 December. Margaret relict of William More (CV) was granted administration on his estate. Richard Fenwick (g) to administer oath.

Cropper vs. Faucitt. Gartrude relict of John Crapper (SO) exhibited release to Rhoda Faucett (SO) executrix of said Crapper.

14:122 Date: 20 April 1687. Witnesses: John Deane, John Collins, William Whittington. Said Gartrude also gave PoA to William Whittington. Date: 20 April 1687. Said Whittington attested to these proceedings. Date: 20 March 1687/8. Ro. Carvile exhibited request of cease & desist on any proceedings. Date: 7 April 1688. Exhibited will of John Cropper, constituting Rhoda Faucett executrix. Samuel Hopkins (g) to prove said will. Said Faucett was granted administration. Appraisers: Charles Ratcliff, Mathew Scarborough. Said Hopkins to administer oath.

Exhibited verbal will of Thomas Griffin (SM), proved.

14:123 Richard Hill (SO) exhibited list, taken by John Smock, of things not inventoried in estate of Ann Smith. John Vigerous is administrator. Legacies to: her daughter Elisabeth Smith, her daughter Martha, Samuel Sewall.

4 December. Deborah Boyden widow of John Boyden (chirurgeon) exhibited renunciation on his estate. Date: 10 September 1688 at Choptank. Witnesses: Edward Pollard, Jere. Simpson. Arthur Parserell (Chester Run) petitioned for LoA. Appraisers: Mr. Thomas Harman (merchant, Chester, TA), Mr. Vesaills (chirurgeon, KE). Date: 10 September 1688 at Wye. Said Parserell was granted administration, as principle creditor. Appraisers: Thomas Harman, (N) Vesials. George Robotham (g) to administer oath.

Clement Hill, Esq. executor of Stephen Murty exhibited additional accounts.

William Langworth (g) exhibited oath of Elisabeth Bremer administratrix of James Bremer (SM). Securities: John Hilton, Thomas Reeves. Also exhibited oath of John Hilton & Thomas Reeves, appraisers.

Court Session: 1688

8 December. Exhibited inventory of
Peter Phipheard (CV), by appraisers John
Wiseman & William Kirbey.

Robert Benson was granted administration
on estate of John Francis (CH), as
greatest creditor. Appraisers: Thomas
Crackstone, John Godshall. Capt.
Ignatius Causeene to administer oath.

14:124   (N) Underwood procurator for Robert
Winsmore vs. Edward Cooke who married
Katherine executrix of Robert Winsmore
(DO). To be rendered his portion of
said estate.

19 December. Exhibited will of Edward
Reeves (BA), constituting his widow Mary
executrix. Miles Gibson (g) to prove
said will. Said Mary was granted
administration. Appraisers: John
Walston, Robert Kemble. Said Gibson to
administer oath.

Richard Ascue who married Mary relict of
John Hamond (BA) was granted
administration on his estate.
Appraisers: John Walston, Robert Kemble.
Miles Gibson (g) to administer oath.

Richard Ascue who married Mary relict of
Samuel Brande (BA) was granted
administration on his estate.
Appraisers: John Walston, Robert Kemble.
Miles Gibson (g) to administer oath.

21 December. Exhibited inventory of
John Parsons (SM), by appraisers Abraham
Rhodes & William Aisquith.

22 December. Exhibited will of John
Parsons (SM), bequeathing to: wife Mary,
son Edward, son John, son Cosmo,
daughter. Children are under age 21.
Mentions: land in freshes of Great
Choptank, land bought of Thomas Stroud &
John Lane & John Edmondson.
14:125   Said Mary has since married John
Thompson (cooper, SM).

Exhibited will of Basil Warring (CV),
constituting his widow Sarah executrix,

Page 132

Court Session: 1688

Richard Marsham in right of his 2 sons Marsham Waring & Basill Waring, & John Hance in right of his son Sampson Waring executors. Thomas Brooke (g) to prove said will. Said executors were granted administration. Appraisers: Thomas Greenfield, Thomas Gant. Said Brooke to administer oath.

3 January. Exhibited will of Thomas Pew, which is unsigned & Ann Pew widow is unwilling to prove. Said Ann was granted administration.

9 January. Mrs. Hester Nicholson relict of Nicholas Nicholson (merchant, AA) was granted administration on his estate. Appraisers (neighbors & housekeepers): John Elsey, John Miles. Maj. Nicholas Gassaway to administer oath. Petition from Henry Bonner, mentions my cousin your wife. Date: 1 January 1688 at AA.

Thomas Taylor for Roger Troton who married a daughter of Thomas Scott (dec'd) was granted administration on his estate. Both father & mother are dec'd & there is no other relation. **14:126** Appraisers: Henry Wilmott, Charles Powell. Maj. Thomas Taylor (DO) to administer oath.

10 January. Exhibited bond of Capt. Edward Burford administrator of John Baker (AA). Security: Maj. Nicholas Gassaway. Also exhibited inventory, by appraisers Walter Phelps & Leonard Wayman.

Exhibited will of John Cropper (SO), proved before Samuel Hopkins (g). Also exhibited oath of Rhoda Faucett executrix. Also exhibited oath of Charles Ratcliff & Mathew Scarborough, appraisers.

Exhibited bond of John Vigerous administrator of Ann Smith (SO). Securities: William Richardson, William Innis. Also exhibited inventory, by appraisers John Smock & William

Court Session: 1688

Richardson.

Exhibited will of Arnold Paramore (SO), proved in VA.

Mr. Richard Fenwick exhibited oath of Margery Moore administratrix of William Moore (CV). Securities: John Miles, Peter Joy.

11 January. Exhibited will of Capt. Justinian Gerard (SM), constituting his widow Sarah executrix. Kenelm Cheseldyn (g) to prove said will. Said Sarah was granted administration. Appraisers: Richard Clouds, Samuel Cooksey. Said Cheseldyn to administer oath.

Exhibited inventory of Bryan OBryan (SM), by appraisers Derick Browne & Robert Ford, Sr.

Ro. Carvile petitioned for Henry Mitchell for LoA on estate of Charles Parvey (CV), as principle creditor. Date: 1 January 1688. Said Mitchell was granted administration. Appraisers: John Hollins, Richard Leake. Capt. Richard Ladd to administer oath. Mentions: John Browne.

Ro. Carvile petitioned for Richard Leake & his wife Frances relict & executrix of Daniel Bloyd for LoA on his estate. Date: 1 January 1688. Said Richard & Frances were granted administration. Appraisers: Henry Mitchell, William Martin. Capt. Richard Ladd to administer oath.

14:127 Exhibited will of Martha Pennock (CV), constituting Maj. Nicholas Sewall executor. Said Sewall was granted administration. Appraisers: Joseph Edloe, Andrew Abington. Col. Darnall to administer oath.

Samuel Thomas was granted administration on estate of Sarah Thomas (AA). Thomas Knighton to administer oath.

Court Session: 1688

Margaret Holland sister to Francis
Holland was granted administration on
his estate. Thomas Knighton to
administer oath.

Sheriff (AA) to summon Joseph Chew to
render accounts on estate of Francis
Holland, at request of Mr. Richard
Johns.

Exhibited will of Morgan Pranch (SM),
but no executor was named. Mr. Robert
Carvile to prove said will. Thomas
Guither was granted administration.
Appraisers: William Twisden, Anthony
Evans. Said Carvile to administer oath.

16 January. Exhibited will of Samuel
Jackson (SO), proved before Maj.
William Brereton. Also exhibited oath
of John Davis administrator.
Securities: Thomas Divies, Thomas
Gordon. Also exhibited oath of Simon
Perkins, Sr. & James Wetherley,
appraisers. Also exhibited inventory.

Maj. William Brereton exhibited oath of
Thomas Gordon administrator of Jenkin
Morris (SO). Securities: James Givan,
Thomas Ackworth. Also exhibited oath of
Capt. John Winder & James Weatherly,
appraisers. Also exhibited inventory.

Exhibited will of Alexander Addison
(SO), proved before Maj. William
Brereton.

14:128   Also exhibited oath of Ann Addison
administratrix. Securities: George
Bayly, John Moore. Also exhibited oath
of Philip Ascue & Thomas Horsman,
appraisers. Also exhibited inventory.

Exhibited will of Thomas Willin (SO),
proved before Maj. William Brereton.
Also exhibited oath of Alice Willin
executrix. Also exhibited oath of James
Dasheile & Daniel Hast, appraisers.
Also exhibited inventory.

William Wheatley (SO) son-in-law to
Jenkin Morris (SO) was granted
administration on 28 August last. James

Court Session: 1688

Dashiele (g) to administer oath. LoA
were never given since when the Court
offered it to him, he refused & the
Court offered it to another.

Exhibited will of William Hathley (SO),
proved before James Dashiell (g).
Reason for delay: Thomas Edwards was
gone out of the country & it was felt he
would return but he did not. William
Piper did attest to the will. Date: 30
November 1688. Signed: James Dashiell.
Also exhibited bond of Katherine Hathley
relict. Securities: John Hanley,
Richard Jefferson. Also exhibited
inventory, by appraisers Daniel Hast &
Christopher Nutter.

18 January. Exhibited will of Nicholas
White (SM), constituting James Cullen
executor. James Pattison (g) to prove
said will. Said Cullen was granted
administration. Appraisers: Thomas
Haddock, Thomas Williams. Said Pattison
to administer oath.

19 January. Exhibited inventory of
Denis Husculoe (SM), by appraisers
Richard Edelen & Marmaduke Semme.

Francis Hutchins (g) exhibited oath of
William Turner administrator of James
Stritch (CV). Securities: William
Holland, William Whittington.

26 January. Anthony Underwood for Ann
Hopewell widow vs. estate of Hugh
Hopewell, Sr. Caveat exhibited.

George Hawes (CV) attorney for Edward &
Dubley Carleton were granted
administration on estates of William
Shaw (CV) & his wife, as principle
creditors. Appraisers: John Gale,
Michael Ball. Francis Collier (g) to
administer oath.

Thomas Tench (g) & Thomas Knighton (g)
to examine accounts of Joseph Chew
administrator of Francis Holland (AA).

Court Session: 1688

14:129 Exhibited inventory of James Bremer
(SM), by appraisers John Hilton & Thomas
Reeves.

Mary Stratford administratrix of Joseph
Stratford (SM) exhibited accounts.
Continuance was granted.

Anthony Neale one of executors of Capt.
James Neale (CH) exhibited accounts &
additional accounts.

Col. Henry Jowles exhibited oath of
Richard Clarke & Joseph Fry
administrators of Thomas Brayne (CV).
Securities: Thomas Pearson, Thomas
Davis. Also exhibited oath of Thomas
Pierson & Thomas Davis, appraisers.

29 January. Moses Jones who married
Katherine relict & executrix of James
Wheeler (CH) was granted continuance.

Elisabeth relict of John Portwood (SM)
was granted administration on his
estate. Appraisers: Thomas Carvile,
John Hilton. William Langworth (g) to
administer oath.

Executrix of William Young (TA)
exhibited accounts, proved before
William Finney (g).

Executor of Richard Jackson (TA)
exhibited accounts, proved before
William Finney (g).

William Finney (g) exhibited oath of
John Glandining & Edward Tomlins,
appraisers of William Dundedale (TA).
Also exhibited bond of Margarett relict
& administratrix. Securities: Nicholas
Broadway, Jacob Seth. Also exhibited
inventory.

William Finney (g) exhibited oath of
William Hemsley & John Aleridge,
appraisers of Richard Hedger (TA). Also
exhibited bond of Charles Hemsley
administrator. Securities: Anthony
Maile, Thomas Collins. Also exhibited
inventory.

William Finney (g) exhibited oath of John Glandining & Nicholas Broadway, appraisers of Christopher Thomas (TA). Also exhibited bond of Thomas Thomas administrator. Securities: John Glandining, John King. Also exhibited inventory.

Richard Isles who married Elisabeth relict of Demindigoe Gambra (CH) was granted administration on his estate. Appraisers: Cleborne Lomax, Thomas Jones. Henry Hawkins (g) to administer oath.

30 January. Exhibited inventory of Thomas Brayne (CV), by appraisers Thomas Peirson & Thomas Davis.

14:130 Grace Goddard vs. Ann Cooper (alias Ann Goddard). Sheriff (TA) to subpoena Samuel Creyker to testify for Grace Goddard.

Henry Darnall exhibited bond of Ann Pew. Securities: Hugh Hopewell, William Haimes. Also exhibited will of Capt. Roger Baker. LoA to Thomas Bowman revoked. LoA to Mr. Thomas Johnson who married Mary Baker only daughter & surviving legatee of said Roger. Also exhibited oath of Andrew Abington & Joseph Edloe, appraisers.

Exhibited inventory of Guy Finch (CV), by appraisers Michael Ball & Thomas Kineston.

31 January. Exhibited inventory of John Vines (TA), by appraisers Richard Haseldyne & Nicholas Bishopp.

James Murphey (g) exhibited oath of Thomas Mason administrator of Robert Wild (TA). Securities: David Farbank, Thomas Lurke. Also exhibited oath of Hugh Sherwood & James Sedgwick, appraisers. Also exhibited inventory.

Exhibited will of John Mitchell (TA), proved before James Murphy (g). Also exhibited oath of Ann Mitchell

Court Session: 1688

executrix. Also exhibited oath of James
Scott & William Scott, appraisers. Also
exhibited inventory.

2 February. Capt. Richard Hill to
examine additional accounts of Ursula
Moore (alias Ursula Burges) executrix of
Col. William Burges executor of
Nicholas Painter (AA).

Exhibited will of John Dew (CV),
constituting Derby Sullivant executor.
Said Sullivant was granted
administration. Mr. George Lingan to
prove said will & administer oath.

LoA were granted to Mary Johnson (alias
Mary Baker) (CV) on estate of Roger
Baker (CV). On 8 February last, Thomas
Bowman (merchant, London) was granted
administration on estate of said Roger
Baker (CV), as next-of-kin as his
sister's son. Also William Archbishop
of Canterbury granted LoA to Mary
Johnson (alias Mary Baker) (daughter &
surviving legatee in will of said Roger)
wife of Thomas Johnson.
14:131 LoA to said Bowman revoked, & said Mary
was granted administration.

5 February. Exhibited inventory of
Christopher Goodson (SM), by appraisers
Thomas Kirtley & William Husband.

12 February. Exhibited will of Joseph
Isaake (CV), constituting his widow
Margaret executrix. Mr. Francis
Collier to prove said will. Said
Margaret was granted administration.
Appraisers: Maj. Ninian Beall, William
Dawes. Said Collier to administer oath.

Henry Darnall petitioned that Benjamin
Evans lately married Sarah widow of
William Routs. Date: 7 February 1688/9
at Mattapony. Said Benjamin & Sarah
were granted administration.
Appraisers: Thomas Greenfield, Charles
Bibins. Richard Marsham (g) to
administer oath.

Exhibited bond of Philip Kennard administrator of Thomas Wilham (CE). Securities: Swithin Wells, Ezekiel Jackson. Also exhibited inventory, by appraisers Edward Beck & Ezekiel Jackson.

Exhibited bond ob James Wilson administrator of William Jones (CE). Securities: Henry Pennington, Sr., Nathaniel Pearce.

John Steward for Thomas Christian (age 19) son of Lawrence Christian was granted administration on estate of said Lawrence. Appraisers: John Stoope, Philip Holleadger. Mr. William Ward (g, CE) to administer oath.

Exhibited will of John Kennimont (TA), proved before James Murphy (g).

Alexander Mackfarland & his wife Elisabeth executrix of Mathew Seley (AA) exhibited additional accounts, proved before Capt. Hanslap.

14:132 William Harris renounced administration on estate of Francis Davis. Estate is so small. Mentions: children, Francis Billingsley. Ja. Martin renounced administration. Estate is so small & much indebted. Said Martin is attorney for Richard Durham. Date: 8 February 1688/9.

13 February. Francis Billingsley & John Leach, Jr. were granted administration on said estate of Francis Davis, as greatest creditors. Appraisers: MM Edward Isaak, Richard Starling. Mr. John Craycroft to administer oath.

Exhibited will of Richard Edmonds (BA), proved before Col. George Wells. Also exhibited oath of Elisabeth Edmonds executrix, sworn 7 January last. Also exhibited oath of Henry Johnson & Edward Beedle, sworn same day.

14 February. Elias Lowry brother of Henry Lowrey (CV) was granted

Court Session: 1688

administration on his estate.
Appraisers: John Wilmott, William
Nedham. Francis Hutchins (g) to
administer oath.

Mr. Batson for Daniel Sheredine
petitioned for LoA on estate of William
Keepe (CV). Date: 25 Janaury 1688.
Said Sheredine was granted
administration. Appraisers (CV): Mr.
Hugh Ellis, James Sawell. Francis
Hutchins (g) to administer oath.

15 February. Honor relict of John
Durdon (AA) was granted administration
on his estate. Capt. Henry Hanslap to
administer oath.

Joseph Chew (AA) was granted LoA on
estate of Francis Holland, on behalf of
his daughter. Said infant is now dec'd.
(N) Underwood procurator for William
Meares (CV) grandfather to said infant
petitioned for administration.

14:133 Exhibited will of Thomas Pattison (AA),
constituting his widow Jane executrix.
Capt. Henry Hanslap to prove said will.
Said Jane was granted administration.
Appraisers: Thomas Planner, William
Williams. Said Hanslap to administer
oath.

Samuell Young who married Mary widow &
administratrix of Maj. Thomas Francis
(AA) petitioned for Capt. Richard Hill
to examine accounts. The dec'd died
suddenly, much in debt in ENG & MD.
Said Young had several houses burn on
"this day". Date: 15 March 1687/8.

William Smith (CV) made his will,
constituting his wife Elisabeth
executrix. She died before exhibiting
accounts. Simon Nichols who married
Jane Gaskin (legatee) was granted
administration. Appraisers: Maj.
Ninian Beall, James Moore. Francis
Collier to administer oath.

Maj. William Brereton to examine
accounts of William Elgatt administrator

Court Session: 1688

of William Elgatt (SO).

Maj. William Brereton to examine
accounts of William Jones executor of
Cornelius Johnson (SO).

16 February. William Langworth (g)
exhibited oath of Elisabeth Portwood
administratrix of John Portwood (SM),
sworn 8 February instant. Securities:
Thomas Melton, James Capline. Also
exhibited oath of Thomas Carvile & John
Hilton, appraisers.

18 February. Thomas Griffin son of
Thomas Griffin, Sr. (SM) exhibited his
verbal will. Appraisers: William
Guither, Elias Beech. James Pattison
(g) to administer oath.

14:134   19 February. Henry Hawkins (g)
exhibited oath of Richard Isles & his
wife Elisabeth relict of Domindigo
Gambra (CH), sworn 5 February 1688.
Securities: William Thompson, Charles
Garrett. Also exhibited oath of
Cleborne Lomax (CH) & Thomas Jones (CH),
appraisers.

Capt. Ignatius Causeene exhibited oath
of Robert Benson administrator of John
Frances (CH), sworn 20 December last.
Securities: Thomas Crackstone, John
Godshall. Also exhibited oath of Thomas
Crackstone & John Godshall, appraisers,
sworn same day.

Exhibited inventory of Charles Steward
(KE), by appraisers Henry Carter & Lewis
Meredith.

William Smoote vs. Robert Yates & his
wife Rebecca executrix of James Tyre
executor of John Bowles who married
relict & executrix of William Batten.
Answer to libel exhibited.

Capt. Richard Hill exhibited oath of
William Freeman administrator of Thomas
Bowles (AA), sworn 12 December last.
Security: Jacob Harnis. Also exhibited
oath of Jacob Harnis & John Whitehead,

appraisers, sworn same day. Also
exhibited inventory.

John Meconikin executor of John
Meconikin (KE) exhibited further
accounts.

James Phillips exhibited judgement
against John Lillington, being the
greatest creditor. Elisabeth Lillington
is relict of said John.

Sarah Hawlton relict of William Hawlton
(cordwinder, CH) renounced
administration on his estate,
recommending Philip Lynes (CH), as
principle creditor. Date: 24 December
1688. Witnesses: Edward Till, James
Miller.

14:135 Gideon Gundry exhibited:
- LoA of Nicholas Jones returned,
  since it was a mistake. Said Jones
  made a will, previously sent down by
  Capt. Pearce.
- bond of (N) Kennard & (N) Wilson.
- inventory of Thomas Wilham.
- inventory of William Jones.
Date: 15 December 1688 at CE.

21 February. Richard Bayly (AA) who
married Mary widow of Mark Johnson (AA)
was granted administration on his
estate. Appraisers: Robert Eagle, John
Smart. Capt. Richard Hill to
administer oath. Mentions: Mr. Henry
Constable, Mr. Greenbury.

Richard Agambra son of Domindigo Agambra
(dec'd) vs. Richard Isles (taylor, CH)
administrator of said Gambra. Summon to
said Isles to show cause why LoA should
not be revoked.

Ann Pullen administratrix of Richard
Pullen (CE) summoned to show cause why
LoA should not be revoked.

Edward Selby, John Cross, & James
Haskett executors of Edward Selby (AA)
summoned to render accounts.

Elisabeth Hall executrix of Richard Hall (CV) summoned to show cause why she does not administer said estate.

James Henny relict of John Henny (SO) summoned to show cause why she does not administer said estate.

Capt. Henry Hanslap to examine additional accounts of Patrick Murfey (AA) & his wife Mary relict & administratrix of John Gray (AA).

Mary Howell relict & executrix of Nathaniell Howell (CE) & Martha Pope & his wife Mary late relict & administratrix of
14:136 John Howell. Said John & Nathaniel were executors of John Vanhack & administrators of Sarah Vanhack relict of said John, in trust for Sarah Vanhack (sole daughter, infant).

22 February. Exhibited bond of Margarett Holland administratrix of Francis Holland (AA). Securities: Hugh Gill, Garrett Hopkins. Thomas Knighton exhibited oath of William Holland & Garret Hopkins, appraisers, sworn 21 January last.

Thomas Knighton (g) exhibited oath of Richard Lockwood & John Waters, appraisers of Sarah Thomas (AA). Also exhibited bond of Samuel Thomas, administrator. Securities: James Ellis, Job Evans. Also exhibited inventory.

27 February. John Craycroft (g) exhibited oath of William Howes administrator of William Edmonds (CV), sworn 26 January last. Securities: John Willymott, James Berry. Also oath of John Willymott & James Willymott, appraisers, sworn same day.

Exhibited will of Capt. John Cobreath (CV), constituting his son John executor, with assistance from Mark Clare, William Meades, & John Hunt. They are also the guardians for the children. Said Hunt & Clare renounced

administration. Date: 13 February 1689.
Witnesses: John Hume, John Bennett.
John Craycroft (g) to prove said will.
William Meades was granted
administration, as guardian to said
John. Appraisers: John Sunderland,
Abraham Clarke. Said Craycroft to
administer oath.

Katherine relict of Hugh Floyd (CV) was
granted administration on his estate.
Appraisers: Thomas Hillary, John
Sunderland. Thomas Tasker to administer
oath.

28 February. Exhibited will of John
Moffett (CV), constituting Andrew
Tenehill & Elisha Hall executors.
George Lingam (g) to prove said will.
Said Tenehill & Hall were granted
administration. Appraisers: Thomas
Hillary, Timothy Sowell. Said Lingam to
administer oath.

1 March. Sarah relict of William Hawton
exhibited her renunciation. [See f.
134.] Philip Lynes was granted
administration, as principle creditor.
Appraisers: Ignatius Wheeler, James
Miller. Maj. John Wheeler to
administer oath.

7 March. William Moss was granted
administration on estate of John Clarke
(CH), as principle creditor.
Appraisers: Edward Rookwood, William
Spikman. Randolph Hanson (g) to
administer oath.

14:137 Anne relict of George Goer (CH) was
granted administration on his estate.
Appraisers: Cleborne Lomax, William
Thompson. Capt. Ignatius Causeene to
administer oath.

8 March. Exhibited will of Thomas Green
(CV), constituting his widow Ann
executrix. Thomas Tasker (g) to prove
said will by oaths of Henry Deackes,
Priscilla Dale, & John Baty.

Court Session: 1688

Exhibited inventory of William Moore
(CV), by appraisers David Davis & John
Miles.

9 March. John Londey for Margaret
Lafeild was granted administration on
estate of Bartholomew Ramsey, a bachelor
who died at her house & was formerly
partner with her husband John Lafeild.
Cites verbal will bequeathing to said
Margaret & 1 godchild. Estate is very
considerable. Date: 15 December 1688 at
house of Capt. James Murphey in St.
Michael's River. Said Margaret was
granted administration. George Robotham
(g) to administer oath.

11 March. Ann Thompson widow of Joseph
Thompson petitioned for LoA. Date: 20
August 1688. Appraisers: John Booth,
Anguish Marrow. Charles Hutchins (DO)
to administer oath.

At request of Robert Carvile, summons
issued to sheriff (CV) on 14 March 1688.
On 9 July 1686, Thomas Brayne (CV) who
married Elisabeth eldest daughter of
Arthur Ludford (dec'd) was granted
administration on estate of said
Ludford. Thomas Brooke (g) to
administer oath. On 1 October
following, an inventory was exhibited.
Thomas Brayne is now dec'd. Securities:
Richard Clarke, Joseph Fry. Samuel
Hickman who married Elisabeth relict of
said Brayne was granted administration
on estate of said Ludford.

14:138   15 March. Anthony Underwood procurator
for John Mackdowell vs. John Hambleton
executor of Elisabeth Mackdowell. Reply
to answer exhibited.

1 October. Elisabeth Coursey relict &
executrix of Maj. William Coursey (TA)
exhibited accounts, proved before Thomas
Smithson (g).

Col. William Burges executor of
Nicholas Painter exhibited accounts.

Court Session: 1688

Col. William Burges administrator of John Barker exhibited receipts.

Thomas Simonds & his wife Margaret relict & executrix of John Walker (TA) exhibited accounts. Continuance was granted.

10 October. Anthony Neale one of executors of Capt. James Neale (CH) exhibited additional accounts.

8 December. Henry Constable administrator of Rowland Nance (BA) exhibited accounts.

Henry Constable administrator of Rowland Nance administrator of James Wells exhibited accounts.

Thomas Stone administrator of Giles Tomkins (CH) exhibited accounts.

22 March. Ursula Moore (alias Ursula Burges) relict of Col. William Burges executor of Nicholas Painter (AA) exhibited additional accounts, proved before Richard Hill.

Exhibited will of Phineas Blackwood (DO), proved before Jacob Lockermane (g). Also exhibited oath of John Woodward & Anthony Tayler, appraisers.

23 March. Exhibited will of Capt. Justinian Gerard (SM), proved before Kenelm Cheseldyne (g). Also exhibited oath of Sarah relict. Also exhibited oath of Richard Clouds & Samuel Cooksey.

Court Session: 1689

27 March. Exhibited will of John Dew (AA), proved by 2 witnesses before George Lingan (g) on 5th instant. Other witness is dec'd. Also exhibited oath of Andrew Tennehill & Timothy Seawell, appraisers. Also exhibited inventory.

Exhibited will of Thomas Green (CV), proved before Thomas Tasker (g).

28 March. Exhibited inventory of Thomas Griffin (SM), by appraisers William Guyther & Elias Beech.

30 March. Joachim Kiestead (CV) exhibited will of Numan Barber (CV), constituting him executor. Francis Hutchins (g) to prove said will. Said Kiestead was granted administration. Appraisers: John Willymott, William Whittington. Said Hutchins to administer oath.

14:139   Exhibited inventory of Roblet Thompson (CH), by appraisers John Wildes, Thomas Whichaley. John Courts, Jr. exhibited will of Roblet Thompson, proved. Also exhibited of Humphry Warren executor & oath of appraisers.

Exhibited inventory of John Portwood (SM), by appraisers Thomas Carvile & Thomas Hilton.

Exhibited will of Mathew Cartwright (SM), proved before Clement Hill, Esq., constituting John Turlinge, Sr. & his wife Sarah Cartwright executors. John Turlinge exhibited his renunciation on 13 March 1688. Witness: Edward Farr. Said Sarah was granted administration. Appraisers: Samuel Berry, John Carvile. Clement Hill, Esq. to administer oath.

1 April. Exhibited will of Arnold Parramore (SO), but no executor was named. Sarah widow was granted administration, per Capt. William Whittington. Appraisers: Mathew Scarborough, John Terry. Samuel Hopkins (g) to administer oath.

2 April. William Dent procurator for Richard Agambra (son of Domindigo Agambra, CH) vs. Richard Isles (taylor). Libel exhibited.

Ignatius Causeene exhibited oath of Ann relict of George Grer (CH), sworn 5 March last. Securities: John Bracher, James Latimore. Also exhibited oath of Cleborne Lomax & William Thompson,

Court Session: 1689

appraisers, sworn same day.

Michael Taney & his wife Margaret vs.
Ann Denis (alias Ann Banks) executrix of
Thomas Bankes (CV). Answer exhibited.

Michael Taney (sheriff, CV) to summon
Richard Clarke & Joseph Fry to render
accounts on estates of Arthur Ludford &
Thomas Brayne. Said Clarke & Fry
exhibited accounts & additional accounts
on estate of said Ludford.
14:140 Distribution: orphans. Also exhibited
accounts on estate of said Brayne.

Per Maj. Thomas Long, Abigail Scudamore
administratrix of Thomas Scudamore (BA)
was granted discharge.

3 April. Charles Ashcom executor of
Samuel Ashcom (CV) exhibited inventory,
by appraisers Samuel Bourne & Thomas
Parslow.

Mary Sarson widow of Edward Searson (AA)
petitioned for LoA, as she is a weekly
woman. Date: 22 February 1688. Said
Mary was granted administration. Capt.
Henry Hanslap to administer oath.

Exhibited inventory of John Francis
(CH), by appraisers Thomas Craxton &
John Godshall.

Ann Fairloe (CV) was granted
administration on estate of John Goud
(CV). George Royston exhibited bands of
matrimony. Appraisers: James Crafford,
John Turner. Mr. Roger Brooke to
administer oath.

Exhibited will of John Russell (CV), but
no executor was named. John Craycroft
(g) to prove said will. James Wood for
Margaret widow was granted
administration. Said Craycroft to
administer oath.

14:141 Capt. James Murphey exhibited will of
William Leeds (TA), proved. Also
exhibited oath of Michael Leeds
administrator. Securities: Hugh

Sherwood, William Hambleton. Also
exhibited oath of Hugh Sherwood & James
Sedgwick, appraisers. Also exhibited
inventory.

Exhibited bond of Philip Lynes
administrator of William Hawton (CH).
Securities: Joseph Bullutt, Ignatius
Wheeler.

Robert Yates & wife executrix of James
Tyre executor of Peter Carr exhibited
additional accounts.

Thomas Peirson & wife administratrix of
John Golaish (CV) exhibited accounts.

4 April. Joseph Sempille for Margaret
Henry relict of John Henry (SO),
exhibited that her husband left no
estate. Said Margaret was granted
administration. Appraisers: Lawrence
Craffort, James Hinderson. Edmond
Howard (g) to administer oath.

Exhibited was bond of Hugh Ellis
administrator dbn of Thomas Cosden (CV).
Securities: John Bigger, Samuel
Copeland.

Exhibited was bond of John Galwith
administrator of Richard Barton (CV).
Security: Thomas Robinson. Date: 28
April 1683.

Exhibited was bond of Michael Taney
administrator of Thomas Jackson (CV).
Securities: John Grover, Joseph
Williams. Date: 24 May 1684.

Exhibited will of John Clarke (CV),
proved before Roger Brooke (g) on 26
February 1680.

Exhibit bond of Fridua Gardner widow of
James Gardner (CV). Securities: Michael
Taney, Thomas Arnold. Date: 17 May
1682.

Mentions: John Woodcock (Registrar, Land
Office).

Court Session: 1689

William Ward (g) exhibited bond of
Thomas Christian son of Lawrence
Christian (CE), to be transported by
Capt. William Pearce (sheriff, CE).
Securities: John Stoope, William Drake.
Also exhibited inventory
14:142   by appraisers John Stoop & Philip
Holledger.

5 April. Exhibited will of Edward
Mariarte (AA), proved, constituting his
widow Honor executrix. Said Honor is
Quaker. Said Honor was granted
administration. Capt. Henry Hanslap to
administer oath.

William Barton (g) exhibited oath of
John Bracher administrator of Hugh
Thomas, sworn 17 November last.
Securities: Charles Garrett, Alexander
Curre. Also exhibited oath of John
Courts & Cleborne Lomax, appraisers,
sworn same day.

Exhibited inventory of Richard Gardiner
(SM), by appraisers Capt. Joseph Piles
& James Bowling (g).

John Gardner administrator of Thomas
Rigge (CH) exhibited accounts.

6 April. James Thompson administrator
of Andrew Clarke (CH) exhibited
accounts. Continuance was granted.

Henry Costin administrator of George
Buxton (TA) exhibited accounts &
additional accounts.

Edward Sweatnam (KE) administrator of
John Abrahams was granted continuance.
Exhibited was will of said Abrahams,
constituting George Vinson (TA)
executor. Said Vinson has renounced
executorship. Date: 23 November 1688.
Witnesses: John Hynson, Chris. Goodhand.

Exhibited inventory of Thomas Rigge, by
appraisers John Clements & Francis
Adams.

Court Session: 1689

Edward Man exhibited that Mary Drumple
relict of James Drumple (TA) refused to
take the oath. Date: 6 April 1689.

Exhibited will of John Younger (TA),
proved before Edward Man (g). Also
exhibited inventory, by appraisers
Thomas Martin & Henry Alexander.

Exhibited inventory of William Hawton
(CH), by appraisers Ignatius Wheeler &
James Miller.

Exhibited accounts & additional accounts
on estate of Col. Philemon Lloyd (TA)
by Mr. Richard Bennit. Continuance was
granted.

14:143 Exhibited will of Nicholas White (SM),
proved before James Pattison (g). Also
exhibited oath of James Cullen executor
sworn 25 January last. Also exhibited
oath of Thomas Haddock & Thomas
Williams, appraisers, sworn same day.

8 April. William Holland for Joseph
Sanders & his wife Elisabeth relict of
John Troaton (TA) was granted
administration on his estate.
Appraisers: Richard Gover, Richard
Tucker. Thomas Tench (g) to administer
oath.

Richard Sweatnam exhibited will of
Edward Stevenson (TA), constituting John
Browne & his relict Letitea Stevenson
executors. George Robotham (g) to prove
said will. Said executors were granted
administration. Appraisers: Isaac
Winchester, Joseph Hacker. Said
Robotham to administer oath.

9 April. William Dent for William
Holland & his wife Margaret sole heiress
at law of Francis Holland (AA) exhibited
caveat.

Capt. Henry Hanslap exhibited oath of
Honor Durdon administratrix of John
Durdon (AA), sworn 8 March 1688. Said
Honor is a Quaker. Securities: Walter
Phelps, John Gray. Also exhibited

inventory.

Exhibited will of John Stimson (AA),
proved before Edward Burges (g). Also
exhibited oath of William Roper & Walter
Phelps, appraisers. Also exhibited
inventory.

Richard Galloway who married relict of
Benjamin Lawrence (AA) petitioned for
LoA on his estate. Date: 5 April 1689.
Thomas Knighton (g) to administer oath.

Edward Pindar (g, DO) was granted
administration on estate of Nathan Jones
(DO), on behalf of orphan (infant).
Appraisers: Philip Pitt, William Mishey.
Maj. Thomas Taylor to administer oath.

14:144 10 April. Daniel Longman administrator
of Richard Arnold (AA) exhibited
additional accounts.

Exhibited inventory of William Marshall
(CV), by appraisers John Sunderland &
George Cole.

Richard Bennett (g) for Henrietta Maria
Loyd administratrix of Edward Inman (TA)
petitioned for Col. Vincent Lowe to
examine accounts.

James Cranford exhibited will of Thomas
Crowder (CV), constituting his widow
Mary executrix. John Craycroft (g) to
prove said will. Said Mary was granted
administration. Appraisers: Edward
Isaake, Thomas Hinton. Said Craycroft
to administer oath.

Capt. Henry Hanslap to examine accounts
of:
• Joseph Chew & his wife Elisabeth
  executrix of Seaborne Battee (AA).
• James Pindle & his wife Elinor
  administratrix of Richard Cheyney
  (AA).

Exhibited inventory of William Edmonds
(CV), by appraisers John Willymot &
James Willymot.

Court Session: 1689

Capt. Richard Ladd exhibited will of Daniel Bloyd (CV), proved. Also exhibited oath of Richard Leake & his wife Frances executors. Also exhibited oath of Henry Mitchell & William Martin, appraisers.

Capt. Richard Ladd exhibited oath of Henry Mitchell administrator of Charles Parey (CV). Securities: John Hollins, Richard Leake. Also exhibited oath of John Hollins & Richard Leake, appraisers.

11 April. Priscilla widow of William Lisle (CV) was granted administration on his estate. Appraisers: Maj. Ninian Beale, John Chittam. George Lingan to administer oath.

Exhibited will of Thomas Ellis (CV), but no executor was named. Francis Collier (g) to prove said will. Dorothy the widow was granted administration. Appraisers: John Edmondson, John Chittam. Said Collier to administer oath.

Sarah relict & administratrix of John Evans (carpenter, CV) exhibited that appraisers Richard Fenwick & Charles Ashcom have refused to appraise said estate. New appraisers: Richard Keene, John Read.

14:145 13 April. Pocomoke, 21 January 1688/9. Petition of Jane Cooper (widow). Col. Vincent Lowe was granted administration on estate of Samuel Cooper (SO). Security: George Lafield. Appraisers: William Whittington, Francis Jenkins. Col. William Coleborne to administer oath.

15 April. Ann relict & administratrix of Richard Weaver (CV) exhibited accounts.

Rebecca relict of Timothy Pedan (SM) was granted administration on his estate. Appraisers: Joseph Semple, John Powell. Kenelm Cheseldyn (g) to administer oath.

Page 154

Court Session: 1689

Exhibited inventory of David Bloyd (CV),
by appraisers Henry Mitchell & William
Martin.

Exhibited inventory of Charles Parvey
(CV), by appraisers John Hollins &
Richard Leake.

16 April. Kenelm Cheseldyn (g)
exhibited oath of Rebecca Pedan
administratrix of Timothy Pedan (SM).
Securities: Joseph Sempille, John
Powell. Also exhibited oath of Joseph
Sempille & John Powell, appraisers.

William Dent procurator for Richard
Agambra son of Domindego Agambra vs.
Richard Isles. Said Isles married
Elisabeth relict of said Domindego. No
answer to libel. Ruling: former
administration was declared void.
Complainant was granted administration
on said estate. Exhibited was
inventory, by appraisers Cleborne Lomax
& Richard Jones.

Ann Dance relict of Denis Sullivant (SM)
exhibited that she could find no
security. James Pattison (g) to
administer oath to said Ann. Said Ann
is now wife of Thomas Dance (SM).
14:146 James Pattison exhibited that Ann
Sullivant could not obtain bond. Date:
27 February 1687.

William Dent procurator for Robert
Macklin son of Robert Macklin (TA,
dec'd) petitioned for the administration
bond of William Bishopp & Mathew Ward
who were administrators for the interest
of the orphan be assigned to him.
Ruling: granted.

Robert Carvile procurator for Mary,
Elisabeth, Ann, & Katherine Cooksey
orphans of Philip Cooksey vs. William
Dent procurator for Richard Brightwell &
Richard Southerne administrators of Mary
Truman. Ruling: surplus of said estate
to be "redouned" to next of kin.

Robert Carvile procurator for Stephen
Luff vs. Arnold Elzey administrator of
Charles Ballard. Ruling: Capt. William
Whittington & James Round (g) to make
division of estate.

John Mackdowell sole brother of Henry
Mackdowell vs. John Hambleton executor
of Elisabeth Mackdowell relict &
administratrix of said Henry. Ruling:
plaintiff to have administration dbn on
estate of said Henry. Defendant to pay
costs & charges. On 24 May, said John
was granted administration. Appraisers:
John Manning, Samuel Holdsworth. Capt.
Richard Ladd to administer oath.

Exhibited inventory of Timothy Pedan
(SM), by appraisers Joseph Sempille &
John Powell.

17 April. James Yore who married
Patience administratrix of Daniel
Clocker exhibited accounts. Continuance
was granted.

Henry Lowe (g) who married Susannah
relict & administratrix of John Darnall,
Esq. exhibited accounts. Continuance
was granted.

14:147   20 April. LoA to Richard Isles who
married Katherine relict of Domindigo
Agambra (CH) were revoked. Richard son
of said Domindigo was granted
administration. Appraisers: Thomas
Lewis, William Clarkson. John Addison
(g) to administer oath.

26 April. Exhibited inventory of Thomas
Pew (CV), by appraisers Joseph Edloe &
Andrew Abington.

2 May. William Elmes (CE) brother of
Thomas Elmes (TA) was granted
administration on his estate.
Appraisers: Henry Price, Nathaniel
Tucker. William Harris (KE) to
administer oath.

3 May. Lambert Wilmer petitioned for
payment of debt due Mr. Edward Halsey.

Court Session: 1689

Date: 29 April 1689. Oliver Bornewall to Mr. Butler (sheriff, TA) to take into his possession all items belonging to Edward Halsey (TA, dec'd).

6 May. Exhibited will of John Cobreath (CV), proved before John Craycroft (g). Also exhibited oath of William Meades guardian of John Cobreath executor. Also exhibited oath of John Sunderland & Abraham Clarke, appraisers. Also exhibited inventory.

John Craycroft (g) exhibited oath of Edward Isaake & Richard Sterling, appraisers of Francis Davis (CV). Also exhibited inventory. Also exhibited bond of Francis Billingsley & John Leach, Jr., administrators.

8 May. Exhibited inventory of Hugh Floyd (CV), by appraisers Thomas Hillary & John Sunderland. Also exhibited bond of Katherine relict & administratrix. Securities: John Sunderland, John Hance.

Francis Hutchins (g) exhibited oath of Daniel Sheredine administrator of William Keepe (CV). Securities: Jeremiah Sheredine, Edward Cowdery. Also exhibited oath of Hugh Ellis & James Seawall, appraisers. Also exhibited inventory.

Exhibited will of Human Barber (CV), proved before Francis Hutchins (g). Also exhibited oath of Joachim Kirkstead executor. Also exhibited oath of William Whittington & John Willymott, appraisers. Also exhibited inventory.

Francis Hutchins (g) exhibited oath of Elias Lowry administrator of Mary Lowry (CV). Securities: Henry Cox, William Howes. Also exhibited oath of William Nedham & John Willymott, appraisers.

14:148 Exhibited inventory of John Moffett (CV), by appraisers Thomas Hillary & Timothy. Seawell.

Court Session: 1689

Exhibited inventory of Frances Brookes
(TA), by appraisers John Scott &
Alexander Ray. Also exhibited accounts.

13 May. Exhibited inventory of Morgan
Pranch (SM), by appraisers Anthony Evans
& Zachariah Vansweringen.

14 May. Justinian Tennison, Sr.
administrator of Vincent Mansfeild &
administrator of Justinian Tennison, Jr.
exhibited accounts on both estates.

16 May. Capt. David Browne exhibited
accounts of Samuel Heyden administrator
of Somer Adams (SO).

Exhibited will of John Russell (CV),
proved before John Craycroft (g). Also
exhibited oath of Margarett relict &
administratrix. Sureties: Abraham
Clarke, John Bennet. Also exhibited
oath of Abraham Clarke & John Hunt,
appraisers. Also exhibited inventory.

18 May. Gilbert Clarke for Mrs.
Beaumont petitioned for LoA on estate of
her husband. Date: 29 April 1689. Mary
relict of Richard Beaumont (CH) was
granted administration on his estate.
Appraisers: Anthony Neale, Gilbert
Clarke. Capt. Humphry Warren to
administer oath.

21 May. Exhibited inventory of Martha
Pennock (CV), by appraisers Joseph Edloe
& Andrew Abington.

23 May. Robert Carvile (g) exhibited
oath of Thomas Guither administrator of
Morgan Pranch (SM). Securities: William
Guither, Anthony Evans. Also exhibited
oath of Anthony Evans & Zachariah
Vansweringen, appraisers.

Exhibited inventory of Capt. Justinian
Gerard (SM), by appraisers Richard
Clouds & Samuel Cooksey.

Elisabeth Lillington (BA), now wife of
John Lillington, exhibited that she
remarried shortly after the death of her

former husband John Taylor (BA) &
petitioned for LoA. Appraisers: John
Hall, James Maxfeild. Mr. Thomas Staly
to administer oath. Date: 6 May 1689.
Said Elisabeth was granted
administration. Appraisers: William
Westbury, Nicholas Rogier. Mr. Francis
Watkins to administer oath.

14:149   24 May. Elisabeth Lillington relict of
John Taylor (BA) was granted
administration on his estate.
Appraisers: William Westbury, Nicholas
Rogier. Francis Watkins (g) to
administer oath.

Johanna Legg petitioned for LoA on
estate of her husband, who left no real
estate. She is a poor widow with 3
children. Date: 25 April 1689 at KI.
Said Johanna was granted administration
on estate of William Legg (KE).
Appraisers: Alexander Walters, Lewis
Meredith. Christopher Goodhand (g) to
administer oath.

Exhibited will of William Rhamsey (AA),
constituting his widow Pretiosia
executrix. Capt. Henry Hanslap to
administer oath.

Exhibited will of Thomas Bloyce (SO),
but no executor was named & only 2
witnesses. Maj. William Brereton to
prove said will. William Wright was
granted administration. Appraisers:
Richard Whittey, George Betts. Said
Brereton to administer oath.

Exhibited will of Allan Smith (KE),
constituting his widow Mary executrix,
now wife of John Copedge. Said Mary was
granted administration. Appraisers:
Michael Miller, Richard Jones.
Christopher Goodhand (g) to administer
oath.

Edward Boothby letter to Mr. Cheseldyn.
Exhibited will of James Philipps (BA),
constituting his son James executor.
Capt. Henry Johnson to prove said will.
Said son was granted administration.

Court Session: 1689

Appraisers: William Osborne, John Hall. Said Johnson to administer oath.

Rando. Brandt petitioned for LoA for Joseph Churnell on the estate of Francis Masson (sojourner at house of said Churnell, CH). Date: ultimate April 1689. Said Joseph Curnell was granted administration. Appraisers: Robert Yates, Richard Land. John Courts (g, CH) to administer oath.

14:150 Petition that Nathaniel Howell, guardian of Sarah Vanheck orphan, is dec'd & greatly indebted. Said Nathaniel's widow had the orphan's estate appraised with that of said Nathaniel. Said widow is not married to Richard Kenard. Col. St. Leger Codd (president of Court in CE) is unwilling to act without direction. Signed: Mary Pope. Date: 16 March 1688/9. Letter to said Codd. Date: 2 April 1689. Regarding estate of Sarah daughter of John Vanheck (CE, dec'd). Mentions: Capt. Pearce, Mrs. Mary Pope, Mr. Stiles. Date: 24 May 1689.

25 May. George Robotham (g) exhibited oath of Arthur Purserell administrator of John Boyden (TA), sworn 2 February last. Securities: Thomas Bruff, Thomas Loggins. Also exhibited oath of Thomas Herman & Gerald Vessialls, appraisers, sworn same day. Also exhibited inventory.

Exhibited inventory of Nicholas Nicholson (AA), by appraisers John Elsey & John Miles. Also exhibited bond of Hester Nicholson administratrix. Securities: John Larkin, John Martin.

28 May. Capt. Henry Hanslapp exhibited oath of Mary Sarson administratrix of Edward Sarson (AA), sworn 23 April last. Securities: James Hackett, James Parnell. Also exhibited oath of James Sanders & James Hackett, appraisers, sworn same day.

14:151 Exhibited will of Mary Shaw (South River, AA), constituting John Gresham executor. Maj. Nicholas Gassaway to prove said will. Said Gresham was granted administration. Said Gassaway to administer oath.

31 May. Exhibited will of William Goodale (AA), constituting his widow Ruth executrix. Said Ruth is also dec'd. Capt. Henry Hanslapp to prove said will. Thomas Lineycomb was granted administration, as greatest creditor. Said Hanslapp to administer oath.

1 June. Katherine relict of William Sergeson (SM) exhibited accounts. Lewis Jones married said Katherine & possessed themselves of the estate, depriving the creditors & orphans. Sheriff (SM) to summon said Lewis & Katherine to Court last October. Said Lewis was not to be found. Said Katherine appeared & was charged to render accounts. Inventory of said Sergeson listed.

4 June. Exhibited inventory of Mathew Cartwright (SM), by appraisers Thomas Carvile & John Nichols.

William Dent exhibited will of John Posey (CH), constituting his widow Susanna executrix. Only 1 witness is alive. Said Susanna was granted administration. Appraisers: William Marshall, Edward Phillpott. Capt. Ignatius Causeene (CH) to administer oath.

14:152 Justinian Tennison, Sr. administrator of Vincent Mansfeild & administrator of Justinian Tennison, Jr. exhibited additional accounts, proved. Continuance was granted.

6 June. Exhibited will of John Moffett (CV), proved before George Lingan (g) on 16 March last. Also exhibited oath of Thomas Hillary & Timothy Seawell, appraisers.

Court Session: 1689

Exhibited inventory of William Rout (CV), by appraisers Thomas Greenfeild & Charles Beavan.

10 June. James Pattison (g) exhibited oath of Thomas Griffin administrator of Thomas Griffin (SM), sworn 19 February last. Securities: William Guither, Elias Beech. Also exhibited oath of William Guither & Elias Beech, appraisers, sworn same day.

Exhibited inventory of George Goer (CH), by appraisers Cleborne Lomax & William Thompson.

12 June. Anthony Underwood petitioned for LoA for Richard Sweatnam administrator of Thomas Browne (bricklayer, TA), as chief creditor. Date: 11 June 1689. Said Sweatnam was granted administration. Appraisers: John Booker, John Whittington. Edward Man to administer oath.

13 June. Exhibited will of Joseph Isaake (CV), proved before Francis Collier (g). Also exhibited inventory, by appraisers Ninean Beall & Joseph Dacres.

Exhibited inventory of William Shaw (CV), by appraisers John Gale & Michael Ball. Also exhibited bond of George Hawes administrator. Securities: James Veitch, Edward Fenwick.

Exhibited inventory of William Smith (CV), by appraisers Ninian Beall & James Moore. Also exhibited bond of Simon Nichols administrator. Securities: James Moore, Edward Phenex.

Exhibited will of John Morgan (TA), constituting Thomas Collins executor. Said Morgan hanged himself.

14 June. Walter Emerton son of Jane Emerton (AA) was granted administration on her estate. Appraisers: Richard Wells, William Holland. Thomas Knighton (g) to administer oath.

Court Session: 1689

Edward Talbot for Elisabeth Hall relict & executrix of Richard Hall (carpenter, CV) was granted administration on his estate. Appraisers: Maj. Ninian Beall, George Cole. George Lingan (g) to administer oath.

14:153 Edward Talbot for Mathew son of Mathew Seley (AA) was granted administration on his estate. Appraisers: Robert Lockwood, John Walters. Thomas Knighton (g) to administer oath.

Dorothy relict of William Rogers (TA) was granted administration on his estate. Appraisers: William Sparkes, (N). George Robotham (g) to administer oath.

Ann relict of William Obrey (CV) was granted administration on his estate. Appraisers: James Drinkwater, William Barton. Capt. Richard Ladd to administer oath.

16 June. John Addison exhibited oath of Richard Agambra administrator of Domindigo Agambra, sworn on 9 May last. Securities: Mr. Philip Mason, George Athey. Also exhibited oath of Thomas Lewis & William Clarkson, appraisers, sworn same day.

17 June. Capt. Henry Hanslapp exhibited oath of Honor Durden (Quaker) administratrix of John Durden (AA), affirmed on 8 March 1688.

Capt. Henry Hanslapp exhibited bond of Honor Mercarte executrix of Edward Mercarte (AA), sworn 17 May. Securities: Joseph Williams, John Beet.

Thomas Hix administrator of Edward Haman (KE) exhibited accounts.

Exhibited inventory of Edward Serson (AA), by appraisers James Sanders & James Hackett.

Gabriell Parrott petitioned for LoA on estate of James Powell (AA), per will of

Page 163

Court Session: 1689

Sarah Powell widow of said James Date:
25 May 1689. Said Parrott was granted
administration. Appraisers: Benjamin
Williams, John Powell. Capt. Henry
Hanslapp to administer oath.

12 November 1688. William Turner was
granted administration on estate of
James Stritch (CV). Appraisers: Thomas
Hughes, William Needham. Francis
Hutchins (g) to administer oath.

14:154 19 June. Exhibited inventory of
Domindigo Agambra (CH), by appraisers
Thomas Lewis & William Clarkson.

Richard Clarke petitioned that the
balance of the estate of Arthur Ludford
to be paid to the orphans is not
correct. the 1/3rd due to Elisabeth
Hickman (alias Elisabeth Brayne) rec'd
by Thomas Brayne, was embezzled by said
Brayne. Said Clarke & Joseph Fry
administrators of said Brayne will be
allowed same.

22 June. Exhibited bond of Dorothy
relict & administratrix of Thomas Ellis
(CV). Securities: John Chittam, Robert
Edmondson. Will was proved by 2
witnesses before Francis Collier (g);
other one is dec'd. Also exhibited
inventory, by appraisers Robert
Edmondson & John Chittam.

Exhibited accounts & additional accounts
of estate of Col. Philemon Loyd (TA).

24 June. Exhibited will of Bartholomew
Ennalls (DO), proved before John Brooke
(g). Said Brooke exhibited oath of
Mary, Thomas, William, & Joseph Ennalls
executors, sworn 14 January last. Also
exhibited oath of Charles Hutchins &
John Woodward, appraisers.

25 June. Thomas Wall for Elisabeth
widow of Lawrence Woodnite (DO) was
granted administration on his estate.
Appraisers: William Dorsey, William
Mishew. John Woodward (g) to administer
oath.

Page 164

Court Session: 1689

Thomas Wall who married Jane relict of
John Walker (DO) was granted
administration on his estate.
Appraisers: Thomas Skinner, John Ford.
John Woodward (g) to administer oath.

28 June. Samuel Young & his wife Mary
administratrix of Maj. Thomas Francis
(AA) exhibited accounts, proved before
Capt. Richard Hill.

Henry Constable & his wife Katherine
executrix of James Rigbie (AA) exhibited
additional accounts, proved before Capt.
Hill.

Exhibited will of Michael Basey (DO),
proved before John Brooke (g). Also
exhibited oath of Jane Basey executrix,
sworn 16 February last. Also exhibited
oath of Richard Willhouse & Edward
Newton, appraisers, sworn same day.

Randolph Hanson (g) exhibited oath of
William Mosse administrator of John
Clarke (CH), sworn 17 April last.
Securities: Edward Rookwood, William
Spikman. Also exhibited oath of Edward
Rookwood & William Spikman, appraisers,
sworn same day.
14:155 William Moss petitioned that he has not
as yet obtained the goods & chattels.
Date: 1 June 1689. Continuance was
granted.

3 July. Letter to Capt. William
Whittington & James Round (g, SO).
Regarding: Anthony Underwood procurator
for Stephen Luffe vs. Arnold Elzey
administrator of Charles Ballard. Date:
20 November 1686. Said Elzey was
summoned several times to render
accounts. Judges ordered said Elzey to
pay said Luffe the 1/3 portion of
appraisal made by David Browne & Roger
Woolford on 10 March 1682. Mentions:
Sarah wife of said Luffe & widow of said
Ballard. Said Whittington & ROund to
executor order.

Ro. Carvile petitioned for copy of libel
of William Meares vs. William Holland

Page 165

(now of AA) & ux & copy of will of
Francis Holland & copy of grounds for
which Joseph Chew had administration on
said estate.

William Coale who married Elisabeth
Skipwith widow of George Skipwith (AA)
was granted administration on his
estate. Will of said George was proved
by 2 witnesses in 1684; 3rd witness
refused to take oath. Said Coale
married said Elisabeth since then.
Appraisers: John Scott, Thomas Tench.
Thomas Knighton (g) to administer oath.

Sarah relict of Richard Bancks (CH) was
granted administration on his estate.
Henry Hawkins (g) to administer oath.

14:156   James Ellis petitioned for LoA on estate
of Henry Welsh. Date: 9 April 1689.
Exhibited will of Henry Welsh. Date: 26
March 1689. Legatee: my brother's son
John. Witnesses: Alex. Chapple, Ellinor
Waren, Sarah Radford. Said Ellis was
granted administration, for said John
(infant). Appraisers: John Chapple,
Thomas Hughes. Thomas Knighton (g) to
administer oath.

4 July. Exhibited will of William
Rhamsey (AA), proved before Henry
Hanslap. Also exhibited oath of
Pretiosa executrix, sworn 20 June last.
Also exhibited oath of James Sanders &
Abel Browne, appraisers, sworn same day.
Also exhibited inventory.

Capt. Henry Hanslap exhibited oath of
James Sanders & Abel Browne, appraisers
of William Goodale (AA), sworn 11 June
last. Also exhibited that Thomas
Lincycomb (Quaker) administrator refused
to take oath. Securities: James
Sanders, Abel Browne. Also exhibited
inventory.

John Boring (g, BA) exhibited oath of
William Cole administrator of David
Adams (BA), sworn 7 December last.
Securities: Christopher Gist, Richard
Cromwell. Also exhibited oath of John

Court Session: 1689

Arden & Edward Mountfort, appraisers.
Also exhibited inventory.

Exhibited will of Richard Tydings (AA),
made on 2 February 1687, constituting
his daughter Charity executrix. Capt.
Henry Hanslap to prove said will. Said
Charity has since married John Jorden.
She is not of age. Said John was
granted administration. Said Hanslap to
administer oath.

6 July. Francis Watkins (g) to examine
accounts of George Ashman & his wife
Elisabeth executrix of William Cromwell
(BA).

Thomas Long petitioned for LoA for John
Hails on estate of John Winley (BA).
Date: 1 July 1689. Said Hails was
granted administration.
14:157 Appraisers: Lewis Barton, John Robinson.
Mr. Francis Watkins to administer oath.

10 July. Exhibited inventory of Thomas
Scott (DO), by appraisers Charles Powell
& Henry Willomott.

Grace Boone relict of John Boone
(Clifts, CV) was granted administration
on his estate. Appraisers: Francis
Freeman, William Drumple. Capt.
Richard Ladd to administer oath.

11 July. Exhibited inventory of Ellinor
Waller (DO), by appraisers Michael Basey
& Obediah King.

Exhibited inventory of Nicholas White
(SM), by appraisers Thomas Williams &
Thomas Haddock.

Exhibited will of John Salisbury (DO),
constituting James Peterkin & Edward
White executors. John Brooke (g) to
prove said will. Said Peterkin & White
were granted administration.
Appraisers: Obediah King, Richard Adams.
Said Brooke to administer oath.

13 July. Exhibited will of Thomas
Crowder (CV), proved before John

Page 167

Court Session: 1689

Craycroft (g). Also exhibited oath of Mary Crowder executrix. Also exhibited oath of Edward Isacke & Thomas Hinton, appraisers. Also exhibited inventory.

George Plowden administrator of Robert Thompson (CV) exhibited inventory, by appraisers Thomas Gant & Walter Smith.

Letter from Charles Lord Baltimore. Date: 23 July 1688. Direction to officers regarding Quakers, many being desirous of settling in MD.

14:274 [This folio is on the reverse side of folio 157, and is upside down. This folio is not on the microfilm.]

Inventory of John Hodgson (CE). Date: 18 October 1700. Amount: £1.0.0. Appraisers: Humphry Tilton, Robert Gibson. Executor: Thomas Reason.

Inventory of John Bromfeild (CE). Date: 19 October 1700. Amount: £10.5.6. Appraisers: Humphry Tilton, Edward Ayers.

Court Session: 1692

14A:1 14 June. John Tyrling (SM) son of John Tyrling (SM) was granted administration on his estate. Sureties: Capt. John Coor, Mr. William Taylard. Appraisers: Thomas Carvile, Edward Tipton. Mr. John Bearecroft to administer oath.

30 June. John Anderson (mariner & master of Releife, New Castle) & Joseph Greene (merchant, TA) exhibited that Michael Taylor, Jr. & Lancelott Smith factors for Michael Taylor (merchant, New Castle, ENG) are dec'd. Said Anderson & Greene were granted administration. Appraisers: Edward Pollard, Thomas Delahay. Edward Mann (g, TA) to administer oath.

13 July. Ann Watts widow of Peter Watts (SM) exhibited his will, constituting her executrix. Said will to be proved by oaths of Robert Ferguson, William

Court Session: 1692

Thomas, & Peter Watts (witnesses). Said
Ann was granted administration. Kenelme
Cheseldyne (SM) to administer oath.

29 July. Exhibited will of Michael
Taney (CV), proved by Joachim Kiestead,
George Young, & William Staring (?).
DateL 21 June 1692.
14A:2   Signed: Henry Fernley (clerk, CV).

Thomas Jones son of Robert Jones (St.
George's Hundred, SM) exhibited his
will, but no executor was named,
witnessed by Joseph Waters, Francis
Cole, John Cheverill. Said Thomas was
granted administration. Appraisers:
John Cheverill, Joseph Walters.

Sheriff (SM) to summon Thomas Courtney &
his wife Eleanor to answer libel of
Philip Cocks & his wife Sarah
administratrix of John Johnson (SM).

6 August. Mary Reniger widow of Samuel
Reniger (AA) exhibited his will,
constituting her executrix, witnessed by
George Fipps, Isabell Capell, & John
Meriton. Said Mary was granted
administration. Appraisers: Robert
Lockwood, Benjamin Capell.

23 August. Exhibited inventory of
Anthony Underwood (SM), by appraisers
Garret Vansweringen & Henry Denton.

John Bearecroft (g) exhibited oath of
Thomas Carvile & Edward Tipton,
appraisers of John Tyrling.

14A:3   Lionel Copley, Esq. (Commissary General
& Chief Judge) to Nicholas Greenbury
(AA). Appointment as Deputy Commissary
in AA. Date: 9 August 1692. cc: Mr.
Charles James (CE), Mr. Elias King
(KE), Maj. William Finney (TA), Dr.
John Brooke (DO), Mr. Francis Jenkins
(SO) & Mr. Samuel Hopkins (SO), Col.
Nehemiah Blakiston (SM).

1 September. Exhibited inventory of
James Yore (SM), by appraisers Thomas
Grunwin & Richard Benton.

Court Session: 1692

3 September. Exhibited inventory of Robert Jones (SM), by appraisers John Cheverill & Joseph Walters.

Sheriff (AA) to summon Nathaniel Heathcott (g, AA) administrator of Elisabeth Brewer to answer complaint of William Brewer.

14A:4 Sheriff (CH) to summon Edward Pye (CH) to answer complaint of Roger Brooke & his wife Mary executrix of Winifred Mullett.

6 September. Exhibited inventory of John Tyrling (clerk, SM), by appraisers Thomas Carvile & Edward Tipton.

10 September. Edward Pye vs. estate of Thomas Toft (CH). Caveat exhibited. cc: John Llewellin.

19 September. John Baptista Carbery (g, SM) who married Elisabeth relict & administratrix of Cuthbert Scott (SM) exhibited that she is now dec'd, not having fully administered said estate. Said Carbery was granted administration dbn on estate of said Scott. Said Carbery was granted administration on estate of said Elisabeth. Surety: Charles Carroll (SM). Appraisers: William Rosewell, Stephen Goff. Mr. Richard Clouds (SM) to administer oath.

Petition to Mr. John Llewellin by Ann Medley, wife of William Medley, for LoA on estate of George Reynolds.

Elias King (KE) petitioned for Hester Benton widow of Mark Benton (KI) for LoA on his estate. Date: 15 September 1692 at Yarmouth, KE. Said Hester was granted administration. Appraisers: Lewis Meredith, John Doynes.

3 October. John Copedge (KE) exhibited oath of Ann Barnes executrix of Francis Barnes (KE), sworn 29 July 1692. Sureties: Henry Carter, Ann Downes. Also exhibited oath of Walter Kerby & John Downes, appraisers. Also exhibited

Page 170

inventory.

14A:5   Exhibited inventory of Michael Taney (CV).

Exhibited additional inventory of John Tyrling (SM).

7 October. Edward Jones (CE) was summoned to answer libel of Garrat Murray & his wife Susannah, only surviving issue of William Brockus (CE).

17 October. Appointment of Nehemiah Blakiston, Esq. as Commissary General & Chief Judge. Signed: L. Copley.

14A:6   Thomas Williams (taylor, SM) & his wife Elisabeth daughter of Elisabeth D'Costa (SM, dec'd) exhibited that William Hall (chirurgeon, CH) & his wife Mary, witnesses to will of said Elisabeth, live far distant from the Office. Maj. James Smallwood (CH) to administer oath to them.

22 October. John Hynson (KE) one of executors of Joseph Wicks (KE) exhibited that he & Mr. Robert Burman were constituted executors of said will. Said Burman refused to take oath as executor. Ruling: said Hynson was granted sole administration. Mentions: Mrs. Anne Wicks widow. Appraisers: Hanse Hanson, Thomas Smith. Mr. Elias King to administer oath.

Memorandum: with the Revolution, county courts for probate were established. County clerks are to transmit transcripts to SM.

Mr. James Browne (Glasgow, Scotland) exhibited PoA from Mr. William Arbuckle (merchant, Glasgow, Scotland) brother & heir of Robert Arbuckle (merchant, MD, dec'd). Said Browne was granted administration on said estate, for said William.

14A:7   Exhibited inventory of Tobias Mills (CV).

Philip Cox & his wife Sarah widow of
John Johnson (SM) one of legatees of
Fobbe Roberts (who has not been heard of
for 20 years) petitioned. Said Cox
married the widow & maintained the
orphan of the dec'd. Thomas Courtney
who married Elleanor niece of said
Roberts in opposition to said petition
by said Cox, alleged to have received
several letters written within the last
8/9 years. Said Courtney could not find
said letters, except for one dated 8
September 1675, which was exhibited.
Witnesses to the will of said Roberts
are dec'd. The letter & the will were
examined by Mr. Robert Carvile, Mr.
William Taylard, John Llewellin, & said
Courtney & judged to be written by the
same hand. Said Thomas & Elleanor were
granted administration on estate of said
Roberts.

29 October. Sheriff (KE) to summon John
Hinson one of executors of Maj. Joseph
Wicks to answer libel of Mr. Robert
Burman another executor of said Wicks.

31 October. Sheriff (CH) to summon Col.
Edward Pye administrator of Col.
Benjamin Rozer to render accounts.

Mordecai Moore (AA) & his wife Ursula
executrix of Col. William Burges
executor of Nicholas Painter who married
Judith Parker (alias Judith Cumber)
executrix of John Cumber to answer
complaint of John Cumber grandchild &
legatee of said John Cumber (dec'd).

5 November. John Taunt (SM)
brother-in-law to John Blomfield (SM)
was granted administration on his
estate, in right of orphans. Sureties:
Stephen Gough, William Husbands.
Appraisers: Philip Clark, John Heard.

8 November. Exhibited will of Joseph
Pile (SM), proved by William Langworth,
Robert Mastin, & Philip Briscoe (3 of
witnesses).
14A:8   Anthony Neale & Thomas Turner executors
were granted administration. Surety:

William Langworth. Appraisers: William
Rosewell, Thomas Clark. Mr. John
Bearecroft to administer oath.

10 November. Sheriff (CH) to summon
William Serjeant & his wife Damoras
executrix of John Ward to answer
complaint of Edward Milstead & his wife
Elisabeth one of daughters of said Ward.

Sheriff (CH) to summon Edward Pye (g,
CH) to answer complaint of Roger Brooke
& his wife Mary executrix of Winifred
Mullett.

Mr. John Bearecroft exhibited oath of
William Rosewell & Thomas Clark,
appraisers of Joseph Pile (g).

24 November. Anne Medley wife of George
Medley (SM) & sister to George Reynolds
(SM) has managed said Reynold's estate.
Her husband has been, for several years,
"a person frantick & of unsound mind".
Said Anne was granted administration on
estate of said Reynolds. Sureties (SM):
Richard Burkett, John Baily.
Appraisers: Stephen Gough, Thomas
Kirkley.

Upon examination of inventory of Michael
Taney, certain items are to excluded, as
belonging to the widow. Date: 14
October 1692.

Thomas Tench, Esq. (AA) petitioned for
LoA on estate of George Hawes (merchant,
CV), as principle creditor. Date: 29
October 1692. Said Tench was granted
administration. Appraisers (CV): Thomas
Tasker, Thomas Greenfield. Thomas
Brooke, Esq. to administer oath.

2 December. At the request of John
Llewellin on behalf of Martha Ridgely
daughter & one of the orphans of Robert
Ridgely (dec'd) to whom he is godfather,
Charles Carroll (g, SM) administrator of
Anthony Underwood & his wife Martha
executrix of said Ridgely moved that
according to her father's will, she
14A:9   be educated as a Protestant. She is now

Court Session: 1692

placed in School of Romish Religion.
Ruling: orphan to be placed with her
aunt Mrs. Sarah Clagett until she come
of age to choose her guardian.

Mr. George Plater procurator for Philip
Cox who married Sarah widow of John
Johnson (SM) petitioned for LoA on
estate of said Johnson. Also Thomas
Courtney & his wife Eleanor to be
summoned on LoA on estate of Fobbe
Roberts. If they do not reply,
administration on estate of said Roberts
will be granted to said Philip Cox & his
wife as next-of-kin.

Sheriff (CH) exhibited that Col. Edward
Pye responded to neither summons to
answer complaints of Roger Brooke & his
wife executrix of Winifred Mullett & to
render accounts on estate of Col.
Benjamin Rozer. New summons issued.

Thomas Griffin administrator of Thomas
Griffin was granted continuance.

Robert Cooper (SM) who married Patience
widow of James Yore & widow of Daniel
Clocker petitioned for LoA on estate of
said Clocker.

Mr. Robert Carvile summoned to answer
complaint of Daniel Moy son & legatee of
Richard Moy. New summons issued.

John Watson (SM) & Philip Clark (SM)
administrators of Robert Graham (SM)
were granted continuance. Mr. George
Plater was appointed procurator for
orphan, in lieu of Mr. Robert Carvile.

Robert Cooper & his wife Patience were
granted administration dbn on estate of
Daniel Clocker, unadministered by James
Yore.

Philip Lynes (SM) was granted
administration on estate of Patrick
Connelly (SM), as greatest creditor.

Said Lynes exhibited complaint that he
had LoA on estate of James Yore & that

Court Session: 1692

14A:10 Patience widow conceals all of the estate as belonging to her former husband Daniel Clocker. Said Patience summoned.

John Vowles (CH) who married sister & heiress of Cuthbert Scott (SM) exhibited that John Baptista Carbery has married widow of said Scott, & said widow is since dec'd. Said Carbery has LoA on estate of said Scott & said LoA were illegally obtained. Said Carberry summoned to show cause why LoA should not be revoked.

Elisabeth Mattox relict & administratrix of John Mitchell & of Henry Mattox exhibited accounts, which intermixed both estates.

Philip Lynes (SM) administrator of William Hawton summoned to render accounts, alleges that accounts were tendered. A copy to be produced for the next court.

3 December. Clerk (CH) exhibited transcript of all probate actions.

Clerk (SM) exhibited transcript of all probate actions.

Clerk (KE) exhibited transcript of all probate actions.

Edward Morgan (SM) executor of John Evans (SM) exhibited inventory, by appraisers John Cambell & William Husbands. Also exhibited accounts.

Philip Clark procurator for Robert Burman one of executors of Joseph Wicks (KE) vs. George Plater attorney for John Hinson one of executor of Joseph Wicks (KE). Libel exhibited. Answer exhibited.

14A:11 Philip Clark exhibited that said Wicks made will on 26 March 1688, constituting Mr. Josias Lanham, Mr. John Hynson, & complainant executors, empowering any 2 of them. Said Lanham died soon after said Wicks. Complainant proved said

will & accepted executorship. Said
Hinson "has falsely & deceitfully
suggested that the complainant renounced
executorship & has surreptitiously
obtained executorship". George Plater
exhibited that said Burman renounced
executorship before Mr. Elias King.
Mentions: orphans. Said Burman is no
relation to the orphans, as Burman
married a daughter of the relict by her
former husband. Defendant is an uncle
to orphans. Ruling:

14A:12 joint executorship. Said Burman is to
be guardian of Samuel Wicks (youngest
son). Elias King (g) to administer oath
to widow & other persons.

George Plater for Mordecai Moore (AA)
exhibited that John Cumber grandchild &
legatee of John Cumber (dec'd) had sued
said Moore & his wife Ursula executrix
of Col. William Burges executor of
Nicholas Painter who married Judith
Parker (alias Judith Cumber) executrix
of said John Cumber. Said Moore
appeared & said Cumber did not appear.
Ruling: dismissed.

John Llewellin (SM) exhibited that
George Askin orphan son of John Askin
(SM, dec'd) & Bryan Daly orphan son of
Bryan Daly (SM, dec'd) had been
committed to care of said Llewellin.
Estate of said orphans is in hands of
John Simmonds who married Rebeccah
relict of said dec'ds & mother of said
orphans. Said Simmonds has not
relinquished estate. Furthermore, said
George has privately departed house of
said Llewellin & is harbored by Thomas
Courtney (SM) without consent of said
Llewellin. Ruling: for said Llewellin.

Clerk (SO) exhibited transcript of all
probate actions, for MM Francis Jenkins
& Samuel Hopkins.

Clerk (CE) exhibited transcript of all
probate actions.

Philip Cox (SM) who married Sarah widow
of John Johnson (SM) was granted

administration on his estate. Security:
Thomas Batson. Appraisers: Robert
Taylor, Richard Wise.

14A:13 3 December. List of executors &
administrators due to render accounts.

St. Mary's Co.:
- John Bullock executor of Thomas
  Oakely.
- James Swann administrator of William
  Ninyfinger.
- Thomas Orman & wife executrix of
  John Tong.
- Kath. Obryan administratrix of Bryan
  Obryan.
- Elisabeth Brimmer administratrix of
  James Brimmer.
- John VanReswick & his wife
  administratrix of Christopher
  Goodson.
- Michael Curtis & his wife executrix
  of Just. Gerard.
- Thomas Gwither administrator of
  Morgan Prance.
- James Cullen executor of Nicholas
  White.
- Elisabeth Portwood administratrix of
  John Portwood.
- Francis Greene & Thomas Clark
  executors of Leonard Green.
- James Browne & wife administratrix
  of Thomas Pue.
- Thomas Griffin administrator of
  Thomas Griffin.
- Thomas Courtney & his wife
  administratrix of Fobbe Roberts ats:
  of Philip Cox & wife legatee of John
  Johnson.
- John Baptista Carberry having
  obtained LoA dbn on estate of
  Cuthbert Scott at complaint of John
  Bowles & his wife heiress of said
  Scott.
- Thomas Orrel & his wife & Thomas
  Carvile & his wife to answer libel
  of John Tyrling administrator of
  John Tyrling.
- Thomas Waughob administrator of
  Robert Graham.
- Robert Cooper & his wife Patience at
  complaint of Philip Lynes,

concerning estate of James Yore.
- Charles Carroll administrator of his wife Martha executrix of Robert Ridgely & of Anthony Underwood.
- Edward Morgan administrator of John Evans.
- John Watson & Philip Clark to answer to orphans of Robert Graham.
- Philip Lynes administrator of William Hawton.
- William Moss administrator of John Clark.

Baltimore Co.:
- William Cave administrator of John Dimond.
- William Cole administrator of David Adams.
- Elisabeth Edwards executrix of Richard Edwards.
- Mary Pottel administratrix of Francis Pottel.
- Jenkin Griffith administrator of James Collier.
- Michael Hastings administrator of Francis Pettit.
- Mary Reeve executrix of Edward Reeve.
- Richard Askue administrator of John Hammond.
- Said Richard Askue administrator of Samuel Brand.

Charles Co.:
- Philip Hoskins & his wife administratrix of Margaret Lemaire.
- John Godshall administrator of Mary Weyman.
- Robert Thompson, Jr. administrator of Thomas Elwes.
- Ann Burford executrix of Thomas Burford.
- John Bracker administrator of Hugh Thomas.
- Humphrey Warren executor of Robert Thompson.
- Robert Benson administrator of John Francis.
- Richard Isles administrator of Domindigo Agambra.
- Ann Slade administratrix of George Gore.

Court Session: 1692

- Edward Pye administrator of Col. Benjamin Rozer.
- Said Edward Pye to answer complaint of Roger Brooke & his wife executrix of Winifred Mullett.
- William Serjeant & his wife executrix of John Ward to answer libel of Edward Milstead & wife one of daughters of said Ward.

Anne Arundel Co.:
- Edward & John Dorsey executors of Joshua Dorsey.
- John Marriot executor of John Acton.
- Christian Wheeler administratrix of John Wheeler.
- Eleanor Chiney administratrix of Richard Chiney.
- Mary Giles administratrix of John Giles.
- John Howard & his wife administratrix of John Maccubin.
- Thomas Tench, Esq. administrator of William Marshall.
- John Pettibone administrator of Thomas Pettibone.
- Jane Ferguson administratrix of William Ferguson.
- Edward Selby, John Cross, & James Haggat executors of Edward Selby.
- Nicholas Nicholson administrator of John Baker.
- Elisabeth Vassine administratrix of Francis Vassine.
- Walter Phelps administrator of George Benson.
- Susanna Sewick executrix of John Sewick.
- Thomas Longman administrator of John Longman.
- Rachel Stimpson (alias Rachel Proctor) executrix of John Stimpson.
- William Freeman administrator of Thomas Bowles.
- Esther Nicholson administratrix of Nicholas Nicholson.
- Samuel Thomas administrator of Sarah Thomas.
- Joseph Chew & his wife Margaret administratrix of Francis Holland.
- Honor Durdan administratrix of John Durdan.

- Jane Pattison executrix of Thomas Pattison.
- Samuel Young & his wife administratrix of Thomas Francis.
- Richard Baily administrator of Mark Johnson.
- Patrick Murphy & wife administratrix of John Gray.

Cecil Co.:
- Sarah Meekes executrix of Walter Meekes.
- Thomas Bostick executor of Thomas Bostick.
- Martha Gibson executrix of William O'Derry.
- Mary Howel executrix of Nathaniel Howell.
- Olley Ollison administrator of Peter Ollison.
- James Wilson administrator of William Jones.
- Thomas Webb administrator of Nicholas Jones.
- Philip Kennard administrator of Thomas Williams.
- Elisabeth Yerberry executrix of Thomas Yerberry.
- Thomas Christian administrator of Lawrence Christian.

14A:14 Calvert Co.:
- John Holloway & wife executrix of Samuel Vines.
- Hugh Montgomery & wife executrix of George Parker.
- Sarah Winfen administratrix of Jonas Winfen.
- Hugh Ellis administrator of Thomas Cosden.
- Benjamin Evans & wife administratrix of William Rout.
- Francis Collins & wife administratrix of John Evans.
- Rebeccah Finch administratrix of Guy Finch.
- Margaret Moore administratrix of William Moore.
- Sarah Waring et. al. executors of Basil Waring.
- Henry Mitchell administrator of Charles Parvy.

Court Session: 1692

- Richard Leeke executor of David Bloyd.
- Nicholas Sewall executor of Martha Pennick.
- Darby Sullivan executor of John Dew.
- Thomas Johnson & wife administratrix of Roger Baker.
- Margaret Isaacks executrix of Joseph Isaacks.
- Francis Billingsley & John Leach administrators of Francis Davis.
- Elias Lowry administrator of Henry Lowry.
- Daniel Sheridin administrator of William Keepe.
- Simon Nichols administrator of William Smith.
- William Meads executor of John Cobreath.
- Joseph Edloe administrator of Peter Pheppard.
- William Howes administrator of William Edwards.
- George Hawes administrator of William Shaw.
- Katherine Lloyd administratrix of Hugh Lloyd.
- Andrew Tanyhill & Elisha Hall executors of John Muffet.
- Ann Green executrix of Thomas Greene.

Kent Co.:
- Thomas Parker administrator of James Parker.
- William Harris & John Hynson administrators of Hen. Kennit.
- Samuel Wheeler administrator of John Bouchier.
- Kath. Playne (alias Kath. Inglish) executrix of William Inglish.
- Said Kath. Playne administratrix of Edward Inglish.
- Edward Cox & his wife executrix of Charles Stuart.
- William Harris administrator of Charles Turner.
- Cornelius Comegys & his wife administratrix of John Cambell.
- Edward Swetnam administrator of John Abrams.

Dorchester Co.:
- John Ford administrator of Edward Creeke.
- Thomas Wall administrator of John Walker.
- Henry, Thomas, William, & Joseph Ennals executors of Bartholomew Ennals.
- Walter Cambell & his wife executrix of John Edwards & of Phineas Blackwood.
- Joane Bassey executrix of Michael Bassey.
- Roger Trotton administrator of Thomas Scott.
- Ann Thompson administratrix of Joseph Thompson.

Somerset Co.:
- Thomas Morris administrator of John Murfue.
- Mary Dixon executrix of Ambrose Dixon.
- William Whittington & wife executrix of Thomas Osborne.
- Cornelius Ward administrator of Nathaniel Dougherty.
- Donnough Dennis executor of Roger Ocane.
- Thomas Piles administrator of John Steery.
- Mary Cottingham administratrix of Thomas Cottingham.
- Elisabeth Wilson executrix of Robert Wilson.
- Elisabeth Roberts administratrix of John Roberts.
- Elisabeth Lampin administratrix of Thomas Lampin.
- John Davis administrator of Samuel Jackson.
- Edward Fowler & Alice Willin executors of Thomas Willin.
- Thomas Delahide & his wife Ann Adison administratrix of Alexander Adison.
- Thomas Gourdon administrator of Jenckin Morris.
- John Vigorous administrator of Ann Smith.
- Katharine Heathley administratrix of William Heathley.

Court Session: 1692

- William Jenkinson administrator of Amos Cooke.
- Mary Carroll administratrix of Thomas Carrol.
- Thomas Bramley & his wife executrix of Thomas Osborne.
- Rhoda Francis executrix of John Cropper.
- William Elgate administrator of William Elgate.
- William Jones executor of Cornelius Johnson.

Talbot Co.:
- William Burton administrator of Thomas Young.
- James Sedgewick administrator of Thomas Collins.
- Elisabeth Carman administratrix of Thomas Carman.
- Charles Hemsley administrator of Richard Hedger.
- Frances Kennimont executrix of John Kennimont.
- Ann Mitchell executrix of John Mitchell.
- Thomas Mason administrator of Robert Wild.
- Michael Leeds administrator of William Leeds.
- Thomas Thomas administrator of Christopher Thomas.
- Margaret Dunderdale administratrix of William Dunderdale.
- Thomas Bruff & his wife executrix of James Earle.
- Ann Smith (alias Ann Bonham) administratrix of William Bonham.
- Edmond ODwyer administrator of John Steward.
- William Welsh executor of John Younger.
- Margaret Layfield administratrix of Bartholomew Ramsey.
- William Dixon & his wife & William Sharp executors of Winlock Christison to answer libel of Murty Horney & his wife daughter & legatee of said Christison.

20 December. John Courts (CH) exhibited will of William Butterham (CH), proved

Court Session: 1692

before Cleborne Lomax (CH) by Randolph Brandt & Jeoffry Cole, witnesses.

17 January. William Dent procurator for Roger Brooke (CV) & his wife Mary executrix of Winifred Mullett (widow) vs. Edward Pye (g, CH). Libel exhibited.

14A:15 Said Mullett on 20 April 1685 at Portobacco (CH) possessed in her right goods, etc., & sojourned at house of said Pye at Portobacco. Value: £150.0.0.

On 12 December, Mary Payne widow of Henry Payne (SM) was granted administration on his estate. Security: Capt. Thomas Attoway. Appraisers: Richard Vowles, John Baily.

15A:1 7 January. John Tyrling (SM) administrator of John Tyrling (SM) vs. Thomas Orrell (SM) & his wife & Thomas Carvile (SM) & his wife. Libel exhibited.

William Dent procurator for Edward Milstead & his wife Elisabeth vs. William Serjeant (CH) & his wife Damarus executrix of John Ward (CH). Libel exhibited.

2 January. John Tyrling (SM) administrator of John Tyrling (SM) vs. Thomas Orrell (SM) & his wife Isabella & Thomas Carvile (SM) & his wife. Defendants summoned.

13 January. William Turnor (CV) administrator of James Stritch (CV) exhibited inventory.

Fortune Semme (SM) widow of Marmaduke Semme (SM) exhibited his will, constituting her executrix. Philip Brisco (g, SM) to prove said will. Said Fortune was granted administration. Security: Thomas Medford. Appraisers: John Vaudry, Robert Hagar. Said Brisco to administer oath.

Court Session: 1692

16 January. Thomas Smith (TA) who married Anne widow & administratrix of William Boanam exhibited accounts, proved before Mr. William Finney (TA).

15A:2 28 January. Ant. Neale & Thomas Turner executors of Capt. Joseph Pile petitioned to deliver to Mr. Nicholas Power who married a daughter of said Pile her portion. Date: 12 December 1692. Mentions: Mr. Hill, Mr. Brisco, Mr. Thomas Clark. N. Blakiston directed MM Joshua Guibert (SM) & William Langworth (SM), first sworn by either MM John Bearecroft or Philip Briscoe, to divide said estate into 5 equal portions.

30 January. George Plater procurator for Daniel Moy son of Richard Moy vs. Robert Carvile executor of Elisabeth Moy widow & executrix of said Richard. Libel exhibited.

15A:3 13 February. Court at St. John's. Thomas Blackwell who married widow of Mr. Joshua Dorsey (AA) petitioned that said Dorsey made will bequeathing 1/3rd to his wife & other legacies. Said executrix paid the legacies without bringing said items to appraisement. Ruling: case dismissed. Edward & John Dorsey executors of said Joshua exhibited accounts.
15A:4 Payments to (legacies): Henry Constable, Ralph Jackson, John Larkin, Francis Downes, Robert Proctor, Daniel Macoone. Receipts for legacies to: John Howard, Mathias Howard, Sarah Worthington.

Benjamin Clark who married relict of James Hagget one of executors of Edward Selby summoned to render accounts. Clark exhibited that said Hagget was not concerned with it. The other executors Edward Selby & John Cross are only persons concerned. Ruling: case dismissed.

William Foreman exhibited accounts on estate of Thomas Bowles (AA).

Page 185

Court Session: 1692

John Marriot executor of John Acton (AA) exhibited accounts. Payments to be proved: Robert Norris, William Hopkins, Thomas Philips.

Richard Baily administrator of Mark Johnson (AA) exhibited inventory, by appraisers Robert Eagle & John Stuart. Also exhibited were accounts.

15A:5 John Howard (AA) & his wife Eleanor executrix of John Macubin (AA) exhibited that said Macubin bequeathed all to his wife & that there are no debts to exhibit. Ruling: case dismissed.

William Bateman (AA) & his wife Christian administratrix of her son John Wheeler (AA) exhibited that there are no debts to exhibit. Ruling: case dismissed.

Jacob Lookerman (g, DO) to summon widow of Edward Pindar (g, DO) to take administration on said estate, for benefit of orphans.

15A:6 Thomas Ennalls (DO) one of executors of Bartholomew Ennalls (DO) was granted continuance.

Sheriff (DO) exhibited the following summons:
* Thomas & Joseph Ennalls executors of Bartholomew Ennalls.
* Walter Cambell executor of John Edwards & of Phineas Blackwood.
* Thomas Wall administrator of John Walker.
* Roger Trotten administrator of Thomas Scott.
* Anne Thompson administratrix of Joseph Thompson. (not to be found).
Date: 5 February 1692/3.

Sheriff (SO) exhibited the following summons:
* Thomas Norris, Mary Dixon, William Whittington, Cornelius Ward, Donnough Dennis, Mary Cottingham, Elisabeth Wilson, John Davis, Thomas Gordon, John Vigerous, William

Page 186

Jenkinson, Mary Caroll, Thomas
Bramley, Rhoda Fausit, William
Elgate, William Jones.

- Cited as "non invent.": Thomas
Piles, Elisabeth Roberts, Elisabeth
Lampin, Alice Willin, Ann Addison,
Katharine Heathley.

St. Luffe petitioned for the people to
appear when the weather is warmer due to
the distance & time of the year. Date:
5 February 1692/3 at Manoakin.

Sheriff (TA) exhibited the following
summons:

15A:7   ...

- Summoned: William Barton, James
Sedgewick, Thomas Mason, Thomas
Thomas, Margaret Dunderdale, Thomas
Bruff & his wife, Ann Smith (alias
Ann Bonham), William Welch.
- Cited as dec'd: Elisabeth Carman,
Frances Kennimont, Anne Mitchell,
Michael Leeds, Edmond O'Dwyer,
Margarett Layfield.
- Cited "non est invent": Charles
Hemsely.
- Second summons: William Dixon & his
wife Elisabeth. William Shay
executor of Winlock Christison.

Signed: S. Withers.

Sheriff (SM) exhibited the following
summons:

- Summoned: John Bullock, James Swann,
Thomas Orman, John VanReswick & his
wife, Michael Curtis & his wife,
Elisabeth Portwood, Francis Greene,
Thomas Clark.
- Second summons: Thomas Courtney &
his wife Eleanor administratrix of
Fobbe Roberts, Robert Carvile
executor of Richard Moy, Thomas
Waughob administrator of Robert
Graham (Summons to John Watson &
Philip Clark.), Robert Cooper & his
wife Patience, John Baptista
Carberry.

Signed: Robert Mason.

Sheriff (AA) exhibited the following
summons:

- Summoned: Edward & John Dorsey, John

Court Session: 1692

Marriott, Christian Wheeler, Eleanor
Chiney, John Howard, Thomas Tench,
Esq., John Pettibone, Jane Ferguson,
Walter Felps, Susannah Sewick,
Rachell Stimpson, William Foreman,
Esther Nicholson, Samuel Thomas,
Joseph Chew & his wife, Honor
Durden, Samuel Yong & his wife,
Richard Baily, Patrick Murphy & his
wife.
- Mary Giles – cited but languid.
- Edward Selby, John Cross, & John
  Hagget – said Hagget summoned.
- Elisabeth Vasina – non est invent.
- Nicholas Nicholson – dec'd.
- Jane Pattison – dec'd.
Signed: Benjamin Scrivner (sheriff).

15A:8   Sheriff (BA) exhibited the following
summons:
- Elisabeth Edmonds executrix of
  Richard Edmonds.
- Richard Askue & his wife Mary Reeves
  executrix of Edward Reeves.
- Richard Askue administrator of James
  Hammond.
- Richard Askue administrator of
  Samuel Brandt.
- Persons not found: William Kane,
  William Cole, Mary Petit, Michael
  Hastings.
Signed: John Hall (sheriff).

Sheriff (SM) exhibited the following
summons:
- Thomas Orrell & his wife Isabel &
  Thomas Carvile & his wife.
Signed: Robert Mason (sheriff).

Mr. William Finney (TA) exhibited:
- will of Michael Paul Vanderford,
  constituting George Vanderford &
  John Jackson executors. Said George
  was granted administration.
- will of Thomas Anderson,
  constituting his wife Rebecca
  executrix.
- will of John Newman, constituting
  his wife Judith executrix. Maj.
  John Brooke & his wife Judith were
  granted administration.
- will of Col. Vincent Lowe,

constituting Capt. James Murphy &
Michael Turbut executors. Said
Murphy & Turbut were granted
administration.

- will of Charles Cartwright,
  constituting his wife Sarah
  executrix. Said Sarah was granted
  administration.
- will of Alice Rich (widow),
  constituting her son William Rich
  executor. Said William was granted
  administration.
- bond of Andrew Tonnard administrator
  of Thomas Tonnard. LoA were granted
  on 20 September 1692. Sureties:
  John Edmondson, Edward Pollard.
- bond of Daniel Ingerson
  administrator of Henry Pratt. LoA
  were dated 17 January last.
  Sureties: William Hatfield, William
  Clayton.

Capt. Henry Hanslap (former high
sheriff, AA) exhibited:
- LoA for James Warren administrator
  of Robert French, dated 20 June
  1689.

15A:9   ...
- LoA for Rebecca Lightfoote executrix
  of Thomas Lightfoote, granted 20
  June 1689.
- LoA for Margaret Holland
  administratrix of Francis Holland,
  granted 20 June 1689.
- LoA for Richard Powell executor of
  John Wilkinson, granted 20 June
  1689. Non est inventor.
- LoA for John Watkins administrator
  of John Watkins, granted 20 June
  1689.
- LoA for Joanna Longman
  administratrix of John Longman,
  granted 20 June 1689.
- LoA for Elisabeth Vassine
  administratrix of Francis Vassine,
  granted 20 June 1689.
- LoA for Rebecca Smith executrix of
  Benjamin Smith, granted 20 June
  1689. Non est inventor.
- LoA for James Warry administrator of
  George Lee, granted 20 June 1689.
- LoA for Ursula Burges executrix of

Court Session: 1692

William Burges, granted 20 June
1689.
- will of Richard Tydings, dated 2
February 1687. To be proved on 4
July 1689; actually proved on 13
July 1689. John Jordan who married
Charety executrix was granted
administration during her minority.
Sureties: John Belt, Jos. Williams.
Appraisers: John Sanders, John
Gressam. Also exhibited inventory.
Date: 20 July 1689.
- inventory of James Powell, by
appraisers Benjamin Williams & John
Powell.
- accounts of Walter Felps
administrator of George Bawstock.
To be proved on 6 October 1688;
proved on 8 March 1688.
- LoA for Joanna Longman
administratrix of John Longman.
Said Joanna was granted
administration on 9 October 1688.
- inventory of Thomas Pattison, by
appraisers William Roper & Benjamin
Williams.
- examined accounts of Alexander
Mackfarland who married widow of
Mathew Selly, to be done 9 October
1688.
- accounts of Seaborne Batty, by
Joseph Chew & his wife Elisabeth
executrix. To be done on 10 April
1689; proved on 10 July 1689.

15A:10 George Plater procurator for Philip Cox
& his wife Sarah (CV) widow of John
Johnson (SM) vs. estate of Foble
Roberts. Libel exhibited.

Griffith Jones procurator for Murty
Horney & his wife Elisabeth one of
daughters of Winlock Christison (TA) vs.
William Dixon & his wife & William
Sharp. Libel exhibited.

14 February. Rachel Stimpson (alias
Rachel Proctor) executrix of John
Stimpson (AA) exhibited accounts. Debts
not yet allowed: Henry Ridgely, Gabriel
Parrot.

Court Session: 1692

Patrick Murphy (AA) administrator of John Gary (AA) exhibited accounts. Receipts (in equal amounts): John Kendall for his wife's portion, Zachariah Gary.

William Dent procurator for William Smoote vs. Robert Yates & his wife Rebecca executrix of James Tyre. Commission to examine witnesses: John Courts, Esq. (g, CH), Robert Thompson, Jr. (g, CH), Capt. Randolph Brandt (g, CH), Anthony Neale (g, CH). Subpoenas issued to: Margery wife of Col. Humphry Warren (CH), Thomas Stone (CH),
15A:11 Jane Witchaley wife of Thomas Wichaley (CH), Col. Humphry Warren, Ellanor Beane, William Browne & his wife Mary, Lydia Money, Clebourne Lomax.

15A:12 Daniel Moy vs. William Dent (g) procurator for Robert Carvile. Answer exhibited.

William Dent procurator for Edward Milstead (CH) vs. William Serjeant & his wife executrix of John Ward. Attachment to defendants.

George Plater attorney for Philip Cox & his wife vs. Samuell Watkyns procurator for Thomas Courtney & his wife. Petition for copy of libel.

William Dent procurator for Roger Brooke (CV) & his wife Mary executrix of Winifred Mullett vs. Col. Edward Pye (CH). Attachment to defendant.

John Tyrling (SM) administrator of his father John Tyrling (SM) vs. Thomas Orrell & his wife & Thomas Carvile & his wife. Attachment to defendants.

Murty Horney & his wife vs. George Plater procurator for William Dixon (TA). Answer exhibited.

George Plater procurator for John Currier (merchant) vs. estate of William Hill (DO). Caveat exhibited.

Page 191

Court Session: 1692

15A:13 Samuell Watkins procurator for John Edmondson (TA) vs. estate of William Hill (DO). Caveat exhibited.

Thomas Gourdon (SO) administrator of Jenkin Morris (SO) exhibited accounts.

Robert Yates (CH) who married Rebecca executrix of James Toyer (CH) executor of Peter Carr (CH) exhibited additional accounts on estate of said Carr.

James Sedgewick (TA) administrator of Thomas Collins (TA) exhibited accounts. Estate is overpaid.

William Elgate (SO) administrator of his father William Elgate exhibited accounts.

John Davis (SO) administrator of Samuel Jackson (SO) exhibited accounts.

Elisabeth Wilson (SO) widow & executrix of Robert Wilson (SO) exhibited that estate is clear & there are no debts. Discharge was granted.

15A:14 William Jenkins (SO) administrator of Anne Cooke (SO) exhibited accounts.

George Plater procurator for John Bould (SM) petitioned for LoA on estate of Cuthbert Scott (SM). Said Bould married sister of said Scott. LoA formerly granted to John Baptista Carberry who married relict. William Dent is attorney for said Carberry. Mentions: Elisabeth Davis. Ruling: for Carberry.

Mr. Robert Carvile procurator for orphans of Robert Graham (SM) delivered papers to Mr. George Plater now appointed attorney for said orphans. Mr. Philip Clark to satisfy
15A:15 for his fees on the accounts.

15 February. (N) procurator for William Dixon (TA) petitioned for commission to examine witnesses between Murty Horney & his reputed wife Elisabeth daughter of Winlock Christison (dec'd) & said

William Dixon & his wife Elisabeth &
William Sharp executors of said dec'd.
Commission to Edward Mann (g, TA) &
Thomas Bowdle (g, TA).

John Currier & John Edmondson were
granted administration on estate of
William Hill (DO) yesterday. Said dec'd
left a will, constituting Edward Pindar
& Hugh Eccleston executors. Said Pindar
is also dec'd. Procurator for said
Currier petitioned for said Eccleston to
come & prove the will.

15A:16   At the request of Mr. Charles Caroll,
John Watson (SM) proved an account from
books of Thomas Cuik (dec'd), wherein he
is charged for accounts for Mr. Anthony
Underwood (dec'd).

Mary Dixon (SO) executrix of Ambrose
Dixon (SO) was granted continuance.

Thomas Waughob, John Watson, & Philip
Clark (SM) appeared, in response to a
summons on behalf of the orphans of
Robert Graham.

At the request of James Browne & his
wife Ann widow & administratrix of
Thomas Pue, Philip Clark attested to
receipt passed by Mr. Henry Lowe to
said Ann.

At the request of Thomas Griffin,
William Dent proved a debt due to said
Dent from Thomas Griffin (dec'd), paid
by Thomas Griffin son & administrator.
Accounts were exhibited. Payments yet
to be proved: John Taunt, Daniel Lowry,
William Twisdell, Mr. Vansweringen, Mr.
Philip Lynes. Also exhibited was
receipt from his brother Richard Griffin
for his legacy.

Samuel Watkyns procurator for Robert
Cooper (SM) who married widow of James
Yore appeared, due to a summons by
Philip Lynes. Said Lynes did not
appear, nor was libel exhibited.
Ruling: case dismissed.

15A:17　James Cullen (SM) executor of Nicholas
White (SM) exhibited accounts.
Desperate debts (assigned to dec'd):
- Henry Fox bill to William Lowry.
- Edmund Dwyer to Hen. Denton.

Wife of Cornelius Ward (SO)
administrator of Nathaniel Dougherty
(SO) was granted continuance.

Mary Cottingham (SO) administratrix of
Thomas Cottingham (SO) was granted
continuance.

Charles Caroll (g, SM) administrator of
Anthony Underwood & his wife Martha
exhibited accounts. (Said Caroll was
formerly married to said Martha.)
Payments suspended: John Willymott (CV),
Symon Perkins. Payments to be proved:
Mr. Brant, Edward Miller, Richard
Atwood, John Heard, Joshua Doyne, widow
Evans, Roger Toll, William Twisden,
Robert Edmondson, John Bright, Richard
Clouds, Capt. Greenhall, William
Taylard, estate of John Skipper.

15A:18　Edward Morgan executor of John Evans
(SM) exhibited inventory & accounts.

William Aisquith (SM) administrator of
Edward Home (SM) exhibited accounts.

William Serjeant (CH) administrator of
Charles Shepard exhibited inventory.

William Harris (CE) one of
administrators of Henry Kennet &
administrator of Charles Turnor was
granted continuance.

Precepts issued:
- contempt against William Serjeant &
  his wife executrix of John Ward (CH)
  at suit of Edward Milstead & his
  wife (daughter of said Ward).
- contempt against Edward Pye (CH) at
  suit of Roger Brooke & his wife Mary
  executrix of Winifred Mullet.
- contempt against Thomas Orrell & his
  wife & Thomas Carvile & his wife at
  suit of John Tyrling (SM)

administrator of his father John
Tyrling.
* summons to Hugh Eccleston (DO) one
of executors of William Hill (DO).

15A:19 26 February. Col. William Digges
executor of Rice Williams (CH) exhibited
inventory.

28 February. Joseph Ball (g, Lancaster
Co. VA) petitioned for LoA on estate of
Alexander Atkyns, as principle creditor.
Date: 27 February 1692 before Sir Thomas
Lawrence. Said Ball was granted
administration. Sureties: William
Taylard, Thomas Waughob (SM).
Appraisers: John Bouge.

Court Session: 1693

27 March. Charles Beckwith vs. Henry
Fernley (CV) executor of Anne Bankes
(CV) widow & executrix of Thomas Bankes.
Said Fernley summoned to answer
complaint.

Samuel Watkyns procurator for Elisabeth
Nichols widow of John Nichols (CV)
exhibited caveat against his estate.

Samuel Watkyns procurator for Elisabeth
Nichols vs. estate of Henry Caswell
(CV). Caveat exhibited.

Mr. Philip Brisco (SM) exhibited oath
of John Vaudry & Robert Hagar,
appraisers of Marmaduke Semme, sworn on
20th instant. Also exhibited oath of
Fortune Semme executrix of said
Marmaduke, sworn same day. Also
exhibited will & inventory.

15A:20 4 April. Baker Brooke & Charles Brooke
(orphans of Baker Brooke (dec'd)) vs.
Henry Brent & his wife executrix of said
Baker Brooke, Esq. Said Brent summoned
to answer libel.

11 April. Philip Cox & his wife vs.
Thomas Courtney. Summons to Thomas Beal
& William Aisquith (SM) to testify for

said Cox.

William Sharp letter to John Llewellin.
John Pitts petitioned for LoA on estate
of Thomas Taylor. Said Pitts is
guardian for one of the children.
Mentions: Maj. Finney, Col. Blakiston.
Date: 2 April 1693.

13 April. William Sharp & John Pitts
(surviving overseers of estate of Thomas
Taylor (TA)) exhibited caveat on behalf
of orphans.

Sheriff (SM) to summon:
- John Bullock executor of Thomas
  Oakely.
- James Swan administrator of William
  Ningfinger.
- John Orman & his wife Penelope
  executrix of John Tong.
- Katharine Obryan administratrix of
  Bryan Obryan.
- Elisabeth Brimmer administratrix of
  James Brimmer.
- John VanReswick & his wife Frances
  administratrix of Christopher
  Goodson.
- Michael Curtis & his wife Sarah
  executrix of Justinian Gerard.
- Thomas Gwither administrator of
  Morgan Prance.
- Elisabeth Portwood administratrix of
  John Portwood.
- Francis Green & Thomas Clark
  executors of Leonard Green.
- James Brown & his wife
  administrators of Thomas Pue.
- Philip Lynes administrator of
  William Hawton.
- William Moss administrator of John
  Clark.
- Sarah Cartwright executrix of Mathew
  Cartwright.
- Rebeccah Pean administratrix of
  Henry Pean.
- Peter Johnson executor of Francis
  Johnson.
- Thomas Warren & his wife executrix
  of Robert Cole.
- Sarah Evans executrix of Thomas
  Evans.

Court Session: 1693

- Ignatius Warren administrator of John Warren.
- Robert Philips & his wife administratrix of John Martin.
- Jane Spink executrix of Thomas Spink.
- John Dash executor of Thomas Reynolds.
- Anthony Lambrosy administrator of John Shackler.

15A:21 Jane Long (BA) administratrix of Thomas Long (BA) petitioned for Col. Nicholas Greenbury to examine accounts. She lives 150 miles from "this city" SMC.

Philip Kennard (SO) exhibited accounts on estate of (N).

Robert Gibson (SO) exhibited accounts on estate of (N).

Richard Kennard (SO) exhibited accounts on estate of (N).

15A:22 23 April. Robert Cooper (SM) & his wife Patience Yore relict of Daniel Clocker (SM) was granted administration on his estate, unadministered by James Yore late husband of said Patience. Security: William Taylard (SM). Appraisers: Thomas Price, Daniel Moy.

28 April. Henry Bonner (AA) exhibited:
- inventories: Christopher Skoates, Daniel Longman, Samuel Brothers, Jarvis Winterbottam, George Skipwith, Andrew Allein.
- wills: Thomas Knighton, Edward Talbott, Francis Johnson, Mary Celin, Elisabeth Burnett.
- inventory: Elisabeth Burnett.
- bonds: Richard Gotts administrator of Christopher Skoates, John Bennet administrator of Andrew Allim, Gabriel Parrot administrator of (N) Longman, Richard Chesheir administrator of Samuel Brother, Solomon Sparrow administrator of Jarvis Winterbotom.

Court Session: 1693

Murty Horney & his wife vs. William
Dixon & his wife & William Sharp. MM
Edward Mann (TA) & Thomas Bowdle (TA)
exhibited testimony.
- Mr. Leach deposed that he married in
  the Church of ENG Henry Horney &
  Elisabeth Horney (alias Elisabeth
  Christison) before 15 January 1691.

15A:23 ...
Present: Samuel Payne, Adam Missett,
Elisabeth Mercer, Mary Tutell, et.
al.
- Peter Sydes deposed that he knew
  nothing of the marriage, but after
  that said Murty demanded of said
  Dixon for his wife's portion. Dixon
  replied for Murty to prove the
  marriage.
- John Long deposed that said Dixon
  said to Murty to prove the marriage.
- John Newman deposed the same. [Said
  Newman did not swear.]
Date: 21 April 1693.

Philip Briscoe (SM) exhibited oath of
John Vaudry & Robert Hagar, appraisers
of Marmaduke Semme, sworn 20 March
1692/3. Signed: Philip Brisco.

Ro. Mason (sheriff, SM) exhibited the
following summons:
- Mr. John Watson & his wife
  executrix of Thomas Spink.
- Mr. Philip Lynes administrator of
  William Hawton.
- Robert Philips & his wife
  administratrix of John Martingdal.
- Thomas Gwither administrator of
  Morgan Pearce.
- James Browne & his wife
  administratrix of Thomas Pue.
- Anthony Lambrose administrator of
  John Shaklee.

Rebecca Culver wife of Henry Culver
administratrix of Guy Finch (SO)
exhibited accounts.

15A:24 Joshua Hall who married widow &
administratrix of Joseph Isaacks (CV)
exhibited accounts. Payment to be
proved: Edward Batson.

Court Session: 1693

Petition of Capt. Thomas Claget (CV) on
behalf of Martha Ridgely (under age, one
of orphans of Robert Ridgely (SM)) to
whom he is guardian.

Robert Philips (SM) who married widow of
John Martingdal (SM) exhibited accounts.
Payments to be proved: Mr. Garret
Vansweringen.

15A:25   John Tyrling administrator of his father
John Tyrling (SM) exhibited additional
inventory & accounts. Payments to be
proved: Mr. Rosewell, Thomas Orrell
having custody of a Negro girl, Maj.
Boareman, Mr. Richard Clouds, Capt.
John Courts, Peter Johnson, Mr. Clarol,
Mr. Henry Hawkins, Mr. Thomas Orrell,
Capt. John Addison & Mr. William
Hatton & John Wincoll.

Richard Askue (BA) who married widow of
Edward Reeves (BA) exhibited accounts.

29 April. Said Richard Askue
administrator of James Hammond (BA)
exhibited accounts. Payments to be
proved: George Gunnell, Mr. Miles
Gibson,
15A:26   chattel disposed of by Samuel Brand who
married widow of said Hammond, chattel
in suit with Mr. Thomas Thurston,
Daniel Lovan (died insolvent).

Said Richard Askue who married widow of
Samuel Brand (BA) exhibited accounts.
Payments to be proved: Mr. Miles
Gibson, Capt. Henry Johnson (dec'd).

Thomas Gwither executor of Morgan Prance
(SM) was granted continuance.

15A:27   3 May. [f. 41 to be entered here.]

Mr. Clement Hill vs. estate of Thomas
Long (BA). Caveat exhibited. Mentions:
widow of said Hill is considerable
creditor.

4 May. Samuel Watkyns procurator for
Henry Fernley (CV) vs. Charles
Beckwith. Summons to said Beckwith to

Page 199

answer libel.

5 May. Robert Burman & his wife Anne relict of Henry Staples (KE) exhibited additional accounts. Payments to be proved: William Read, James Howe. Sperate debts: Maj. Ringold, Walter Meeks.

15A:28 Continuance was granted.

8 May. Ann Edwards widow of John Edwards (CV) exhibited his will, proved by Richard Keene & Samuel Watkyns. Said Ann & Samuel Watkyns were granted administration. Mathew Lewis (other executor) renounced administration.

10 May. Moses Jones (CH) who married Katharine relict & executrix of James Wheeler (CH) exhibited additional accounts.

13 May. Exhibited was the will of Thomas Taylor (TA), constituting his wife executrix & PoA to Men's Meeting of Quakers to appoint appraisers. Said wife died some days before him in his time of sickness. Said Thomas did nominate four friends to care for his children: William Berry, John Pitt,

15A:29 William Sharp, Henry Parrot. Said Berry & Parrot are also dec'd. Thomas Taylor (eldest son) seeks LoA on his father's estate to disposed of his brothers' & sister's lands.

15A:30 Signed (from Meeting): John Edmondson, George Joult, Thomas Skillington, Henry Wilchurch, William Stevens, Francis Armstrong, James Ridley, William Stephens, William Edmondson, Walter Dickason, William Dickinson, William Stevens, Jr., John Hodson, William Troth, George Pratt, John Boram, Peter Harwood, Howell Powell, Jr., William Cannydee, William Berry, Joseph Kennerly, Seth Garrett, Howell Powell. Christopher Denny (TA) was granted administration. Appraisers: Edward Mann (g), Walter Quinton. William Bexley (TA) to administer oath.

15A:31 9 June. Nathaniel Davis (mariner,
Londonderry, IRE) was granted
administration on estate of Robert
Arbuckle (merchant, SM). Security:
Gilbert Clark (g, CH).

Summons to Martha Goldsmith (BA) & Mary
Beedle (alias Mary Uty, BA) issued on 20
May. Re: estate of James Fendall.

Summons to Margaret Walston
administratrix of John Walston was
issued on 20 May. Re: estate of her
husband said John Walston.

11 June. John Bayne (g, SM) was granted
administration on estate of William Ladg
(SM), as principle creditor. Security:
Mr. William Dent. Appraisers: John
Bracher, Thomas Simpson.

26 June. Exhibited inventory of Peter
Watts (SM), by appraisers John Lowe &
Thomas Hebb.

15A:32 S. Watkyns for Charles Beckwith vs. G.
Plater for Henry Fernly executor of Ann
Dennis executrix of Thomas Banks.
Continuance was granted.

William Smoote vs. Robert Yates & his
wife executrix of James Yore executor of
John Bowles who married Margery relict &
executrix of William Baker. Depositions
exhibited.

Philip Lynes vs. Robert Cooper & his
wife. Libel exhibited.

Procurator for Henry Lowe (g, CV)
petitioned that Mary Darnall (widow, CV,
dec'd) made her will bequeathing to her
son John Darnall (now dec'd). Said will
is possessed by Col. Henry Darnall & is
not proved. Said Lowe married the widow
of said John Darnall. Said Henry
Darnall summoned.

Ann Edwards widow & executrix of Andrew
Abington administrator of John Payne
15A:33 (CV) was summoned to render accounts.

Court Session: 1693

William Dent for Roger Brooke & his wife executrix of Winifred Mullet vs. George Plater for Col. Edward Pye. Exhibited was original will of said Mullet, unproved.

Baker Brooke & Charles Brooke orphans of Baker Brooke vs. Henry Brent & his wife Ann executrix of said dec'd. Defendant did not appear. Resummoned to next court.

George Plater for Philip Cox & his wife Sarah administratrix of John Johnson vs. Thomas Courtney & his wife executrix of Fobbe Roberts. Answer & accounts exhibited.

Daniel Moy son & heir of Richard Moy vs. Robert Carvile executor of Elisabeth Moy executrix of said Richard Moy. Defendant must file answer.

Edward Milstead vs. William Serjeant & his wife executrix of John Ward. Defendant was attached.

Summons to Mordecai Moore (AA) & his wife Ursula executrix of Col. William Burges executor of Nicholas Painter who married Judith Parker (alias Judith Cumber) executrix of John Cumber to answer
15A:34   libel of John Cumber (grandchild of dec'd).

Mr. Henry Lowe & his wife Susanna relict & administratrix of Mr. John Darnall petitioned for allowance from accounts, allowed at March Court in 1686 at CV. Signed: Caecil Butler (clerk). Further allowed. Date: 17 April 1689.

John Griggs sent papers in his possession, as they were done before the Revolution & Change of Government & the office was not open:
• Commission dated 19 November 1688 to summon Sarah Evans widow & relict of John Evans
15A:35   ...
      (CV) to administer oath. Said Sarah

Court Session: 1693

was sworn 3 July 1689.

John Hall (sheriff, BA) exhibited that
he had served summons to:
- Margaret Goldsmith & Mary Beedle
  (alias Mary Uty) regarding estate of
  James Fendall.
- Margaret Walston administratrix of
  John Walston regarding estate of
  James Fendall.
Date: 3 June 1693.

15A:36   Mr. Thomas Hedge (clerk, BA) exhibited:
proceedings from beginning of the
Revolution.

Mr. Henry Bonner (AA) exhibited
proceedings from June 1690 to November
1692. Said Bonner also exhibited:
- John Wooden deposed that he heard
  Jarvis Winterbotham (AA) about
  October 1692 say that Solomon
  Sparrow & John Taillor shall have
  all.
- William Denseen deposed that he
  heard Jarvis Winterbottam declared
  about January 1692/3 the same.
- Richard Welch deposed the same.

15A:37   ...
- William Cooper deposed the same.
- Mathias Halstead deposed that Jarvis
  Winterbottam in 1678 said that
  Solomon Spencer should have all.
- Richard Butts deposed the same.
Date: 17 February 1692. Inventory was
exhibited, by appraisers John Wooden &
Richard Welch, dated 1 June 1693.

Sheriff (SM) to summon:
- John Bullock executor of Thomas
  Oakley.
- James Swan administrator of William
  Ningfinger.
- Thomas Orman & his wife executrix of
  John Tong.
- Kath. Obryan administratrix of Bryan
  Obryan.
- Elisabeth Breamer administratrix of
  James Bremer.
- John VanReswick & his wife
  administratrix of Christopher
  Goodson.

Page 203

Court Session: 1693

- Michael Curtis & his wife executrix of Justinian Gerard.
- Thomas Gwither administrator of Morgan Prance.
- Elisabeth Portwood administratrix of John Portwood.
- Fran. Greene & Thomas Clark executors of Leonard Greene.
- James Brown & his wife administratrix of Thomas Pue.
- Philip Lynes administrator of William Hawton.
- William Moss administrator of John Clark.

15A:38 Sheriff (KE) to summon:
- Thomas Parker administrator of James Parker.
- William Harris & John Hinson administrators of Henry Kennet.
- Samuel Wheeler administrator of John Boucheir.
- Katharine Playne (alias Katharine English) executrix of William Inglish.
- Katharine Playne administratrix of Edward Inglish.
- William Harris administrator of Charles Turnor.
- Edward Cox executor of Charles Stewart.
- Cornelius Comegys & his wife administratrix of John Cambell.
- Edward Sweatnam administrator of John Abrahams.

Sheriff (CV) to summon:
- John Holloway executor of John Vines.
- Hugh Montgomery & his wife executrix of George Parker.
- George Plowden administrator of Robert Thompson.
- Elisha Hall & his wife Sarah administratrix of Jonas Winfield.
- Hugh Ellis administrator of Thomas Cosden.
- Benjamin Evans & his wife Sarah administratrix of William Rout.
- Francis Collier & his wife administratrix of John Evans.
- Rebecca Finch administratrix of Guy

Page 204

Court Session: 1693

Finch.
- Margaret Moore administratrix of William Moore.
- Sarah Waring et. al. executors of Basil Waring.
- Henry Mitchell administrator of Charles Parry.
- Richard Leeke & his wife executrix of Daniel Boyd.
- Nicholas Sewall executor of Martha Pennick.
- Darby Sulivant executor of John Daw.
- Thomas Johnson & his wife administratrix of Roger Baker.
- Margaret Isaacks executrix of Joseph Isaacks.
- Francis Billingsley & John Leach administrators of Francis Davis.
- Elias Lowry administrator of Henry Lowry.
- Daniel Sherridin administrator of William Keep.
- Symon Nichols administrator of William Smith.
- William Mead executor of John Cobrath.
- Joseph Edloe administrator of Peter Pheppard.
- William Howes administrator of William Edwards.
- George Hews administrator of William Shaw & his wife.
- Katharine Floyd administratrix of Hugh Floyd.
- Andrew Tanyhill & Elisha Hall executors of John Muffet.
- Ann Greene executrix of Thomas Greene.

15A:39 Sheriff (CH) to summon:
- Philip Hoskins & his wife administratrix of Margaret Lemaire.
- John Godshall administrator of Mary Weyman.
- Robert Thompson, Jr. administrator of Thomas Elwes.
- Anne Burford executrix of Thomas Burford.
- John Bracher administrator of Hugh Thomas.
- Robert Benton administrator of John Francis.

Page 205

Court Session: 1693

- Richard Isles administrator of Domindigo Agambra.

Sheriff (TA) to summon:
- William Burton administrator of Thomas Young.
- Charles Hemsley administrator of Richard Hedger.
- Thomas Mason administrator of Robert Wild.
- Thomas Thomas administrator of Christopher Thomas.
- Margaret Dunderdale administratrix of William Dunderdale.
- Thomas Bruff & his wife executrix of James Earle.
- Ann Smith (alias Ann Bonham) administratrix of William Bonham.
- William Welch executor of John Younger.
- Margaret Layfield administratrix of Bartholomew Ramsey.

Sheriff (CE) to summon:
- Sarah Meekes executrix of Walter Meekes.
- Thomas Bostick executor of Thomas Bostick.
- Martha Gibson executrix of William Odery.
- Mary Howell executrix of Nathaniel Howell.
- Olley Ollison administrator of Peter Olison.
- James Wilson administrator of William Jones.
- Thomas Webb administrator of Nicholas Jones.
- Philip Kennard administrator of Thomas Willham.
- Elisabeth Yerberry executrix of Thomas Yerberry.
- Thomas Christian administrator of Thomas Christian.

Sheriff (BA) to summon:
- Elisabeth Edmonds executrix of Richard Edmonds.
- Mary Pottel administratrix of Francis Pottel.
- Jackin Griffith administrator of James Collier.

Court Session: 1693

- Michael Hastings administrator of Francis Pettit.

15A:40 Sheriff (DO) to summon:
- Thomas Wall administrator of John Walker.
- Mary, Thomas, William, & Joseph Ennalls executors of Bartholomew Ennalls.
- Walter Cambell & Susanna executrix of John Edwards & of Phineas Blackwood.
- Joan Bassey executrix of Michael Bassey.
- Roger Trotten administrator of Thomas Scott.
- Ann Thompson administratrix of Joseph Thompson.

Sheriff (SO) to summon:
- Thomas Morris administrator of John Murfue.
- William Whittington & his wife executrix of Thomas Osborn.
- Donnough Dennis executor of Roger Ocane.
- Thomas Piles administrator of John Steery.
- Elisabeth Roberts administratrix of John Roberts.
- Elisabeth Lampin administratrix of Thomas Lampin.
- Alice Willin executrix of Thomas Willin.
- Ann Adison administratrix of Alexander Addison.
- John Vigorous administrator of Ann Smith.
- Katharine Heathley administratrix of William Heathley.
- Mary Carrol administratrix of Thomas Carrol.
- Thom. Bramley & his wife administratrix of Thomas Osborn.
- Rhoda Fraucis executrix of John Cropper.
- William Jones executor of Cornelius Johnson.

Exhibited was inventory of Peter Watts.

Court Session: 1693

Edward Morgan administrator of John
Evans (SM) exhibited was additional
inventory.

Exhibited was inventory of Philip Deyzer
(CH).

15A:41   2 May. Thomas Lawrence (AA) exhibited
inventory of his father Benjamin
Lawrence.

15 May. Richard Bennet (TA) for his
mother Madam Henrietta Maria Lloyd
executrix of Col. Philemon Lloyd
exhibited accounts.

Richard Bennet (TA) for his mother Madam
Henrietta Maria Lloyd administratrix of
Edward Inman (TA) exhibited accounts.

William Turnor (CV) administrator of
James Stritch (CV) exhibited accounts.

Exhibited was inventory of Col. Vincent
Lowe (CV).

15A:42   20 May. Baker Brooke & Charles Brooke
orphans of Baker Brooke (CV) vs. Henry
Brent & his wife executrix of said
Brooke. Libel exhibited.

26 May. William Dent procurator for
William Smoote (CH) vs. Robert Yates &
his wife executrix of James Tyer
executor of John Bowles who married
Margery relict & executrix of William
Baker. Libel exhibited. Answer
exhibited.

6 July. Robert Douglas (CH) & his wife
Mary administratrix of Richard Beaumont
summoned.

21 July. Ne. Blakiston exhibited that
John Rose, William, Christopher Knight,
George Perry, & William Hether proved
will of John Bearecroft. Date: 20 July
1693.

Capt. John Bigger (CV)
15A:43   exhibited:
    • will of Ann Banks (CV), proved on 28

Court Session: 1693

March last, constituting Henry
Fernley executor.
* will of George Bussey, proved on 8
April last, constituting his widow
Ann executrix. Also exhibited
inventory.
* will of William Kid, proved on 20
April last, constituting Samuel
Fowler executor.
* will of William Crauley, proved on
10 June last, constituting his widow
Sarah executrix.
* inventory of Thomas Bennet (CV), by
John Bennet administrator.
* inventory of James Veach.
* inventory of Thomas West.
* inventory of John Veach.

29 July. Mr. Kenelm Cheseldine
procurator for George Short vs. John
Bayne (g, SM). Summons to said Bayne to
answer lebel to reverse administration
on estate of William Lang.

Summons to Richard Clouds, John Baily, &
Joseph Hanniford regarding estate of
Robert Arbuckle.

Mr. Edward Boothby (BA) appointed
Deputy Commissary for BA.
15A:44 Signed: Ne. Blakiston.

Benjamin Hall who married Mary widow of
James Bowling (SM) exhibited his will.
Witnesses live remotely from Office.
Mr. John Bayne
15A:45 to examine said witnesses.

Col. Edward Pye who married Anne widow
& administratrix of Col. Benjamin Rozer
summoned to render accounts.

CH County Court at Portobacco. 13
September last. Capt. William Barton,
Mr. Henry Hawkins, Maj. James
Smallwood, Capt. Philip Hoskins & Maj.
Nicholas Sewall to examine estate of
Notley Rozer orphan son of Col.
Benjamin Rozer (CH) & to deliver to said
Sewall estate of said orphan, as next
relation & guardian.
15A:46 Capt. Philip Hoskins is very sick & did

Page 209

not appear. Col. William Diggs
appeared with said Sewall. Ruling:
transfer to Prerogative Court.

15A:47 Thomas Heath, age 50, deposed that he
keeps a house of entertainment & ferry
in BA for Maj. Thomas Long (SM).
Mentions: Mr. Mark Richardson, Jane
Long widow & administratrix of said
Thomas. Before: Nicholas Greeneberry.

15A:48 William Dent procurator for Penelope
Waters (SM) widow of John Waters (SM)
exhibited his will, constituting her
executrix. She is very "antient" &
feeble. Mr. John Dent to prove said
will. Said Penelope was granted
administration. Appraisers: Giles
Wilson, Henry Norris. Said John Dent to
administer oath.

John Newman (SM) & his wife Rebecca
exhibited will of John Bearecroft (SM),
constituting said John & Rebecca
15A:49 executors. Mr. John Bayne to prove
said will. Said John & Rebecca were
granted administration. Appraisers:
Thomas Clark, James Swann. Said John
Bayn to administer oath.

Richard Clouds & his wife Judith
executrix of John Goldsmith (SM)
summoned to render accounts.

Gilbert Clark (g, CH) exhibited PoA from
Mr. John Fendall son & heir of Capt.
Josias Fendall (CH, dec'd) &
administrator of Mary Fendall
administratrix of said Josias.
Mentions: Col. William Diggs (g, SM).
15A:50 Date: 21 July 1693. Witnesses: Ne.
Blakiston, Mark Gendron. Said Clark was
granted administration, as attorney for
said Fendall. Security: Mr. John
Bayne. Appraisers: Joshua Guibert,
Robert Carse.

Hugh Eccleston (g, DO) executor of
William Hill (g, DO) summoned to prove
said will.

Court Session: 1693

Edward Milstead & his wife vs. William
Serjeant & his wife (CH). Summons to
said Serjeant to answer libel & charge
of contempt.

Daniel Moy son & heir of Richard Moy vs.
Robert Carvile (SM) executor of
Elisabeth Moy executrix of said Richard.
Summons to said Carvile to answer libel
& charge of contempt.

15A:51   Elisabeth Talbot (SM) was granted
administration on estate of Charles Cox
(clerk, SM), as next of kin.
Securities: John Llewellin, William
Taylard. Appraisers: Mr. William
Harpam, William Bladen.

Samuel Fendall (g, BA) exhibited that
Edward Beedle & John Walston overseers &
administrators of James Fendall are also
dec'd. Said Samuel petitioned for LoA
on said estate, for his kinswoman
Elisabeth Fendall widow. Date: 12 May
1691 at Cork. Said James died September
1689. John Fendall had employed a
person to administer the estate; said
person is gone to VA.
15A:52   Said Samuel was granted administration,
on behalf of said Elisabeth. Mr.
Edward Boothby (BA) to administer oath.

Sheriff (CH) to summon:
• William Moss administrator of John
  Clark.
• Ann Slade administratrix of George
  Gore.
• Edward Pye administrator of Col.
  Benjamin Rozer.
• Robert Douglas & his wife
  administratrix of Richard Beaumont.
• Joseph Curnell administrator of
  Francis Massam.
• Susanna Posey executrix of John
  Posey.
• Sarah Bankes administratrix of
  Richard Bankes.
• Henry Hawkins & his wife executrix
  of Alexander Smith.
• Mary Fendall administratrix of
  Josias Fendall.
• John Booker & his wife executrix of

Richard Price.
- Henry Hawkins administrator of Henry Reynolds.
- Dorothy Minock executrix of Michael Minock.
- Charles Garret administrator of Thomas Patrick.
- Eleanor Bayne administratrix of Philip Deyrer.
- Elisabeth Delahay wife of Thomas Delahay administratrix of Michael Halstead.
- Robert Yates & his wife executrix of Lawrence Hoskins.
- Susanna Thomas executrix of William Thomas.
- Damoras Shipard administratrix of Charles Shipard.

15A:53 10 August. Hugh Hopewell (CV) exhibited verbal will of John Thatcher (CV), constituting him executor. Philip Cocks, Peter Collison, & his wife Martha attested before Thomas Parslow. Said Hopewell was granted administration. Security: Mr. William Taylard. Appraisers: William Haines, John Wiseman. Mr. Samuel Watkyns to administer oath.

Mr. John Dent (SM) exhibited will of John Waters (SM), proved by witnesses John Harrison (g) & George Dymond on 10 August 1693. Also exhibited was oath of Penelope Waters executrix,
15A:54 sworn on same day. Also exhibited was oath of George Wilson & Henry Norris, appraisers sworn same day.

16 August. Summons to Hugh Montgomery & his wife Katharine executrix of George Parker one of executors of Thomas Cosden (CV) & for Hugh Ellis executor of Mordecai Hunton other executor of said Cosden, to render accounts on estate of said Cosden.

21 August at SMC. Returns from SM.
- Cited Bullock, Swann, Orurdie, non est inventor his wife, cited O'bryan, non est inventor Bruimer, cited VReswick & wife, Curtis &

Court Session: 1693

wife, Gwither, Portwood, & Clark,
non est Greene, cited Browne & wife,
Lynes, Moss. Signed:

15A:55 Charles Tilden (sheriff, KE) to summon:
* Thomas Parker administrator of James Parker.
* William Harris & John Hynson administrators of Henry Kennet.
* Samuel Wheeler administrator of John Boucher.
* Kath. Playn (alias Kath. English) executrix of William Inglish. [absent]
* Kath. Playn (alias Kath. English) administratrix of Edward Inglish. [absent]
* Edward Cox, et. al. executors of Charles Steward. [in AA]
* William Harris administrator of Charles Turnor.
* Cornelius Comegys & his wife administratrix of John Cambell.
* Edward Sweatnam administrator of John Abrams.

Ninion Beal (sheriff, CV) to summon:
* John Holloway & his wife executrix of John Vines.
* Hugh Montgomery & his wife executrix of George Parker.
* Eliasha Hall & his wife executrix of Jonas Winfield.
* Hugh Ellis administrator of Thomas Cosden.
* Henry Michell administrator of Charles Parvy.
* Richard Leeke administrator of Daniel Floyd.
* Francis Billingsley & John Leech administrators of Francis Davis.
* Darby Sullivan executor of John Dew.
* Daniel Sheiridin administrator of William Keep.
* William Meeds executor of John Cobreth.
* Elisha Hall executor of John Muffet.
* George Plowden administrator of Robert Thompson.
* Francis Collier & his wife administratrix of John Evans.
* Rebecca Finch administratrix of Guy

Page 213

Finch.
- Margaret Moore administratrix of William Moore
- Sarah Waring executrix of Basil Waring.
- Nicholas Sewall executor of Martha Pennich.
- Margaret Isaacks executrix of John Isaacks.
- Symon Nichols administrator of William Smith.
- Joseph Edloe administrator of Peter Pheppard.
- Benjamin Evans & his wife Sarah administratrix of William Rout. [runaway]
- Elias Lowry administrator of Henry Lowry. [runaway]
- William Howes administrator of William Edwards. [disowned is not found]
- George Hewes administrator of William Shaw & his wife. [dec'd & no executor]
- Andrew Tanyhill & Elisha Hall executors of John Muffet. [Tanyhill is dec'd]
- Katharine Lloyd administratrix of Hugh Lloyd. [not found]
- Anne Green executrix of Thomas Green. [dec'd]
- Thomas Johnson & his wife administratrix of Roger Baker. [gone for ENG]

15A:56 Humph. Warren (sheriff, CH) to summon:
- Philip Hoskins & his wife administratrix of Margaret Lemaire.
- John Godshall administrator of Mary Weyman.
- Robert Thompson, Jr. administrator of Thomas Elwes.
- Ann Burford executrix of Thomas Burford.
- John Bracher administrator of Hugh Thomas.
- Robert Benson administrator of John Francis.
- Richard Iles administrator of Domindigo Agambra.
- William Moss administrator of John Clark.

Court Session: 1693

- Ann Slade administratrix of George Gore.
- Edward Pye administrator of Col. Benjamin Rozer.
- Robert Douglass & his wife administratrix of Richard Beaumont.
- Joseph Curnell administrator of Francis Massam.
- Susanna Posey executrix of John Posey.
- Sarah Bankes administratrix of Richard Bankes.
- Henry Hawkins & his wife executrix of Alexander Smith.
- Mary Fendall administratrix of Josias Fendall.
- John Booker & his wife executrix of Richard Price.
- Henry Hawkins administrator of Henry Reynolds.
- Dorothy Minock executrix of Michael Minock.
- Charles Garrat administrator of Thomas Patrick.
- Eleanor Bayne administratrix of Philip Deyrer.
- Elisabeth Delahide wife of Thomas Delahide executrix of Lawrence Hoskins.
- Susanna Thomas executrix of William Thomas.
- Damoras Shepard administratrix of Charles Shepard.

Sam. Withers (sheriff, TA) to summon:
- William Burton administrator of Thomas Young.
- Charles Hemsley administrator of Richard Hedger. [non est inventor]
- Thomas Mason administrator of Robert Wild.
- Thomas Thomas administrator of Christopher Thomas.
- Margaret Dunderdale administratrix of William Dunderdale.
- Thomas Bruff & his wife executrix of James Earle.
- Ann Smith (alias Ann Bonham) administratrix of William Bonham.
- William Welsh executor of John Younger.
- Margaret Layfield administratrix of

Court Session: 1693

Bartholomew Ramsey.

15A:57   Ebenezar Blackiston (sheriff, CE) to
summon:
- Sarah Meekes executrix of Walter
  Meekes.
- Thomas Bostick executor of Thomas
  Bostick.
- Oley Olison administrator of Peter
  Ollison. [not to be found]
- James Wilson administrator of
  William Jones.
- Thomas Webb administrator of
  Nicholas Jones.
- Elisabeth Yerberry executrix of
  Thomas Yerberry.
- Thomas Christan administrator of
  Lawrence Christan.

John Hall (sheriff, BA) to summon:
- William Kane administrator of John
  Dimond. [I can find no such man]
- William Cole administrator of David
  Adams. [dec'd]
- Elisabeth Edmonds executrix of
  Richard Edmonds.
- Mary Pottel administratrix of
  Francis Pottel. {dec'd]
- Jenkin Griffith administrator of
  James Collier. [in PA]
- Michael Haskings administrator of
  Francis Pettit. [runaway]
- Mary Reeve executrix of Edward
  Reeve.
- Richard Askue administrator of John
  Hammond.
- Richard Askue administrator of
  Samuel Brands.

Jacob Lookerman (sheriff, DO) to summon:
- Thomas Wall administrator of John
  Walker.
- Mary, Thomas, William, & Joseph
  Ennalls executors of Bartholomew
  Ennalls.
- Walter Cambell & his wife executrix
  of John Edwards & executrix of
  Phineas Blackwood.
- John Bassey executor of Michael
  Bassey. [languid]
- Roger Trotten administrator of
  Thomas Scott.

- Ann Thompson administratrix of Joseph Thompson. [non est inventor]

15A:58 Ephraim Wilson (sheriff, SO) to summon:
- Thomas Morris administrator of John Murfy.
- William Whittington executor of Thomas Osborn.
- Donnough Dennis executor of Roger Ocane.
- Thomas Piles administrator of John Sterry.
- Alice Willin executrix of Thomas Willin.
- Anne Adison administratrix of Alexander Adison.
- Katharine Heathley administratrix of William Heathley.
- Thomas Bramley executor of Thomas Osborn.
- Rhoda Francis executrix of John Cropper.
- William Jones executor of Cornelius Jones.
- Elisabeth Lampin administratrix of Thomas Lampin. [not in balywick]
- Elisabeth Roberts administratrix of John Roberts. [lives in DO]
- John Vigorous administrator of Ann Smith. [lives in DO]

Ninion Beal (sheriff, CV) exhibited summons to Col. Henry Darnall to exhibit will of Mary Darnall.

Robert Mason (sheriff, SM) exhibited attachment to Robert Carvile (g) to answer charge of contempt & libel of Daniel Moy.

Ninion Beal (sheriff, CV) exhibited summons to
15A:59 Hugh Montgomery & his wife Katharine executrix of George Parker one of executors of Thomas Cosden & to summon Hugh Ellys executor of Mordecai Hunton other executor of said Cosden to render accounts on estate of said Cosden.

John Holloway who married widow of Samuel Vines (CV) exhibited accounts.

Exhibited was inventory of John
Blomfeild (SM).

Daniel Sheridin administrator of William
Keepe (CV) exhibited inventory &
accounts.

John Pettybone (AA) administrator of
Thomas Pettibone (AA) exhibited
accounts.

Mr. William Dent procurator for Mrs.
Mary Ashcom widow of Nathaniel Ashcom
(CV) appeared.

22 August. Samuel Yong & his wife Mary
administratrix of
15A:60 Maj. Thomas Francis (AA) exhibited
accounts, proved before Mr. Richard
Hill (AA). Mentions: payment to Charles
Whitehead. Continuance was granted.

Edward Fowler & his wife Alice widow &
administratrix of Thomas Willin (SO)
exhibited accounts. Continuance was
granted.

William Jones executor of Cornelius
Johnson (SO)
15A:61 was granted continuance.

Philip Hoskins (CH) who married
administratrix of Margaret Lemaire (CH)
exhibited accounts & additional
inventory. Mentions: Mr. Edward
Sanders.

Thomas Delahide who married Ann widow &
administratrix of Alexander Wilson (SO)
exhibited inventory & accounts.

Hugh Montgomery & his wife Katharine
widow & executrix of George Parker
exhibited accounts.
15A:62 Mentions: Dr. Moore, Col. Taylor.

Hugh Ellis administrator of Thomas
Cosden was granted continuance.

Thomas Gwither administrator of Morgan
Prance (SM) exhibited additional
inventory & accounts. Dismissal was

Court Session: 1693

granted.

John Leach, Jr. & Francis Billingsley
administrators of Francis Davis (CV)
exhibited accounts.

Capt. Henry Mitchell administrator of
Charles Parvy exhibited accounts.

William Moss (CH) administrator of John
Clark (CH) exhibited inventory, by
appraisers Edward Rookwood & William
Spokenal on 18 April 1689.

15A:63 William Meads (CV) administrator of
Capt. John Cobrath (CV) exhibited
accounts.

Joannes Baptista Carberry administrator
of Cuthbert Scot (SM) exhibited that one
of appraisers is sick. Continuance was
granted.

Robert Thompson who married widow &
executrix of Giles Blizard (CH)
exhibited inventory.

Mr. William Dent for John Booker & his
wife executrix of Richard Price (CH)
exhibited that said John Baker is not
well & compelled to stay at home.
Continuance was granted.

Joseph Edloe (CV) administrator of Peter
Pheppard exhibited inventory.

Robert Thompson (CH) attorney for George
Elwes administrator of Thomas Elwes was
granted continuance.

15A:64 William Browne & his wife administratrix
of William Ferguson (CV) exhibited
accounts. Continuance was granted.

Richard Litton & his wife administratrix
of John Durden (AA) exhibited accounts.

Walter Felps administrator of George
Bauston (AA) exhibited accounts, proved
before Mr. Henry Hanslap.

Mr. Philip Lynes (SM) petitioned for Robert Cooper & his wife Patience to be summoned.

Robert King & Samuel Hopkins petitioned for Mr. John Francklyn that his wife's absence is because she is incapacitated to perform a voyage over the bay. Proceedings of John Cropper. Date: 10 August 1693.

15A:65 Exhibited from TA:
- will of Ann Mitchell, dated 8 July 1692, proved before Mr. William Finney on 21 March.
- bond of Mary Hopkins administratrix of John Hopkins dated 15 November 1692. Sureties: Henry Frith, Thomas Hopkins.
- bond of Isaac Drury administrator of John Warner dated 22 February 1692/3. Sureties: Edward Casaway, James Scot.
- bond of Sarah Cartwright administratrix of Charles Cartwright dated 4 March 1692/3. Sureties: Ralph Dawson, Robert Harrison.
- bond of James Benson administrator of Thomas Surcot dated 21 March 1692/3. Sureties: John Edmondson, Nicholas Low.
- bond of Peter Watts administrator of John Ayre dated 3 June 1693. Sureties: William Bexley, William Watts.
- bond of John Salter administrator of John Reeves dated 26 June 1693. Sureties: John Valiant, Anthony Rumball
- bond of John Lambert administrator of John Fleming (mariner, Bedeford), dated 16 August 1693. Sureties: John Lillingston, Robert Macklin.

16 August 1693 at Somerset Co. Thomas Jones & John King petitioned that they were sureties to Mr. Stephen Luff for sheriff. Caveat issued against his estate.

15A:66 Samuel Thomas for his mother Ann petitioned for continuance. Date: 18

Court Session: 1693

August 1693 Anne Arundel Co. Said
petition was granted.

23 August. Robert Mason (sheriff, SM)
exhibited summons to Robert Cooper & his
wife Patience.

Mr. William Dent procurator for Mr.
Thomas Clark who was summoned to render
accounts on estate of Leonard Greene.
Said Clark is only an executor in trust,
& has done division amongst children &
delivered to the widow. Continuance was
granted.

Mr. William Dent exhibited that the
difference between Col. Henry Darnall &
Mr. Henry Lowe was referred to
arbitration. Said Dent for said Darnall
petitioned for LoA on estate of Mrs.
Mary Darnall his mother. Said Lowe
petitioned that the will be produced.
15A:67 Continuance was granted.

Mr. George Plater procurator for
Gilbert Clark (g, CH) exhibited a LaC
from Mr. Richard Clouds, regarding the
estate of Robert Arbuckle (merchant).
Said Clark is obliged to surrender to
Mr. (N) Arbuckle brother & heir of
dec'd. Said Clouds complied.

Thomas Orman & his wife executrix of
John Tong were granted continuance.

Mr. John Bayne (SM) for his mother Mrs.
Eleanor Bayne administratrix of Philip
Deyrer (CH) was granted continuance.

15A:68 24 August. Mr. William Dent procurator
for Edward Milstead & his wife vs.
William Serjeant & his wife executrix of
John Ward. Said Serjeant has not
replied to libel or charge of contempt.
Ruling: proceed as by law.

Mr. William Dent procurator for Roger
Brooke & his wife executrix of Winifred
Mullett vs. Col. Edward Pye. Said Pye
has not replied to libel or charge of
contempt. Ruling: proceed as by law.

Page 221

Court Session: 1693

William Smoote vs. Robert Yates & his
wife executrix of James Tayer executor
of John Bowles who married executrix of
William Baker. Continuance was granted.

Daniel Moy son & heir of Richard Moy vs.
Robert Carvile executor of Elisabeth Moy
executrix of said Richard. Answer
exhibited.

Charles Beckwith vs. Mr. Kenelm
Cheseldine for Henry Fernley executor of
Ann Dennis executrix of Thomas Bankes.
Libel exhibited.

Murty Horney & his wife Elisabeth
daughter of Winlock Christison vs.
William Dixon & his wife Elisabeth &
William Sharp executors of said
Christison. No one appeared for the
plaintiff. Ruling: case dismissed.

15A:69 Philip Lynes Mr. Samuel Watkyns
procurator for Robert Cooper & his wife
Patience.. Continuance was granted.

George Short vs. John Bayne
administrator of John Lang. Libel
exhibited.

Thomas Morris administrator of John
Murfy (SO) exhibited accounts.

Roger Trotten administrator of Thomas
Scott (DO) exhibited accounts.

Philip Cox & his wife Sarah
administratrix of John Johnson vs.
Thomas Courtney & his wife executrix of
Fobbe Roberts. Answer exhibited.

Nicholas Sewall petitioned that he is
unable to ride to Office. Date: 21
August 1693. Continuance was granted.

15A:70 Capt. Thomas Ennals one of executors of
Bartholomew Ennals (DO) petitioned:
• Joseph Ennals (one of children of
dec'd) relinquished his share.
Date: 23 December 1692. Witnesses:
Philip Pitt, William Smith, Francis
Hayward. Attested by Hugh

Page 222

Eccleston.
* John Ennalls

15A:71 ...

relinquished his share. Date: 4
February 1692/3. Witnesses: Henry
Hooper, Roger Woolford.
* Henry Ennalls relinquished his
share. Date: 4 February 1692/3.
Witnesses: Henry Hooper, Roger
Woolford.

Henry Bonner exhibited that widow Giles
is very aged & incapable of rendering
accounts. Date: 18 August 1693 Anne
Arundel Co.

15A:72 She is administratrix of John Giles
(AA). Continuance was granted.

29 August. Samuel Watkyns procurator
for John Cumber grandchild of John
Cumber (AA) vs. Mordecai Moore & his
wife Ursula executrix of Col. William
Burges executor of Nicholas Painter who
married Judith Parker (alias Judith
Cumber) executrix of said Cumber.
Defendants summoned.

William Dent procurator for Edward
Milstead (CH) vs. William Serjeant &
his wife Damoras executrix of John Ward
(CH). Attachment rendered.

2 September. Richard Sowter (g)
exhibited PoA from Dame Letitia Bawdon
relict & executrix of Sir John Bawdon
(knight, London). Also LoA to said
Sowter & Mr. John Gardiner (merchant,
London). Said Sowter was granted
administration. Security: John
Edmondson (g, TA). Appraisers: MM
Garret Vanseringen,

15A:73 Henry Denton.

Francis Armstrong (TA) son & heir of
Francis Armstrong (TA) exhibited that
Frances Armstrong widow & executrix of
said Francis is also dec'd. Said
Francis (son) was granted administration
dbn on estate of Francis (father).
Security: John Edmondson (TA).
Appraisers: Thomas Smithson, Michael
Turbutt. Mr. William Finney to

administer oath.

8 September. Philip Lynes (g, SM)
exhibited that Mary Lewis widow of James
Lewis (SM) relinquished administration
on his estate. & desires her brother
said Lynes to administer the estate.
Witness: Christopher Gregory. Said
Lynes was granted administration.
Security: William Taylard. Appraisers:
Owen Gwither, Philip Brisco. Mr.
Edward Greenhalgh to administer oath.

15A:74 23 September. Hugh Hopewell (CV) was
granted administration on estate of
Jonathon King (wheelwright, CV), as
principle creditor. Mr. Philip Lynes,
also a considerable creditor, renounced
administration. Security: Mr. William
Taylard. Appraisers: William Hames,
John Wiseman. Mr. Samuel Watkyns to
administer oath.

Exhibited nuncupative will of Lionel
Copley, Esq., proved by John Llewellin
who wrote the will. Col. Nehemiah
Blakiston, the Judge & one of trustees,
renounced administration. Col.
Nicholas Greenberry, another trustee,
renounced administration by reason of
age & remoteness of habitation. John
Llewellin is on a voyage to ENG.

15A:75 Thomas Tench, Esq. (AA) & George Plater,
Esq. (CV), the other trustees, were
granted administration, on behalf of the
children.

15A:76 Appraisers: MM Philip Lynes, Gilbert
Clark.

15A:77 27 September. Elias King (KE)
exhibited:
- will of William Thomas, constituting
  Susanna Thomas executrix, proved.
  Also exhibited was oath of
  appraisers.
- will & inventory of Daniel Toaes.
- will & inventory of Philip Davis.
- inventory of Mark Benton, by Hester
  Benton administratrix.
- will of William Pearle, constituting
  Elisabeth Pearle executrix, proved.
- oath of John Hynson administrator of

Court Session: 1693

Jonathon Grafton.
- oath of John Hynson & Robert Burman
  executors of Joseph Wicks.

GENERAL INDEX

124, 133, 179,
219
Mary 138, 139
Roger 62, 66, 72,
96, 138, 139,
181, 205, 214
Thomas 60, 98
William 201, 208,
222
Ball
Henry 60
Joseph 195
Michael 130, 136,
138, 162
Ballard
Charles 156, 165
Bancks
Richard 166
Sarah 166
Bankes
Ann 15, 112
Anne 195
Richard 211, 215
Sarah 211, 215
Thomas 15, 18, 19,
24, 67, 72, 112,
123, 124, 149,
195, 222
Banks
Ann 149, 208
Thomas 13, 71, 201
Barber
Human 157
Numan 148
Barbier
Newman 82
Barker
John 147
Barnes
Ann 170
Francis 2, 170
Barons
John 122
Bartam
Richard 68
Bartlet
Sarah 71
Bartlett
Ralph 1
Sarah 1
Barton
Lewis 167
Nathan 111
Richard 150

William 17, 26,
127, 151, 163,
187, 209
Basey
Jane 165
Michael 4, 165, 167
Bassey
Joan 207
Joane 182
John 216
Jone 129
Michael 129, 182,
207, 216
Bateman
Christian 90, 186
William 90, 186
Batson
Edward 198
Mr. 141
Thomas 177
Battee
Elisabeth 65, 68
Seaborn 68
Seaborne 75, 153
Batten
William 142
Batty
Hierom 37
Hierome 23, 32
Seaborne 190
Baty
John 96, 145
Bauston
George 219
Bawdon
John 223
Letitia 223
Bawstock
George 190
Bayard
Nicholas 6
Bayly
George 135
John 12, 16, 25
Mary 12, 16, 25,
143
Richard 67, 143
Bayn
John 210
Bayne
Ann 122
Eleanor 212, 215,
221
John 122, 201, 209,

210, 221, 222
Beach
    Elias 66
Beal
    Ninion 213, 217
    Thomas 29, 57, 195
Beale
    Ninian 2, 14, 107,
        154
    Thomas 57
Beall
    Ninean 162
    Ninian 139, 141,
        162, 163
Bean
    John 41, 52
Beane
    Ellanor 191
Beanes
    Christopher 33
Beard
    Richard 8
Bearecroft
    John 116, 168, 169,
        173, 185, 208,
        210
Beaumont
    Mary 158
    Mrs. 158
    Rich. 51
    Richard 158, 208,
        211, 215
Beavan
    Charles 162
Beck
    Edward 31, 75, 84,
        97, 117, 127,
        140
Beckwith vs. Fernley
        222 1
Beckwith
    Charles 13, 15,
        195, 199, 201,
        222
    George 13, 15
Bedell
    Edward 29
Bedle
    Ed. 26
    Edward 50
Bedworth
    Richard 28
Beech
    Elias 142, 148, 162

Beedle
    Edward 2, 18, 117,
        120, 140, 211
    Mary 201, 203
Beet
    John 163
Begley
    Thomas 111
Belt
    John 190
Benitt
    John 70
Benjar
    Katherine 95
    Robert 95, 97, 114
Bennet
    Henry 113
    John 158, 197, 209
    Richard 208
    Thomas 209
Bennett
    John 145
    Richard 101, 153
Bennison
    Richard 53, 65, 109
    Susanna 53, 65
Bennisson
    Richard 75
Bennit
    John 56
    Richard 152
Bennitt
    Edward 31
    Henry 2, 40
    John 18, 70
Benson
    George 52, 76, 113,
        179
    Hugh 37, 62
    James 220
    Katharine 37
    Robert 1, 132, 142,
        178, 214
Bentham
    Richard 66
Benton
    Hester 170, 224
    Mark 170, 224
    Richard 69, 169
    Robert 205
Berch
    John 128
Berry
    James 144

Page 229

Samuel 148
William 121, 200
Bery
    James 82
Betts
    George 20, 51, 159
    Richard 51
Bexley
    William 200, 220
Bexsley
    William 2
Bibins
    Charles 139
Bigger
    James 4, 6, 7, 25,
        32, 36, 41, 64,
        65, 66, 67, 115,
        126, 127
    John 150, 208
    Margaret 127
Billingsley
    Francis 140, 157,
        181, 205, 213,
        219
Birens
    John 83
Bisco
    Philip 119
Biscoe
    James 33
    Sarah 33
Bishop
    (N) 35
    Ann 23
    Henry 23, 49, 90,
        110
    James 43
    John 110
    Richard 22, 34, 35,
        36, 37, 43, 44,
        47, 54, 55, 80
    Sarah 49, 110
    William 22, 30, 34,
        35, 37, 44, 47,
        48, 53, 54, 55,
        80
Bishopp
    James 91
    Nicholas 94, 138
    William 155
Bishopston
    xx 54
Blackiston
    Ebenezar 47, 216

Nehea. 67
Blackwell
    Thomas 185
Blackwood
    Phineas 128, 147,
        182, 186, 207,
        216
    Susanna 128
Bladen
    William 211
Blake
    Christian 103
Blakiston
    Col. 196
    Ebenezar 45
    N. 185
    Ne. 61, 208, 209,
        210
    Nehemiah 36, 53,
        169, 171, 224
Blaney
    David 21, 39, 75
Blanfoard
    Thomas 58
Blizard
    Giles 123, 219
Blizzard
    Giles 62
    Mary 62
Blomfeild
    John 218
Blomfield
    John 81, 172
Bloyce
    Thomas 159
Bloyd
    Daniel 134, 154
    David 155, 181
Boanam
    William 185
Boareman
    Maj. 199
Boarman
    William 63, 88
Bohemiah
    Augustine Harman 1
Bonam
    William 86
Bonham
    Ann 86, 116, 183,
        187, 206, 215
    William 86, 111,
        116, 183, 206,
        215

Bonner
    Henry 133, 197,
        203, 223
Bonnman
    Ann 43
    William 43
Booker
    John 162, 211, 215,
        219
Boone
    Grace 167
    Humphry 45, 54, 65,
        77, 93, 108
    John 167
Booth
    John 59, 146
Boothby
    Edward 159, 209,
        211
Boram
    John 200
Boring
    John 8, 21, 28, 49,
        61, 69, 74, 79,
        122, 166
Bornewall
    Oliver 157
Bostick
    Thomas 111, 180,
        206, 216
Boston
    Samuel 49
Boswell
    John 37, 45
Boswick
    Thomas 84
Boteler
    Edward 96
Boucheir
    John 204
Boucher
    John 76, 97, 105,
        213
    Ruth 76, 97
Bouchier
    John 181
Bouge
    John 195
Boughton
    Richard 1, 65
Bould
    John 192
Bouman
    Thomas 62

Bounsell
    Walter 32
Bourn
    James 49
    Samuell 32, 50
Bourne
    Capt. 125
    James 10, 11, 66,
        107
    Samuel 125, 149
    Samuell 74
Bowdell
    Thomas 71
Bowdle
    Thomas 58, 71, 193,
        198
Bowen
    Richard 25, 39
Bowles
    John 31, 142, 177,
        201, 208, 222
    Margery 201, 208
    Thomas 129, 142,
        179, 185
Bowling
    James 1, 88, 151,
        209
    John 62
Bowman
    Thomas 66, 72, 138,
        139
Boyd
    Daniel 205
Boyden
    Deborah 131
    John 123, 131, 160
Bracher
    Jane 26
    John 26, 148, 151,
        201, 205, 214
Bracker
    John 178
Bradford
    Thomas 123
Braine
    Thomas 78
Bramley
    Thom. 207
    Thomas 183, 187,
        217
Brand
    Samuel 178, 199
Brande
    Samuel 132

Brands
  Samuel 216
Brandt
  Rand. 34
  Rando. 160
  Randolph 184, 191
  Samuel 188
Branock
  Edmond 42
Brant
  Mr. 194
Brayne
  Elisabeth 146, 164
  Thomas 115, 137,
    138, 146, 149,
    164
Breacher
  John 127
Breamer
  Elisabeth 203
Breames
  Christopher 27
Breerton
  William 77
Bregran
  John 102
Bremer
  Elisabeth 131
  James 131, 137, 203
Brent
  Ann 25, 32, 35, 55,
    202
  Henry 25, 32, 35,
    55, 195, 202,
    208
Brereton
  William 9, 10, 13,
    17, 19, 20, 30,
    38, 48, 51, 56,
    100, 103, 104,
    105, 119, 135,
    141, 142, 159
Brerton
  William 18
Brewer
  Elisabeth 123, 170
  James 123
  William 170
Bridgeforth
  Robert 80
Bright
  John 38, 194
Brightwell
  Richard 14, 26, 36,

    41, 50, 126, 155
  Robert 44
Brimmer
  Elisabeth 177, 196
  James 177, 196
Brisco
  Mr. 185
  Philip 99, 119,
    184, 195, 198,
    224
Briscoe
  Philip 172, 185,
    198
Britt
  Thomas 86
Broadaway
  Nicholas 111
Broadrib
  (N) 61
  Isabell 92
  Isabella 109, 126
Broadribb
  Sibilla 75
Broadway
  Nicholas 137, 138
Brockus
  William 171
Bromfeild
  John 168
Bromley
  Elisabeth 129
  Thomas 129
Brook
  Thomas 3
Brooke
  Baker 32, 35, 55,
    195, 202, 208
  Charles 195, 202,
    208
  Francis 41, 75, 102
  John 74, 129, 164,
    165, 167, 169,
    188
  Judith 188
  Mary 170, 173, 184,
    191, 194
  Roger 6, 117, 149,
    150, 170, 173,
    174, 179, 184,
    191, 194, 202,
    221
  Thomas 3, 50, 130,
    133, 146, 173
Brookes

G. 72
Bussey
Ann 209
George 15, 39, 209
Hezekiah 15
Bussy
George 74
Michael 64
Busy
Paul 39, 53
Susanna 39, 53
Butler
Caecil 202
Mr. 157
Butterham
William 183
Button
(N). 79
Buttram
Jane 15
Nicholas 15, 31
Buttrum
Nicholas 32
Butts
Richard 203
Buxton
George 9, 151

Cade
Robert 57
Cagge
Robert 48, 69
Calke
Isaack 40
Callahan
Martha 72
Cambell
John 82, 87, 100,
113, 175, 181,
204, 213
Walter 182, 186,
207, 216
Cammell
John 1
Campell
John 70
Cannon
Stephen 26, 38, 95,
100
Cannydee
William 200
Capell
Benjamin 28, 169

Isabell 169
Capill
Benjamin 8
Capline
James 142
Carberry
Joannes Baptista
219
John Baptista 177,
187, 192
Carbery
Elisabeth 170
John Baptista 170,
175
Carleton
Dubley 136
Edward 136
Carman
Elisabeth 89, 111,
183, 187
Thomas 89, 111,
115, 183
Carnell
Daniell 48
Deborah 48
Carnoll
Daniel 91
Deborah 91
Caroll
Charles 193, 194
Mary 187
Carpenter
Ann 86
Francis 20
Mary 86
William 86
Carr
Mary 83
Peter 12, 16, 71,
150, 192
Walter 2, 28
William 83
Carrington
John 8, 28
Carrol
Mary 207
Thomas 183, 207
Carroll
Charles 124, 170,
173, 178
Martha 178
Mary 127, 183
Rebeckah 72
Thomas 127

Carse
    Robert 210
Carter
    Henry 102, 105,
        142, 170
    John 14
Cartwright
    Charles 189, 220
    Mathew 148, 161,
        196
    Sarah 148, 189,
        196, 220
Carvile
    John 148
    Ro. 102, 131, 134,
        165
    Robert 10, 11, 26,
        34, 35, 36, 41,
        47, 49, 55, 61,
        62, 64, 66, 68,
        70, 72, 80, 93,
        105, 107, 109,
        124, 126, 135,
        146, 155, 156,
        158, 172, 174,
        185, 187, 191,
        192, 202, 211,
        217, 222
    Thomas 50, 63, 137,
        142, 148, 161,
        168, 169, 170,
        177, 184, 188,
        191, 194
Cary
    Jane 9, 19, 48
    Thomas 9, 19, 48
Casaway
    Edward 220
Casey
    Thomas 89
Caske
    Isaac 97
    Isaak 78
Castleton
    Robert 101
Caswell
    Henry 195
Catterson
    Francis 124
Catterton
    Michaell 65
Causeene
    Ignatius 132, 142,
        145, 148, 161

Cave
    William 178
Celin
    Mary 197
Chadwell
    John 114
Chadwill
    Elisabeth 83
    John 83
Chafe
    John 86, 111
    Richard 54
Chaffe
    John 81
Chaires
    John 43
Chairs
    John 86, 111
Chamberlain
    Samuell 29
Chamberlin
    Samuell 75
Chambers
    Richard 38
Chaplin
    William 73, 74, 126
Chapline
    William 59
Chappell
    John 73, 90, 94
Chapple
    Alex. 166
    John 166
Charlett
    Richard 4, 6
Chaspell
    John 59
Cheseldin
    Kenelm 68
Cheseldine
    Kenelm 209, 222
Cheseldyn
    Kenelm 50, 96, 99,
        134, 154, 155
    Kenelme 4, 36
    Mr. 159
Cheseldyne
    Kenelm 147
    Kenelme 169
    Mr. 124
Chesheir
    Richard 197
Chesly
    Elisabeth 64

Chetham
  John 60
Cheverill
  John 169, 170
Chew
  Ann 73
  Elisabeth 153, 190
  Jos. 59
  Joseph 59, 73, 135,
    136, 141, 153,
    166, 179, 188,
    190
  Margaret 179
  Samuell 73
Cheyney
  Ellinor 90, 108
  Richard 90, 108,
    153
Chilcot
  Anthony 42
Child
  Mark 48, 69
Chilman
  Richard 36, 41
Chiney
  Eleanor 179, 188
  Richard 179
Chittam
  John 2, 31, 154,
    164
Christan
  Lawrence 216
  Thomas 216
Christian
  John 80
  Lawrence 97, 140,
    151, 180
  Thomas 140, 151,
    180, 206
Christison
  Elisabeth 198
  Winlock 183, 187,
    190, 192, 222
Churchyard
  Herman 80
Churnell
  Joseph 160
Claget
  Thomas 199
Clagett
  Sarah 174
Clare
  Mark 70, 144
  Marke 5, 57, 70

Clark
  (N) 213
  Abraham 2, 40
  Benjamin 185
  Gilbert 201, 210,
    221, 224
  John 23, 178, 196,
    204, 211, 214,
    219
  Philip 172, 174,
    175, 178, 187,
    192, 193
  Thomas 173, 177,
    185, 187, 196,
    204, 210, 221
Clarke
  Abraham 113, 145,
    157, 158
  Andrew 68, 74, 88,
    151
  Ann 2
  Gilbert 49, 158
  Hannagh 72
  John 2, 83, 84,
    118, 145, 150,
    165
  Ph. 72
  Richard 115, 137,
    146, 149, 164
  Robert 91, 96
  Thomas 91
Clarkson
  William 156, 163,
    164
Clarol
  Mr. 199
Clayton
  William 189
Cleave
  Nathaniel 121
Clegate
  Thomas 112
Clegatt
  Thomas 62, 66, 96
Clement
  Andrew 24, 42
  John 95, 101
Clements
  Andres 45
  Andrew 119
  John 151
Clementson
  Andrew 77
Cleverly

Ann 23, 34
Thomas 23, 34
Clocker
Daniel 124, 156,
174, 175, 197
Cloud
Nicholas 34
Cloude
Richard 7
Clouds
Judith 210
Nicholas 22, 33,
34, 35, 36, 37,
43, 44, 45, 47,
48, 53, 54, 55,
56
Richard 134, 147,
158, 170, 194,
199, 209, 210,
221
Cluely
Elisabeth 48, 98
Samuel 98
Samuell 48
Coale
William 166
Coate
George 48
Coates
John 127, 128
Cobrath
John 205, 219
Cobreath
John 144, 145, 157,
181
Cobreth
John 213
Cock
Gibart 78
Griffith 45
Cocke
Gesburde 77
Gisbarde 78
Cockerill
John 43
Cocks
Philip 169, 212
Sarah 169
Thomas 13
William 90
Codd
St. Leger 160
Cole
Ann 112

Francis 169
George 96, 98, 106,
153, 163
Jeoffry 184
John 66, 69
Nicholas 68, 69
Robert 196
William 112, 166,
178, 188, 216
Coleborne
William 93, 104,
154
Colebourne 5
William 85, 117,
120, 122
Colleton
William 39
Collier
Edward 47, 123
Francis 82, 107,
136, 139, 141,
154, 162, 164,
204, 213
James 47, 123, 178,
206, 216
John 78, 89, 114
Collings
Thomas 119
Collins
Frances 46
Francis 180
John 131
Thomas 46, 89, 102,
118, 137, 162,
183, 192
Collison
George 40
Martha 212
Peter 212
Collyer
James 7, 123
John 26
Sarah 7
Colyer
Edward 123
Combes
William 52, 58, 70,
71, 91, 96
Comegys
(N) 34
Cornelius 19, 20,
28, 61, 69, 75,
92, 109, 113,
126, 181, 204,

213

Compton
 John 2
Conant
 Lidia 73
 Lydia 5, 24, 97,
  113
 Robert 5, 24, 97,
  112, 113
Connaway
 Ann 104
 Joseph 109
Connelly
 Patrick 174
Constable
 Catherine 101
 Henry 101, 143,
  147, 165, 185
 Katherine 165
Cooke
 Amos 122, 183
 Anne 192
 Edward 132
 Francis 123
 Katherine 132
 William 38, 39
Cookesey
 Phillip 44
Cooksey
 (N) 36, 41
 Ann 14, 26, 126,
  155
 Catherine 14
 Elisabeth 14, 26,
  126, 155
 Katherine 26, 126,
  155
 Mary 14, 26, 126,
  155
 Philip 126, 155
 Phillip 14, 26
 Samuel 134, 147,
  158
Cooper
 Alice 88
 Ann 94, 125, 138
 Jane 154
 Nicholas 27
 Patience 174, 177,
  187, 220, 221
 Patience. 222
 Robert 174, 177,
  187, 193, 197,
  201, 220, 221,

222

 Samuel 93, 120, 154
 Sarah 93
 Thomas 44, 72, 122
 William 203
Coor
 John 168
Cooy
 Sam. 23
Copedge
 John 159, 170
Copeland
 Samuel 150
Copley
 L. 171
 Lionel 169, 224
Coppper
 Grace 70
Corbin
 Nicholas 130
Cord
 William 72, 95, 130
Cornell
 Joseph 11, 12, 25,
  112
Cosden
 Thomas 34, 68, 70,
  96, 117, 125,
  150, 180, 204,
  212, 213, 217,
  218
Costin
 Henry 9, 151
Cottingham
 Mary 93, 120, 182,
  186, 194
 THomas 93, 120,
  182, 194
Cottman
 Benjamin 9
 Benjamine 5
Coursey
 Elisabeth 10, 146
 Henry 10, 17, 34,
  42, 43, 54, 58,
  63, 64, 81, 86,
  87
 Mr. 63
 William 10, 46, 86,
  146
Coursy
 William 10
Courtney
 Eleanor 169, 174,

Page 238

223
Judith 172, 176,
  202, 223
Curnell
  Joseph 160, 211,
  215
Curre
  Alexander 151
Currier
  John 191, 193
Curtis
  (N) 213
  Michael 177, 187,
  196, 204
  Sarah 196
Cusack
  Michael 43
Cusacke
  Michaell 28
Cusick
  Michael 17

D'Costa
  Elisabeth 171
Dacres
  Joseph 162
Dafes
  Philip 57
Dakes
  Robert 120
Dakins
  Simon 41
Dale
  Priscilla 145
Daly
  Bryan 176
Dams
  John 21
Dance
  Ann 155
  Thomas 155
Daniel
  Isaack 41
Daniell
  Thomas 41, 43
Dant
  Thomas 78
Dante
  Thomas 33
Darcy
  Thomas 18, 35, 40,
  42
Dare

Nathaniel 1
Nathaniell 23, 65
William 1, 8, 43,
  44, 46, 76, 89
Darnall
  (N) 25
  Col. 61, 134
  Henry 15, 52, 53,
  54, 57, 68, 70,
  108, 138, 139,
  201, 217, 221
  John 156, 201, 202
  Mary 201, 217, 221
Dash
  John 63, 197
Dasheile
  James 95, 100, 103,
  135
Dasheill
  James 101, 108
Dashield
  James 26
Dashiele
  James 136
Dashiell
  James 38, 136
Davies
  Thomas 52
Davis
  Ann 104
  David 34, 146
  Elisabeth 192
  Francis 140, 157,
  181, 205, 213,
  219
  John 73, 104, 112,
  113, 135, 182,
  186, 192
  Nathaniel 201
  Philip 224
  Phillip 13
  Thomas 70, 115,
  118, 137, 138
Daw
  John 205
  Mary 79, 103
Dawes
  William 139
Dawson
  Henry 13
  Ralph 220
  Richard 8
Day
  Edward 111

Robert 96, 114, 124
Deackes
    Henry 145
Deakins
    Thomas 21, 77
Deane
    John 131
    William 20, 69, 85,
        99
Dekreyker
    John 49, 51
Delahay
    (N) 21
    Elisabeth 212
    Thomas 168, 212
Delahide
    Ann 218
    Elisabeth 215
    Thomas 182, 215,
        218
Dellahay
    Mathew 8
Demondidier
    Anthony 8, 28
Demundeder
    Anthony 122
Denis
    Ann 72, 149
    Donagh 85
Dennis
    Ann 13, 15, 18, 22,
        35, 53, 67, 112,
        123, 124, 201,
        222
    Donagh 119
    Donnough 182, 186,
        207, 217
    Edm. 3, 6
    Edmond 4, 22, 35,
        53
    Edmund 19
Denny
    Christopher 200
Denseen
    William 203
Dent
    John 57, 88, 210,
        212
    William 12, 15, 27,
        54, 123, 148,
        152, 155, 161,
        184, 191, 192,
        193, 201, 202,
        208, 210, 218,

219, 221, 223
Denton
    Hen. 194
    Henry 68, 124, 169,
        223
    James 45
Derumple
    James 67, 77
    Mary 77
Devilliard
    Jacob 24, 114
Devillyard
    Jacob 42, 119
Dew
    John 139, 147, 181,
        213
Deyrer
    Philip 212, 215,
        221
Deyzer
    Philip 208
Diamont
    John 83
Dickason
    Walter 200
Dickinson
    William 200
Digges
    William 57, 70, 71,
        195
Diggs
    William 210
Dillon
    Thomas 25
Dimond
    John 178, 216
Divellard
    Jacob 94
Divies
    Thomas 135
Dixon
    Ambrose 84, 117,
        182, 193
    Elisabeth 187, 193,
        222
    Mary 84, 182, 186,
        193
    Thomas 120
    William 183, 187,
        190, 191, 192,
        193, 198, 222
Dobbs
    John 21, 113
Dodd

Peter 37
Done
    Robert 70
Doneuan
    Daniell 57
Donn
    Elisabeth 16
    Obadiah 16
Dorne
    Robert 58
Dorrell
    Chatherine 40
    Nicholas 40
Dorsey
    Edward 29, 43, 52,
        75, 86, 101,
        179, 185, 187
    John 86, 101, 179,
        185, 187
    Joshua 86, 100,
        101, 179, 185
    William 96, 164
Dossett
    John 39
Dossey
    John 42
    William 42
Dougherty
    Nathaniel 182, 194
Doughestie
    Nathaniel 85
Doughterty
    Nathaniel 120
Doughty
    Peter 95, 100
Douglas
    Mary 208
    Robert 208, 211
Douglass
    Robert 215
Dove
    Robert 4, 6, 81, 92
Dowce
    Edward 120
Downes
    Ann 170
    Francis 185
    John 170
Doyne
    Joshua 194
    Robert 8, 16, 25,
        27, 45
Doynes
    John 170

Drake
    William 151
Drew
    Andrew 73
    Anthony 65, 80,
        103, 107
    Mary Ann 65, 80
Drinkwater
    James 163
Drumple
    James 152
    Mary 152
    William 167
Drury
    Isaac 220
Dryden
    Henry 58
    James 93, 122
Dryfeild
    Thomas 4
Duall
    Marin 75
Dudson
    Richard 35
Duhattaway
    Jacob 97
Duncan
    Jane 98
Duncon
    Jane 41
    Patrick 41
Dundedale
    Margaret 112
    Margarett 137
    William 112, 137
Dunderdale
    Margaret 183, 187,
        206, 215
    William 183, 206,
        215
Dunkin
    Patrick 76, 90, 98
Durdan
    Honor 179
    John 179
Durden
    Honor 163, 188
    John 163, 219
Durdon
    Honor 141, 152
    John 141, 152
Durham
    Richard 140
Duvall

Marun 24
Dwyer
   Edmund 194
Dymond
   George 212

Eager
   Mary 94, 100
   Thomas 94
Eagle
   Robert 45, 53, 54,
      65, 75, 77, 93,
      108, 143, 186
Earle
   James 115, 183,
      206, 215
Eason
   John 67
Eastgate
   William 53, 94
Eccleston
   Hugh 193, 195, 210,
      223
Eddlin
   Richard 60
Edelen
   Richard 136
Edelin
   Richard 63, 88
Edlen
   Richard 2
Edloe
   Joseph 35, 107,
      126, 134, 138,
      156, 158, 181,
      205, 214, 219
Edmonds
   Elisabeth 117, 140,
      188, 206, 216
   Richard 29, 55,
      117, 140, 188,
      206, 216
   William 121, 144,
      153
Edmondson
   John 53, 57, 64,
      132, 154, 189,
      192, 193, 200,
      220, 223
   Robert 164, 194
   William 200
Edmunds
   Richard 19, 99

Edwards
   Ann 200, 201
   Elisabeth 178
   John 18, 24, 31,
      42, 52, 68, 69,
      76, 81, 88, 111,
      124, 128, 182,
      186, 200, 207,
      216
   Richard 178
   Susanna 88
   Thomas 136
   William 181, 205,
      214
Eiorne
   John 36
Elgate
   (N) 74
   William 10, 18, 30,
      31, 72, 73, 76,
      107, 126, 183,
      187, 192
Elgatt
   William 141, 142
Ellis
   Dorothy 154, 164
   Elisabeth 50, 117
   Hugh 27, 96, 117,
      141, 150, 157,
      180, 204, 212,
      213, 218
   James 144, 166
   Peter 50
   Rob. 55
   Thomas 2, 107, 154,
      164
Ellys
   Hugh 217
Elmes
   Thomas 156
   William 83, 84, 97,
      127, 156
Elridge
   William 18
Elsey
   John 133, 160
Elwes
   George 122, 219
   Thomas 122, 178,
      205, 214, 219
Elzey
   Arnold 87, 117,
      118, 156, 165
Emerson

Page 244

110, 189
Frisby
  William 10, 77, 79,
    85, 90, 106
Frith
  Henry 220
Fry
  Edward 1, 31, 69,
    115
  Francis 1
  Joseph 70, 81, 92,
    115, 137, 146,
    149, 164
Frye
  Joseph 6
Furlong
  Edward 13, 34, 78
Furnace
  William 61, 119
Furnice
  William 54

Gaforth
  Richard 114
Gaither
  John 75
Gale
  John 136, 162
Galloway
  Richard 153
Galwith
  John 150
Gamball
  George 23
  Richard 1
  William 1
Gambell
  William 71
Gambra
  Demindigoe 138
  Domindigo 142
  Dominidigo 143
Gant
  Thomas 2, 3, 88,
    133, 168
Gardener
  Richard 52
Gardiner
  John 223
  Luke 37, 52, 54, 62
  Richard 21, 37, 53,
    54, 62, 151
Gardner

Capt. 125
Constant 95
Fridua 150
James 150
John 95, 101, 151
Richard 125
Garey
  William 119
Garforth
  Richard 113
Garland
  John 85
  Samuel 85
  Samuell 24, 56
  Thobias 56
Garrat
  Charles 215
  Nathaniel 66
Garret
  Charles 212
  Nathaniel 87
Garrett
  Charles 142, 151
  Nathaniel 97
  Nathaniell 78
  Richard 56
  Seth 200
Gary
  John 191
  William 117
  Zachariah 191
Gasaway
  Nicholas 68
Gaskin
  Jane 141
Gassaway
  Nicholas 4, 5, 65,
    103, 107, 108,
    133, 161
Gather
  John 28, 43, 52
Gendron
  Mark 210
Gerard
  Just. 177
  Justinian 92, 134,
    147, 158, 196,
    204
  Sarah 134, 147
  Thomas 122
Gerrard
  Ann 52
  Justinian 79
  Thomas 1, 41, 52

Thomas 76
Gordon
    Thomas 104, 126,
        135, 186
Gore
    George 178, 211,
        215
Gorley
    John 65
Gottee
    Richard 5, 28
Gotts
    Richard 197
Goud
    John 149
Gough
    Stephen 172, 173
Gouldsmith
    Joanna 18
    John 7
Gourdon
    Thomas 182, 192
Gover
    Richard 152
    Robert 112
Gower
    Robert 24
Grafton
    Jonathon 225
Graham
    Robert 174, 177,
        178, 187, 192,
        193
Grangier
    Christopher 44
Graves
    William 72
Gray
    John 14, 39, 76,
        90, 98, 108,
        109, 144, 152,
        180
    Joseph 41, 76
    William 89
Greeble
    John 55
Green
    Ann 145, 181
    Anne 214
    Christopher 77, 93
    Francis 60, 91, 196
    George 20, 60
    Henry 36, 40, 46,
        55

Leonard 105, 177,
    196
Robert 60
Thomas 145, 147,
    214
Greenberry
    Nicholas 224
Greenbury
    Mr. 143
    Nicholas 45, 53,
        54, 65, 77, 93,
        100, 169, 197
Greene
    (N) 213
    Ann 205
    Fran. 204
    Francis 177, 187
    George 14, 73
    John 103
    Joseph 168
    Lawrence 99
    Leonard 91, 204,
        221
    Thomas 181, 205
Greeneberry
    Nicholas 210
Greenfeild
    Martha 3
    Thomas 3, 162
Greenfield
    Thomas 133, 139,
        173
Greenhalgh
    Edward 224
Greenhall
    Capt. 194
Gregory
    Christopher 224
Grer
    Ann 148
    George 148
Gresham
    John 65, 68, 75,
        161
Gressam
    John 190
Grey
    John 24, 52
    Joseph 30
    Richard 20
    Thomas 30
Gribble
    John 37, 43
Griffeth

Jenkin 123
Griffin
    Richard 193
    Thomas 63, 68, 69,
       131, 142, 148,
       162, 174, 177,
       193
Griffith
    Jackin 206
    Jenkin 178, 216
Griggs
    John 3, 9, 49, 59,
       60, 62, 66, 67,
       70, 71, 74, 76,
       93, 94, 124,
       125, 128, 202
Grome
    Moses 26
Groome
    Moses 7
Grover
    John 150
Grunwin
    Mr. 63
    Thomas 16, 22, 23,
       29, 66, 69, 70,
       71, 91, 169
Guess
    Elisabeth 14
    George 14
Guest
    George 39
Guibert
    Joshua 185, 210
Guist
    Christopher 28
Guither
    Thomas 68, 135, 158
    William 34, 63,
       142, 158, 162
Gundry
    Benjamin 25
    George 56
    Gideon 116, 117,
       143
    Mary 25
Gunnell
    George 199
Gunnery
    Benjamin 7
    Mary 7
Gunter
    Timothy 82
Guyat

John 95, 99, 103
Guyther
    William 66, 148
Guytor
    William 69
Gwither
    (N) 213
    Nicholas 15
    Owen 224
    Thomas 177, 196,
       198, 199, 204,
       218
    William 15
Gwndry
    Giddon 56

Hacker
    John 54
    Joseph 152
Hacket
    Nicholas 58
Hackett
    James 103, 160, 163
    Mary 57
    Nicholas 14, 57, 71
Haddock
    Thomas 136, 152,
       167
Hagar
    Robert 184, 195,
       198
Hager
    Thomas 88
Haggat
    James 179
Hagget
    James 185
    John 188
Hails
    John 167
Haimes
    William 138
Haines
    William 107, 212
Hall
    Benjamin 209
    Eliasha 213
    Elisabeth 95, 144,
       163
    Elisha 114, 126,
       145, 181, 204,
       205, 213, 214
    James 47, 117

John 7, 26, 56, 78,
89, 114, 115,
123, 159, 160,
188, 203, 216
Joshua 198
Mary 171, 209
Richard 95, 144,
163
Sarah 26, 47, 89,
114, 115, 117,
204
William 171
Hallett
Jacob 40
Halsey
Edward 156, 157
Halstead
Mathias 203
Michael 212
Halstine
Richard 94
Haman
Edward 31, 163
Hambleton
John 59, 60, 62,
66, 93, 108,
124, 126, 146,
156
William 150
Hamersley
Francis 111
Hames
William 224
Hamilton
Gilbert 23, 32, 37
Hammond
James 188, 199
John 100, 101, 178,
216
Hamon
Ann 24
Daniell 77
Edward 24
Philip 80
Hamond
John 86, 95, 132
Hance
John 33, 133, 157
Mary 33
Hanley
John 136
Hanlon
Hugh 32, 51
Hanniford

Joseph 209
Hans
John 71
Hanslap
Capt. 78, 140
Henry 24, 69, 75,
79, 90, 98, 99,
100, 108, 109,
110, 113, 116,
141, 144, 149,
151, 152, 153,
159, 166, 167,
189, 219
Hanslapp
Henry 24, 28, 38,
87, 160, 161,
163, 164
Hansliff
Jerimiah 40
Hanslop
Henry 68
Hanson
Hance 2, 13, 16
Hans 31, 106, 127
Hanse 171
Henry 21
Randolph 145, 165
Harden
John 69
Hardgrave
Edward 14
Harding
Joseph 19
Hardy
Henry 12, 16, 25
Hargness
Ann 26
William 26
Hargrave
Edward 27
Harman
Augustine 1
Henry 88
Mary 88
Thomas 131
Harmer
(N) 47
Timothy 47
Harness
Jacob 129
Harnis
Jacob 142
Harpam
William 211

Harper
    Margrett 42
    William 38, 51
Harquest
    Ann 55
    William 55
Harrington
    Charles 6
Harris
    Ann 14, 27
    Henry 14, 27, 109
    John 59
    Richard 101, 127
    Symon 21, 38, 39,
        75
    Thomas 14
    William 4, 13, 14,
        15, 20, 28, 31,
        61, 69, 84, 85,
        90, 99, 100,
        105, 106, 109,
        120, 129, 140,
        156, 181, 194,
        204, 213
Harrison
    Frances 71
    Francis 52, 91, 96,
        113
    John 18, 60, 212
    Robert 220
Harrys
    William 73
Harsfort
    George 73
Harwood
    Peter 200
Haseldyn
    Richard 41
Haseldyne
    Richard 102, 110,
        138
Hasell
    Richard 56
Hasfurt
    George 61, 85
Haskett
    James 143
Haskings
    Michael 216
Haskins
    John 61, 67
Haslewood
    John 92, 120
Hassell

    Richard 36
Hast
    Daniel 103, 108,
        135, 136
Hastings
    Michael 130, 178,
        188, 207
Hatfield
    William 189
Hathley
    Katherine 108, 136
    William 108, 136
Hatteraile
    (N) 12
Hatton
    Elisabeth 58, 71
    Samuel 127
    Samuell 58, 71
    William 49, 51, 82,
        99, 199
Hawes
    George 136, 162,
        173, 181
Hawkins
    Henry 138, 142,
        166, 199, 209,
        211, 212, 215
    John 86
Hawlton
    Sarah 143
    William 143
Hawton
    Sarah 145
    William 75, 145,
        150, 152, 175,
        178, 196, 198,
        204
Hayden
    Francis 102
    Penelope 102
    Samuel 100
Hayman
    Ellinor 100, 104
    Henry 100, 104
Hayward
    Francis 222
    Nicholas 122
Headger
    Mary 102
    Richard 102
Heard
    John 172, 194
Hearn
    Robert 106

Hearne
　　William 18, 30
Heath
　　Abraham 38, 51
　　James 17, 81
　　Thomas 210
Heathcott
　　Nathaniel 170
Heathley
　　Katharine 182, 187,
　　　　207, 217
　　William 182, 207,
　　　　217
Hebb
　　Thomas 5, 201
Hedge
　　Thomas 2, 34, 203
Hedger
　　Richard 137, 183,
　　　　206, 215
　　William 121
Hemsely
　　Charles 187
Hemsley
　　Charles 102, 137,
　　　　183, 206, 215
　　Mr. 55
　　Mrs. 55
　　William 137
Henderson
　　Bartholomew 87
Henning
　　John 23
Henny
　　James 144
　　John 144
Henry
　　John 150
　　Margaret 150
Herman
　　Elisabeth 65, 76
　　Ephraim 65, 76
　　Gasperus 8
　　Thomas 160
Hether
　　William 208
Hewes
　　George 214
Hews
　　George 205
Hewson
　　Richard 42
Heyden
　　Samuel 105, 158

Heydon
　　Samuell 26, 39
Hiccah
　　William 66
Hiccocks
　　William 115
Hickman
　　Elisabeth 115, 146,
　　　　164
　　Samuel 115, 146
Hicks
　　Thomas 24, 31, 129
Hickson
　　Henry 46
Hide
　　Peter 100
Higgins
　　Mary 71
　　Michael 71
Higham
　　Francis 93
Hiland
　　John 1
Hill
　　(N) 61
　　Capt. 165
　　Clement 11, 12, 21,
　　　　26, 32, 37, 50,
　　　　52, 54, 59, 60,
　　　　61, 62, 63, 67,
　　　　68, 79, 102,
　　　　107, 127, 131,
　　　　148, 199
　　Francis 4
　　Mr. 185
　　Richard 1, 7, 13,
　　　　30, 73, 86, 87,
　　　　94, 98, 100,
　　　　101, 104, 108,
　　　　110, 129, 131,
　　　　139, 141, 142,
　　　　143, 147, 165,
　　　　218
　　Willemott 73
　　William 36, 191,
　　　　192, 193, 195,
　　　　210
　　Willmott 110
Hillary
　　Thomas 145, 157,
　　　　161
Hilton
　　John 123, 131, 137,
　　　　142

Thomas 148
Himes
    Thomas 111
Hinderson
    James 150
Hinds
    Thomas 102
Hinson
    Charles 15
    John 2, 4, 13, 58,
        74, 85, 123,
        172, 175, 204
Hinton
    Thomas 44, 153, 168
Hitchcock
    (N) 6
Hix
    Thomas 163
Hobbs
    Thomas 19, 48
Hodges
    William 58, 74
Hodgson
    John 168
Hodson
    John 34, 76, 200
Hogan
    John 6
    Paul 6
Hoggon
    Mary 6
Holbrook
    Thomas 39
Holdsworth
    Robert 113
    Samuel 156
Holladay
    Thomas 3, 14
Holland
    Francis 35, 59, 73,
        135, 136, 141,
        144, 152, 166,
        179, 189
    Margaret 135, 152,
        189
    Margarett 144
    Sarah 59
    William 4, 27, 97,
        98, 136, 144,
        152, 162, 165
Holleadger
    Philip 87, 140
Holledger
    Philip 151

Hollen
    John 26
Holliday
    Samuell 59
Hollins
    John 1, 134, 154,
        155
Hollinsworth
    John 89, 115
Hollis
    Henry 79, 93, 103
Holloway
    James 129
    John 82, 95, 96,
        114, 124, 180,
        204, 213, 217
    Martha 103
Hollyday
    Samuell 73
Holman
    Abraham 89, 115
    Sarah 89, 115
Homan
    Edward 130
Home
    Edward 194
Hooper
    Eleanor 58, 59
    Ellinor 126
    George 89, 114
    Henry 1, 30, 42,
        223
    Richard 126
    Sarah 73, 89, 114
Hopewell
    Ann 33, 136
    Francis 33
    Hugh 3, 4, 7, 9,
        67, 70, 71, 94,
        136, 138, 212,
        224
Hopkins
    Garret 144
    Garrett 144
    John 220
    Joseph 78, 92
    Mary 220
    Sam. 60, 61
    Samuel 23, 83, 84,
        91, 92, 95, 104,
        118, 130, 131,
        133, 148, 169,
        176, 220
    Samuell 22, 30, 57,

72, 73
Thomas 107, 220
William 100, 186
Hopper
    Robert 78, 100, 108
Horney
    Elisabeth 190, 192,
        198, 222
    Henry 198
    Murty 183, 190,
        191, 192, 198,
        222
Horsey
    Samuel 93, 120
    Stephen 113
Horsman
    Thomas 104, 135
Hosier
    Henry 127
    Richard 5, 27
Hoskins
    Elisabeth 84
    John 61
    Laurence 32, 112
    Lawrence 11, 12,
        16, 112, 212,
        215
    Philip 84, 114,
        178, 205, 209,
        214, 218
    Phillip 10
How
    Edmund 52
    Joseph 19
    Obadiah 19, 67
    Thomas 93, 103
Howard
    Edmond 95, 119, 150
    Edmund 49, 61
    Eleanor 186
    Ellinor 95, 100
    Hannah 31
    Henry 31
    John 95, 100, 179,
        185, 186, 188
    Mathias 185
    Michaell 73
    Philip 52, 75
Howe
    Edmond 40
    James 200
    Thomas 79
Howel
    Mary 180

Howell
    John 144
    Mary 84, 97, 144,
        206
    Nathaniel 84, 127,
        160, 180, 206
    Nathaniell 97, 144
Howes
    William 121, 144,
        157, 181, 205,
        214
Hozier
    Henry 19
    Richard 27
Hubart
    John 83
Hudson
    Mathew 21
    Robert 35
Huggins
    Mary 113
    Michael 113
Hughes
    Thomas 164, 166
Hughs
    Thomas 65
Hull
    Richard 103
Hulse
    Meverell 12, 28
Hume
    John 145
Humphereys
    Ellis 85
Humpheryes
    E. 85
Hunt
    Elisabeth 33
    John 33, 144, 158
    Wolfran 21, 68
    Woolfran 13, 38
Hunton
    (N) as creditor of
        47
    Elisabeth 8, 23
    Mordecai 117, 212,
        217
    Mordecay 8, 34, 70,
        96, 125
    Mordicay 23, 27
    Mordicey 32
    Mr. 125
Hurlock
    Edward 3

Hurly
  Dennis 29
Husband
  William 70, 82, 87,
    100, 130, 139
Husbands
  William 172, 175
Huscula
  Dennis 60, 62
Husculaw
  Denis 60
Husculoe
  Denis 88, 136
Hutchins
  Charles 119, 146,
    164
  Francis 5, 15, 85,
    89, 136, 141,
    148, 157, 164
  William 68
Hutchison
  William 74
Hyam
  Fran. 79
  Francis 103
Hynson
  Charles 13, 31, 91
  John 13, 31, 32,
    62, 69, 90, 94,
    106, 121, 151,
    171, 175, 181,
    213, 224, 225

Iles
  Richard 214
Impey
  Deborah 9
  Thomas 9, 120
Ingerson
  Daniel 189
Inglish
  Catherine 99, 121
  Dennis 43
  Edward 47, 56, 100,
    121, 181, 204,
    213
  Kath. 181
  Maj. 69
  Mr. 95
  William 56, 69, 99,
    105, 181, 204,
    213
Ingo

Peter 8
Inman
  Edward 63, 81, 153,
    208
Innes
  Alexander 6, 9, 11,
    30, 77
  Allexander 5
  Patrick 2, 3, 4, 6,
    9
Innis
  Nathaniel 22, 110
  Nathaniell 46
  Patrick 11
  Samuel 104
  William 110, 133
Isaac
  Edward 85, 89
Isaacks
  John 214
  Joseph 181, 198,
    205
  Margaret 181, 205,
    214
Isaak
  Edward 140
Isaake
  Edward 153, 157
  Joseph 139, 162
  Margaret 139
Isacke
  Edward 98, 168
Isles
  Elisabeth 138, 142,
    155
  Katherine 156
  Richard 138, 142,
    143, 148, 155,
    156, 178, 206

Jackson
  Ezehiel 84
  Ezekiel 97, 117,
    140
  John 188
  Margrett 29, 48
  Ralph 185
  Richard 92, 115,
    137
  Samuel 104, 135,
    182, 192
  Simon 83
  Thomas 29, 31, 48,

Page 255

64, 150

James
  Charles 83, 97,
    128, 169
  Edward 14
  Richard 33, 71
  Sarah 49, 61
  Thomas 45, 49, 61,
    83
Jefferson
  Richard 136
  Sam. 62
  Samuel 123
Jegon
  Peter 44
Jenkins
  Ann 72
  Fran. 18
  Francis 154, 169,
    176
  Richard 33, 72
  William 192
Jenkinson
  William 122, 183,
    187
Joce
  Thomas 10, 20
Johns
  Richard 135
  Thomas 80
Johnson
  Capt. 38, 39
  Cornelius 9, 19,
    20, 51, 142,
    183, 207, 218
  David 73
  Francis 196, 197
  Henry 79, 117, 140,
    159, 199
  John 50, 60, 63,
    107, 127, 169,
    172, 174, 176,
    177, 190, 202,
    222
  Mark 143, 180, 186
  Mary 50, 139
  Nicholas 26
  Peter 196, 199
  Thomas 138, 139,
    181, 205, 214
  William 106
Jones
  Ann 8
  Cornelius 217

Daniel 8, 21, 60
David 28
Edward 1, 5, 66,
  76, 77, 93, 171
Elisabeth 122
Griffeth 55
Griffith 44, 69,
  95, 118, 190
Humphry 32
Jane 30
Joseph 72
Katharine 200
Katherine 92, 93,
  128, 137, 161
Lewis 92, 93, 161
Lucy 95
Morgan 27, 58, 74,
  121
Moses 1, 128, 137,
  200
Nathan 153
Nicholas 116, 143,
  180, 206, 216
Phillip 25
Rice 83
Richard 1, 16, 28,
  43, 44, 71, 86,
  109, 111, 122,
  155, 159
Robert 169, 170
Thomas 23, 30, 41,
  46, 48, 61, 76,
  99, 120, 138,
  142, 169, 220
Walter 36, 40, 54,
  55
William 20, 51,
  116, 128, 140,
  142, 143, 180,
  183, 187, 206,
  207, 216, 217,
  218
Jonson
  Albert 46
Jordan
  Charety 190
  John 190
Jorden
  John 167
Joult
  George 200
Jowles
  (N) 125
  Col. 125

Edward 7, 114
Roger 114
Latimore
James 148
Latropp
William 69
Latrupp
William 115
Laurence
Benjamin 61, 100
Daniell 50
Henry 5, 44
Thomas 61
Lawrence
Benjamin 86, 153,
208
Henry 91, 99, 105
John 106
Thomas 195, 208
Lawson
Thomas 83
Lawsson
Thomas 65
Layfeild
George 36, 41
Layfield
Margaret 183, 206,
215
Margarett 187
Leach
John 60, 65, 140,
157, 181, 205,
219
Mr. 198
Leake
Frances 134, 154
Richard 134, 154,
155
Lean
John 106
Leatch
John 65
Lecset
Ann 125
Lee
George 48, 189
Robert 57
Leech
John 213
Leeds
Michael 106, 149,
183, 187
William 106, 149,
183

Leeke
Richard 181, 205,
213
Lefar
Reme 53
LeFarr
Reme 61
LeFeuer
Reme 61
Rene 67
Legg
Johanna 159
William 21, 113,
159
Leisett
Ann 70
Lemaire
John 84
Margaret 84, 178,
205, 214, 218
Margarett 112
Lesson
James 32
Letchworth
Joseph 3
Lewellin
John 70
Lewis
Abigail 34
Abigall 6
Henry 6, 34
James 29, 224
Katharine 29
Mary 224
Mathew 6, 200
Thomas 118, 156,
163, 164
Liesett
John 125
Lightfoote
Rebecca 189
Thomas 189
Lillingston
John 220
Lillington
Elisabeth 143, 158,
159
John 143, 158
Lincycomb
Thomas 166
Lindsey
Jane 27, 71, 109
Thomas 71, 109
Lineycomb

Thomas 161
Lingam
  George 124, 145
Lingan
  George 48, 53, 89,
    96, 98, 106,
    139, 147, 154,
    161, 163
Linsey
  Thomas 87
Lisle
  Priscilla 154
  William 154
Litton
  Richard 219
Llewellin
  John 16, 23, 29,
    170, 172, 173,
    176, 196, 211,
    224
Lloyd
  Henrietta Maria 82,
    208
  Hugh 181, 214
  Katharine 214
  Katherine 181
  Philemon 41, 82,
    152, 208
  Phillomen 27
Lockermaine
  Jacob 111, 128
Lockermane
  Jacob 147
Lockwood
  Richard 144
  Robert 56, 85, 92,
    130, 163, 169
Loggins
  Thomas 160
Lomax
  Cleborn 26
  Cleborne 12, 26,
    127, 138, 142,
    145, 148, 151,
    155, 162, 184
  Clebourne 191
Lonally
  Louis 18
Londey
  John 146
Long
  Jane 197, 210
  John 50, 63, 119,
    198

Mary 44
Thomas 44, 61, 73,
  74, 123, 149,
  167, 197, 199,
  210
Longman
  (N) 197
  Daniel 86, 93, 153,
    197
  Daniell 45, 61
  Joanna 189, 190
  Johanna 116
  John 116, 179, 189,
    190
  Thomas 179
Loockerman
  Jacob 20
Lookerman
  Jacob 88, 186, 216
Looton
  Jacob 123
Lovan
  Daniel 199
Love
  Robert 14
Low
  Nicholas 220
Lowder
  Richard 10, 56
Lowe
  Col. 80
  Henry 63, 122, 156,
    193, 201, 202,
    221
  John 201
  Susanna 202
  Susannah 156
  Vincent 44, 55, 82,
    94, 102, 153,
    154, 188, 208
Lowrey
  Henry 140
Lowry
  Daniel 193
  Elias 140, 157,
    181, 205, 214
  Henry 181, 205, 214
  Mary 157
  William 194
Loyd
  (N) 63
  Hen. Maria 63
  Henrietta Maria 81,
    153

Philemon 106, 164
Luct
    Ann 68
Ludford
    Arthur 78, 115,
        146, 149, 164
Luellin
    John 91
Luff
    Stephen 26, 36,
        104, 156, 220
Luffe
    Joseph 36
    Sarah 165
    St. 187
    Stephen 9, 36, 38,
        81, 86, 87, 117,
        165
Lundin
    Robert 40
Lurke
    Thomas 138
Lyle
    William 25
Lynam
    John 86
Lynes
    (N) 213
    Philip 55, 99, 143,
        145, 150, 174,
        175, 177, 178,
        193, 196, 198,
        201, 204, 220,
        222, 224
    Phillip 17, 22, 24,
        32, 35, 36
Lytfoot
    Rebeckah 28
    Thomas 28, 51

Macall
    George 72
    James 7
Maccubin
    John 95, 100, 179
Macdowell
    Elisabeth 108
Mackall
    Rachell 72
Mackdowell
    Elisabeth 59, 60,
        62, 65, 74, 93,
        124, 126, 146,

156
Henry 62, 93, 113,
    156
James 113
John 62, 66, 93,
    108, 113, 126,
    146, 156
William 113
Mackenny
    Jane 76
Mackfarland
    Alexander 88, 116,
        140, 190
    Elisabeth 116, 140
Mackforland
    Alexander 79
Macklin
    Robert 123, 155,
        220
Macklyn
    Richard 44
    Robert 37, 43, 44,
        48, 55
Macoone
    Daniel 185
Macubin
    John 186
Maddox
    Rachaell 100
    Thomas 100, 108
Madox
    Rachell 78
    Thomas 78
Magruther
    James 3
    John 3
Mahenney
    (N) 74
    Jane 72
Mahenny
    John 73
Maile
    Anthony 137
Makamy
    Jane 126
    John 126
Man
    Edward 48, 67, 77,
        88, 91, 117,
        152, 162
Mann
    Edward 43, 168,
        193, 198, 200
Manning

Medcalfe
  Richard 14
Medford
  Thomas 184
Medley
  Ann 170
  Anne 173
  George 173
  William 170
Meeds
  William 213
Meeke
  Sarah 82
Meekes
  Sarah 180, 206, 216
  Walter 111, 112,
    180, 206, 216
  William 109
Meeks
  Walter 200
Melson
  (N) 82
Melton
  Susanna 76, 94
  Thomas 142
  William 76, 94
Mercarte
  Edward 163
  Honor 163
Mercer
  Elisabeth 198
Meredith
  Henry 93
  Lewis 102, 105,
    142, 159, 170
Meriton
  John 169
Merriday
  Louis 49
Michell
  Ann 103
  Henry 213
  John 103
Middleton
  Robert 74
Midleton
  Robert 68
Mikles
  John 60
Miles
  John 97, 133, 134,
    146, 160
  Peter 78
  Thomas 3, 5

Miller
  Edward 194
  James 14, 27, 143,
    145, 152
  John 70, 81, 91,
    118
  M. 27, 68
  Mich. 61
  Michael 10, 24, 73,
    84, 85, 159
  Michaell 44, 47,
    56, 77, 78
Milles
  James 50
  Peter 33
Mills
  James 49, 50
  Tobias 171
Milstead
  Edward 173, 179,
    184, 191, 194,
    202, 211, 221,
    223
  Elisabeth 173, 184
Minock
  Dorothy 212, 215
  Michael 212, 215
Mirax
  Richard 92, 115
Mishew
  William 76, 96, 164
Mishey
  William 153
Missett
  Adam 198
Mister
  Marmaduke 104
Mitchell
  Ann 138, 183, 220
  Anne 187
  Elisabeth 4, 111
  Henry 134, 154,
    155, 180, 205,
    219
  James 24
  John 4, 49, 111,
    138, 175, 183
  Margaret 113
  Thomas 60
  William 6, 76, 98,
    108, 110
Mockawin
  James 91
Moffett

John 145, 157, 161
Mohany
(N) 107
Moire
James 107
Molines
Edward 35
Money
Lydia 191
Montgomery
Hugh 180, 204, 212, 213, 217, 218
Katharine 212, 217, 218
Moore
Dr. 218
Elisabeth 36
James 30, 141, 162
John 135
Margaret 180, 205, 214
Margery 134
Mordecai 172, 176, 202, 223
Richard 36, 71, 91, 96
Ursula 139, 147, 172, 176, 202, 223
William 134, 146, 180, 205, 214
More
Margaret 130
Richard 58, 71
William 130
Morehouse
Robert 10
Morgan
Edward 4, 82, 87, 100, 175, 178, 194, 208
Henry 30
John 162
Thomas 48
Morray
James 2
Morris
Jenckin 182
Jenkin 101, 104, 135, 192
Thomas 36, 83, 91, 118, 182, 207, 217, 222
Mosely

Thomas 5
Moss
(N) 213
William 145, 165, 178, 196, 204, 211, 214, 219
Mosse
William 39, 165
Mould
John 26, 120
Mount
Thomas 64
Mountford
Edward 112
Thomas 37, 52
Mountfort
Edward 167
John 53, 94
Thomas 53, 64, 94
Moy vs. Carvile
174 1
Moy
Daniel 174, 185, 191, 197, 202, 211, 217, 222
Elisabeth 185, 202, 211, 222
Richard 174, 185, 187, 202, 211, 222
Mudd
Thomas 62, 88
Muffet
John 181, 205, 213, 214
Mugenburgh
Martin 41
Mullet
Winifred 194, 202
Mullett
Winifred 170, 173, 174, 179, 184, 191, 221
Mullins
Edward 126
Murfey
Mary 144
Patrick 144
Murfue
John 83, 91, 182, 207
Murfy
John 217, 222
Murfye

Capt. 67
Murphey
    James 89, 94, 138,
        146, 149
Murphy
    Elisabeth 54, 116
    James 9, 14, 40,
        43, 53, 94, 103,
        106, 117, 119,
        120, 125, 138,
        140, 189
    John 118
    Nicholas 54, 116
    Patrick 180, 188,
        191
Murrah
    Anguish 43
Murray
    Garrat 171
    James 103
    Susannah 171
Murrey
    James 48
Murty
    Anthony 12, 27
    Stephen 68, 131
Musgrove
    Cuthbert 45
    Dorothy 45

Naish
    Henry 20
Nance
    Rowland 101, 147
Naper
    Edward 51
Napper
    Edward 49
Nash
    Alexander 36, 77,
        126
Neale
    Ant. 185
    Antho. 127
    Anthony 7, 49, 51,
        75, 137, 147,
        158, 172, 191
    James 7, 137, 147
    Jonathon 93
Nedham
    William 141, 157
Needham
    William 164

Nelson
    John 65
    Thomas 62, 67, 98
Newboll
    Thomas 85
Newen
    Owen 65
Newman
    George 33, 34, 35
    Henry 67
    John 9, 14, 120,
        188, 198, 210
    Judith 188
    Rebecca 210
    Richard 37
Newton
    Edward 4, 129, 165
    Richard 51
Nicholls
    Humphry 24, 42
    William 5
Nichols
    Elisabeth 195
    Humphry 94, 119
    John 161, 195
    Simon 141, 162, 181
    Symon 205, 214
Nicholson
    Esther 179, 188
    Hester 133, 160
    Humphry 114
    Nicholas 13, 38,
        107, 133, 160,
        179, 188
Ningfinger
    William 196, 203
Ninyfinger
    William 177
Noble
    Dorothy 56
    Isaac 13
    Robert 42
Noris
    Henry 57
Norris
    Daniel 9, 10, 13,
        19, 77, 83, 105,
        106, 113
    Daniell 20, 37, 48,
        57, 69, 80
    Henry 88, 118, 210,
        212
    Robert 186
    Thomas 186

Norwood
  Andrew 43
Nowell
  William 95
Nubald
  Thomas 119
Nuball
  Thomas 127
Nuthall
  Ja. 6
  James 6, 7, 64, 65,
    66, 115, 126,
    127
Nutter
  Christopher 101,
    108, 136
Nutthall
  (N) 41
  James 4, 7, 25, 36
  John 94
Nyfinger
  Judith 99
  William 99, 119

O'bryan
  (N) 213
O'Cane
  Roger 85
O'Derry
  William 180
O'Dwyer
  Edmond 117, 187
Oakely
  Lionell 122
  Lyonell 96
  Thomas 177, 196
Oakley
  Thomas 203
Obrey
  Ann 163
  William 163
OBryan
  Bryan 106, 107,
    134, 177, 196,
    203
  Kath. 177, 203
  Katharine 196
  Katherine 106, 107
Ocaine
  Roger 119
Ocane
  Roger 182, 207, 217
Odain

Dennis 31
Odary
  William 84
Odery
  William 97, 206
Odwine
  Dennis 21, 22, 31
  Rose 21, 31
ODwyer
  Edmond 183
Offly
  Mabell 45
Okridge
  John 56
Oldfeild
  George 1
Olison
  Oley 216
  Peter 206
Ollison
  Ellinor 89
  Olley 89, 180, 206
  Peter 89, 180, 216
Oman
  Mary 73
Omely
  Bryand 64
  Isabella 64
  Mary 64
  Susanna 64
Orick
  James 53, 76
Orman
  John 196
  Penelope 196
  Thomas 177, 187,
    203, 221
Orme
  Robert 28
Orrel
  Thomas 177
Orrell
  Isabel 188
  Isabella 184
  Thomas 184, 188,
    191, 194, 199
Orrick
  James 98
Orruck
  James 65, 75
Orurdie
  (N) 213
Orwick
  James 6

Osborn
  Thomas 207, 217
Osborne
  Attalanta 22, 46
  Elisabeth 91
  John 22, 46, 60
  Thomas 76, 91, 97,
    105, 118, 129,
    182, 183
  William 160
Osbourne
  Elisabeth 84
  John 1
  Thomas 84
Otridge
  John 56
  Thomas 56
Ottridge
  John 13, 15, 16
Owen
  Richard 92, 120
Owing
  Richard 75

Paert
  Bryan 57, 72
Page
  Nicholas 9
Painter
  Nicholas 68, 73,
    139, 146, 147,
    172, 176, 202,
    223
Panter
  John 20
Panther
  John 9, 39, 48, 51
Paramore
  Arnold 134
  Sarah 92
Parey
  Charles 154
Parker
  George 4, 5, 8, 17,
    18, 19, 28, 34,
    60, 70, 80, 85,
    89, 96, 98, 117,
    125, 180, 204,
    212, 213, 217,
    218
  Henry 20, 37, 116
  James 83, 181, 204,
    213

Judith 172, 176,
    202, 223
  Katharine 85
  Katherine 85, 96
  Thomas 10, 20, 83,
    181, 204, 213
  William 5, 27
Parnell
  James 160
Parramore
  Arnold 148
  Sarah 148
Parratt
  Gabriell 47
Parrot
  Gabriel 190, 197
  Henry 200
Parrott
  Gabriell 163
Parry
  Charles 205
Parserell
  Arthur 131
Parslow
  Ellinor 125
  Thomas 50, 125,
    149, 212
Parsons
  Cosmo 132
  David 32
  Edward 132
  Francis 63, 64
  John 93, 129, 132
  Mary 9, 19, 93, 132
  Peter 9, 19
  Thomas 8
Parvey
  Charles 134, 155
Parvy
  Charles 180, 213,
    219
Patrick
  Ann 22, 46
  Roger 22, 46, 72
  Rory 22, 46
  Thomas 212, 215
Pattison
  James 35, 63, 136,
    142, 152, 155,
    162
  Jane 141, 180, 188
  Thomas 141, 180,
    190
Paxton

Hugh 87
Payne
  Henry 184
  John 201
  Mary 184
  Samuel 198
Pean
  Henry 196
  Rebeccah 196
Pearce
  Capt. 143, 160
  Morgan 198
  Nathaniel 116, 128,
    140
  William 151
Pearle
  Elisabeth 224
  William 224
Pearson
  Thomas 137
Peart
  (N) 22
  James 12, 21, 28
Pedan
  Rebecca 154, 155
  Timothy 154, 155,
    156
Peirpoint
  Henry 108
Peirson
  Thomas 115, 138,
    150
Pembrooke
  Jane 11, 12, 17, 26
  John 11, 12, 17, 26
Pennich
  Martha 214
Pennick
  Martha 181, 205
Pennington
  Henry 78, 97, 111,
    112, 116, 128,
    140
  Thomas 40, 111, 112
Pennock
  Martha 134, 158
Perkett
  William 74, 99
Perkins
  Simon 104, 135
  Symon 194
Perry
  George 208
Peterkin

James 167
Peterson
  Andrew 40
  Margaret 86
  Margrett 34
  Mathias 86
Petit
  Mary 188
Petite
  Francis 130
Pettibone
  John 98, 108, 179,
    188
  Thomas 98, 108,
    179, 218
Pettit
  Francis 178, 207,
    216
Pettybone
  Isaack 45
  John 218
  Joseph 45
  Richard 45, 54, 65
Petybone
  Isaack 54
  Joseph 54
Pew
  Ann 133, 138
  Thomas 133, 156
Phelps
  Walter 24, 52, 76,
    90, 98, 107,
    108, 113, 133,
    152, 153, 179
Phenex
  Edward 162
Pheppard
  Peter 181, 205,
    214, 219
Philipps
  Daniel 94
  James 120, 159
Philips
  James 79
  Robert 197, 198,
    199
  Thomas 186
Philks
  James 46
Phillips
  Daniell 42, 76
  James 2, 18, 26,
    120, 143
  John 42

Quinton
  Walter 200

Radford
  Sarah 166
Radney
  William 71
Ragley
  James 64
Ralph
  Thomas 19
Ramsey
  Bartholomew 146,
    183, 206, 216
Randall
  Benjamin 11
Ranger
  Christopher 72
Rapier
  John 70, 71
Rasin
  Elisabeth 79, 87
  John 79
  Mary 79, 87
  Philip 79, 87
  Thomas 79, 87, 96,
    99
Ratcliff
  Charles 22, 46,
    110, 131, 133
  John 49, 51, 102
Rattliff
  Joan 127
Rawlings
  John 4
  Philladelphia 4
Ray
  Alexander 158
Read
  (N) 36
  John 38, 154
  Mathew 118
  Nathaniel 82, 87
  Nathaniell 64
  William 38, 200
Reader
  Benjamin 96, 128
Reason
  Thomas 168
Reed
  George 78
  Nathaniell 63

Reeder
  Benjamin 107
Reeve
  Edward 178, 216
  Mary 178, 216
Reeves
  Edward 132, 188,
    199
  John 220
  Mary 132, 188
  Thomas 123, 131,
    137
Relfe
  Thomas 19
Reniger
  Mary 169
  Samuel 169
Revell
  Katharine 23, 81
  Katherine 87, 90,
    113
  Randall 23, 30, 81,
    87, 113
Reynolds
  George 170, 173
  Henry 212, 215
  Thomas 197
Rhamsey
  Pretiosa 166
  Pretiosia 159
  Samuel 83
  Samuell 62, 80, 81
  William 159, 166
Rhoades
  Abraham 129
Rhoads
  Abraham 93
Rhodes
  Abraham 10, 132
Ricaud
  Benjamin 4, 31, 58,
    69, 79, 85, 99
  Thomas 79
Ricaut
  Joseph 25
Rich
  Alice 189
  William 189
Richardson
  Mark 18, 65, 73,
    80, 89, 103,
    107, 113, 114,
    210
  Susanna 18, 65, 73,

William 162, 180,
204, 214
Routs
William 139
Royston
George 149
Rozer
Benjamin 172, 174,
179, 209, 211,
215
Notley 209
Rumball
Anthony 220
Rumsey
James 33
Russell
John 70, 149, 158
Margaret 149
Margarett 158
Rycutt
Joseph 6

Salesbury
John 64
Salisbury
John 118, 121, 167
Sallesbury
John 58
Salsbury
John 68, 74
Salter
John 220
Sampson
Richard 83
Sander
Jos. 56
Sanders
Edward 218
Elisabeth 152
James 121, 160,
163, 166
John 190
Joseph 152
Santee
Christopher 27
Sargison
William 3
Sarson
Edward 160
Mary 149, 160
Saunders
James 65, 68, 75,
103

Joseph 56
Sawell
James 141
Sayer
Maj. 40, 47, 63
Peter 40, 46, 47,
53, 55, 56
Petter 21
Saywell
James 52, 118
Scafield
Henry 80
Scarborough
Mathew 90, 130,
131, 133, 148
Scarborow
Mathew 23
Scarbrough
Mathew 95
Matth. 72
Scorer
Arthur 21
Scot
Cuthbert 219
James 220
Scott
Cuthbert 170, 175,
177, 192
James 27, 41, 75,
113, 119, 139
John 6, 7, 48, 158,
166
Thomas 133, 167,
182, 186, 207,
216, 222
William 89, 117,
119, 139
Scrivener
Benjamin 73
Scrivner
Benjamin 188
Scudamore
Abigail 74, 149
Abigall 61
Thomas 26, 61, 74,
79, 149
Sealy
George 44
Seamons
John 67
Searson
Edward 149
Seawall
James 157

William 30
Shepard
    Charles 194, 215
    Damoras 215
Sheredine
    Daniel 141, 157
    Jane 32
    Jeremiah 157
    Jerimiah 32
Sheridin
    Daniel 181, 218
Sherridin
    Daniel 205
Shertcliff
    William 19
Sherwood
    Hugh 106, 138, 150
Shipard
    Charles 212
    Damoras 212
Shipwas
    John 38
Shipway
    John 51
Shitup
    Thomas 56
Short
    George 209, 222
Sibthorpe
    Christopher 123
Simes
    Marmaduck 60
Simmonds
    John 176
    Rebeccah 176
Simmons
    James 61, 67
    Thomas 87
Simms
    Samuel 5
Simonds
    Henry 89
    Margaret 147
    Thomas 147
Simons
    Abigail 33
    James 61
Simpers
    Ann 43
    Richard 43
Simpson
    Jere. 131
    Thomas 7, 201
Sims

Richard 79
Sinclere
    William 24
Sinick
    John 70
    Susanna 70
Sinicke
    John 80
    Susanna 80
Sirick
    John 103, 113
    Susanna 113
Skillington
    Thomas 200
Skinner
    Ann 3
    Robert 3, 40
    Thomas 96, 165
Skipper
    John 43, 96, 122,
       194
Skipwith
    Elisabeth 166
    George 166, 197
Skoates
    Christopher 197
Slade
    Ann 178, 211, 215
Sly
    Gerard 36
    Gerrard 36, 41
Smallwood
    James 171, 209
Smart
    John 109, 143
    Susan 109
Smith
    Alexander 12, 27,
       211, 215
    Alice 40, 75, 129
    Allan 159
    Allen 76, 77
    Ann 73, 104, 116,
       130, 131, 133,
       182, 183, 187,
       206, 207, 215,
       217
    Anne 52, 185
    Barbara 15, 45
    Ben. 58
    Benjamin 72, 189
    Charles 81
    Edward 22, 46, 52,
       57, 61, 73, 90,

110
Elisabeth 104, 131,
 141
Henry 5
John 47
Joseph 75
Lancelott 168
Margaret 129
Margret 75
Martha 131
Mary 159
Michael 83
Nathan 5, 8, 75,
 129
Ralph 11, 12, 112
Rebecca 189
Rebeckah 58, 72
Richard 15, 25, 45,
 72, 96
Robert 55, 63, 80,
 86
Sarah 75, 129
Thomas 8, 40, 61,
 69, 75, 94, 129,
 171, 185
Walter 88, 168
William 33, 141,
 162, 181, 205,
 214, 222
Smithson
Richard 15, 34
Thomas 9, 20, 27,
 37, 41, 45, 47,
 75, 110, 117,
 146, 223
William 24, 36
Smock
John 1, 30, 49, 52,
 73, 90, 91, 104,
 118, 129, 130,
 131, 133
Smocke
John 22, 57
Smoote
William 142, 191,
 201, 208, 222
Snowden
John 43
Solesbury
Elisabeth 58
Sollars
John 112
Sollers
John 24, 89

Sone
Joseph 46
Sorbourough
Jane 6
John 6
Southern
Richard 26, 28, 36,
 41, 44, 126
Valentine 44
Southerne
Richard 12, 14,
 114, 155
Sowell
Timothy 145
Sowter
Richard 223
Sparkes
William 163
Sparrow
Solomon 197, 203
Spear
(N) 61
Speare
Richard 73, 85
Spencer
John 80
Solomon 203
Thomas 74, 125
Spendergrass
James 81
Spernon
Alice 44
Joseph 44
Spikman
William 145, 165
Spink
Jane 197
Thomas 197, 198
Spokenal
William 219
Sprigg
Eleanor 66
Elenor 6
Elianor 64, 65
Elioner 6
Ellinor 115
Mr. 4
Squire
Jonathon 5, 36
Squirrel
xx 125
Staly
Thomas 159
Stanberry

John 51
Stanbery
  John 49
Standbury
  John 102, 127
Standy
  John 67
Stanely
  John 14
Stanley
  John 91, 94, 119
Stanly
  John 43, 48, 53
  Robert 25, 39
Stansby
  Mary 26
Stapelford
  Raymond 42
Stapelfort
  Charles 30, 42
  Eleanor 42
  Elinor 30
  Raymond 30
Staples
  Ann 9
  Henry 9, 80, 81,
    105, 200
Staring
  William 169
Starling
  Richard 140
Steery
  John 182, 207
Steevens
  John 44
Stephens
  George 94
  John 27, 118
  Simon 111
  William 200
Sterling
  Richard 157
  Thomas 6
Sterry
  John 18, 30, 217
  Sarah 18
Stery
  John 118
Stevens
  Col. 18, 23, 37
  Edward 78
  Elisabeth 61, 80
  George 45, 77, 114
  Giles 49

Simon 53
Thomas 62, 67
William 11, 13, 22,
  23, 30, 32, 46,
  52, 54, 61, 80,
  99, 111, 200
Stevenson
  Edward 152
  Letitea 152
  Thomas 38
Steward
  Charles 142, 213
  John 117, 120, 140,
    183
Stewart
  Charles 204
Stiles
  Mr. 95, 160
Stimpson
  John 179, 190
  Rachel 179, 190
  Rachell 188
Stimson
  John 128, 153
  Rachael 128
Stoakes
  Peter 13, 88, 96,
    111, 128
Stockett
  Fran. 28
  Francis 12, 38, 39,
    51
Stokes
  John 79
Stone
  Hugh 50
  John 62, 80, 83,
    84, 101, 114,
    122
  Thomas 126, 147,
    191
Stonestreet
  Thomas 66
Stook
  John 78
  Mary 78
Stoop
  John 97, 151
Stoope
  John 140, 151
Storer
  Arthur 3
Storey
  John 92

Stow
    Edmond 53
    Jane 53
Stratford
    Joseph 60, 63, 67,
        137
    Mary 60, 137
    widow 63
Stratton
    Thomas 58
Strawbridge
    Honora 54, 61, 119
    John 54, 61, 119
Stritch
    James 136, 164,
        184, 208
Strong
    Francis 89
    James 119
Stroud
    Thomas 132
Stuart
    Charles 102, 105,
        181
    John 92, 186
Stuarts
    (N) 102
Sulivan
    Ann 63
    Dennis 63
Sulivant
    Darby 205
Sullivan
    Darby 181, 213
Sullivane
    Flo. 102
Sullivant
    Ann 155
    Denis 155
    Derby 139
    Patrick 127
Sumerland
    James 13
Summers
    Benjamin 120
Sunderland
    John 5, 7, 89, 98,
        106, 145, 153,
        157
Sundley
    William 108
Surcot
    Thomas 220
Suthern

Vallentine 72
Sutten
    George 34
Swaine
    John 81, 86, 111
Swan
    James 99, 196, 203
    Judith 99
Swann
    (N) 213
    James 119, 177,
        187, 210
Sweatnam
    Edward 2, 90, 121,
        151, 204, 213
    Richard 52, 53, 55,
        118, 152, 162
Swetnam
    (N) 34
    Edward 181
    Richard 14, 42, 44
Swift
    Mich. 62
    Michael 80
Swinfen
    Fran. 33
    Francis 51, 126
Swinfenn
    Francis 14
Sydes
    Peter 198
Sykes
    John 35
Symons
    Abigail 33
    Henry 65

Taillor
    John 203
    Thomas 34, 86, 92,
        95, 101, 103,
        130
Talbot
    Edward 163
    Elisabeth 211
Talbott
    Edward 93, 197
Talley
    Walter 99, 100, 120
Tally
    Walter 56
Tanehill
    Andrew 124

Ann 96
Taney
   Margaret 123, 149
   Michael 6, 115,
     123, 124, 126,
     149, 150, 169,
     171, 173
   Michaell 19, 25, 67
Tanyhill
   Andrew 181, 205,
     214
Tarner
   John 94
Tasker
   Thomas 2, 8, 23,
     31, 145, 147,
     173
Taunt
   John 172, 193
Tawney
   Margaret 112
   Michael 112
Tayer
   James 222
Taylard
   William 168, 172,
     194, 195, 197,
     211, 212, 224
Tayler
   Anthony 147
Taylor
   Abraham 14
   Anthony 88, 111,
     128
   Arthur 14
   Col. 88, 218
   Daniel 8
   Hope 119
   John 1, 27, 159
   Michael 168
   Robert 177
   Thomas 70, 80, 92,
     120, 133, 153,
     196, 200
   William 14
Temple
   William 14
Tenant
   Nich. 102
Tench
   Margaret 5
   Margrett 8
   Thomas 4, 5, 8, 18,
     28, 98, 106,

     112, 136, 152,
     166, 173, 179,
     188, 224
Tenehill
   Andrew 145
Tennehill
   Andrew 147
Tennison
   Jary 26
   John 5, 26
   Justinian 25, 26,
     31, 59, 63, 66,
     158, 161
Terry
   John 148
Thatcher
   John 212
Thomas
   Alexander 119
   Ann 220
   Christopher 111,
     138, 183, 206,
     215
   Hugh 127, 151, 178,
     205, 214
   John 26, 28, 122,
     130
   Rob. 34
   Robert 6
   Samuel 93, 134,
     144, 179, 188,
     220
   Sarah 134, 144, 179
   Susanna 212, 215,
     224
   Thomas 111, 138,
     183, 187, 206,
     215
   William 9, 20, 31,
     32, 40, 80, 110,
     169, 212, 215,
     224
Thomkins
   Giles 126
Thompson
   Ann 146, 182, 207,
     217
   Anne 186
   George 58
   James 68, 74, 151
   John 97, 132
   Joseph 146, 182,
     186, 207, 217
   Priscilla 86

Richard 10, 49, 66
Robert 88, 122,
   128, 168, 178,
   191, 204, 205,
   213, 214, 219
Roblet 148
Thomas 92, 115
William 142, 145,
   148, 162
Zachary 42, 86, 111
Thomson
  John 73
Thorn
  Thomas 28
Thornbury
  Richard 28
Thornton
  Miles 43, 91
Thrift
  John 39
  Mary 50
Thurston
  Thomas 199
Tike
  William 52, 74
Tilden
  Charles 2, 20, 25,
    31, 32, 106,
    121, 213
Till
  Edward 143
Tillyard
  John 13, 14
Tilton
  Humphry 116, 168
Tippings Plantation
  xx 54
Tipton
  Edward 168, 169,
    170
Toaes
  Daniel 224
Toat
  Frances 79
Toate
  Robert 79, 81, 92
Todd
  Lancelott 76, 98
Toft
  Thomas 170
Toll
  Roger 194
Tomkins
  Giles 147

Tomlins
  Edward 63, 64, 82,
    87, 112, 137
Tompson
  John 78
Tong
  John 177, 196, 203,
    221
Tonge
  John 102, 107, 128
Tonnard
  Andrew 189
  Thomas 189
Tordy
  James Mills 61
Townhill
  Edmond 29
Townsen
  John 72
Townsend
  John 90, 127
Toyer
  James 192
Tracy
  Samuel 50
Trevant
  Robert 50
Troaton
  John 152
Troth
  William 200
Troton
  Roger 133
Trotten
  Roger 186, 207,
    216, 222
Trotton
  Roger 182
True
  William 10, 19, 77
Trueman
  Henry 6
  Mary 2, 14, 26, 36
  Thomas 2
  William 3, 21
Truman
  Henry 117
  Mary 114, 126, 155
Trundell
  John 103
Tucker
  Florence 78
  Nathaniel 156
  Richard 152

Tull
    Richard 68, 69, 81,
        124
Turbut
    Michael 189
Turbutt
    Mary 94
    Michael 223
Turlinge
    John 148
Turnell
    John 66
Turner
    Charles 105, 106,
        181
    Elianor 71
    Elisabeth 82, 98
    John 33, 62, 71,
        76, 82, 96, 98,
        149
    Richard 71
    Thomas 172, 185
    William 136, 164
Turnor
    Charles 194, 204,
        213
    William 184, 208
Turvile
    William 30
Tutell
    Mary 198
Tutstone
    Richard 89
Twisdell
    William 193
Twisden
    William 135, 194
Tydings
    Charity 167
    Richard 109, 167,
        190
Tyer
    James 16, 50, 71,
        112, 208
    Rebeccah 12, 16, 50
Tyler
    Robert 40
Tyre
    James 12, 25, 112,
        142, 150, 191
    Rebecca 112
    Rebeccah 12
Tyrling
    John 168, 169, 170,

        171, 177, 184,
        191, 194, 195,
        199

Underwood
    (N) 92, 123, 132,
        141
    Anthony 6, 26, 29,
        34, 35, 47, 48,
        52, 53, 54, 58,
        59, 62, 64, 65,
        66, 68, 78, 80,
        88, 103, 108,
        126, 136, 146,
        162, 165, 169,
        173, 178, 193,
        194
    Martha 173, 194
Utie
    George 103
Uty
    Elisabeth 10, 11
    George 10, 11, 65,
        80
    Mary 201, 203
    Nathaniel 11
    Nathaniell 10
Utye
    George 107, 114

Vadery
    John 119
Valiant
    John 220
Vanderford
    George 188
    Michael Paul 188
Vanderheydon
    Margaret 116
    Mathias 116
Vanhack
    John 144
    Sarah 144
Vanheck
    John 95, 160
    Sarah 95, 160
VanReswick
    Frances 196
    John 177, 187, 196,
        203
Vanseringen
    Garret 223

Vansweringen
  Gar. 57
  Garrat 48, 68
  Garratt 29
  Garret 23, 124,
    169, 199
  Garrett 57, 78
  Mr. 193
  Zachariah 158
Vasina
  Elisabeth 188
Vasseen
  Elisabeth 112
  Francis 112
Vassine
  Elisabeth 179, 189
  Francis 179, 189
Vaudry
  John 50, 99, 184,
    195, 198
Vaughan
  William 122
Veach
  James 209
  John 209
Veining
  Nathaniel 12, 16
Veitch
  James 82, 95, 99,
    103, 162
Verin
  Nathaniel 112
  Nathaniell 50
Vesaills
  Mr. 131
Vesials
  (N) 131
Vessialls
  Gerald 160
Vigerous
  John 130, 131, 133,
    186
Vigorous
  John 104, 182, 207,
    217
Vine
  Tommesin 72
Viner
  John 43, 94
Vines
  John 138, 204, 213
  Martha 82, 103
  Samuel 82, 95, 99,
    103, 180, 217

Viney
  Henry 39
  Thomason 39
Vinson
  George 151
Vowles
  John 175
  Richard 184
VReswick
  (N) 213

Wade
  John 4
Wale
  Edward 22, 46, 110
Walker
  Daniel 102, 116
  Daniell 20, 37, 46
  John 58, 86, 87,
    96, 147, 165,
    182, 186, 207,
    216
  Margaret 86
  Margrett 58
  Thomas 23
Wall
  Jane 165
  Jone 96
  Thomas 96, 164,
    165, 182, 186,
    207, 216
Wallace
  Jane 37
  widow 37
Waller
  Elianor 64
  Ellinor 167
  Elloner 68
  William 87, 118
Wallis
  William 5
Walston
  John 26, 120, 132,
    201, 203, 211
  Margaret 201, 203
Walters
  Alexander 105, 159
  Allexander 2
  John 116, 163
  Joseph 169, 170
Walton
  Rebecah 60
  William 1, 60, 72,

Wealch
  William 117
Weatherly
  James 10, 135
Weaver
  Ann 82, 107, 154
  Richard 82, 107,
    154
Webb
  Elisabeth 116
  Thomas 116, 180,
    206, 216
  William 119
Weddill
  Mary 86
  Roger 86
Wedell
  Mary 81
  Roger 81
Wedill
  Mary 42
  Roger 42
Weedill
  Roger 111
Weeks
  John 56
Weickes
  Joseph 105
Welch
  Richard 203
  William 187, 206
Welham
  Thomas 36
Wells
  George 29, 38, 41,
    43, 50, 55, 99,
    117, 140
  James 101, 147
  Richard 90, 162
  Swithin 140
Welsh
  Henry 166
  John 166
  Maj. 87
  William 183, 215
Wessells
  Gerardus 121
West
  John 93, 117, 120
  Richard 94
  Thomas 209
  William 101
Westbury
  William 159

Wetherley
  James 135
Wetherly
  James 18, 31, 101,
    104
  John 18
Weyman
  Mary 178, 205, 214
Wheatley
  William 101, 104,
    135
Wheeler
  Christian 87, 90,
    179, 188
  Ignatius 145, 150,
    152
  James 1, 83, 128,
    137, 200
  John 41, 74, 84,
    87, 90, 95, 98,
    108, 112, 128,
    145, 179, 186
  Maj. 68
  Samuel 1, 24, 87,
    97, 105, 126,
    181, 204, 213
  Samuell 36, 77
Whichaley
  Thomas 128, 148
Whinfeild
  Jonah 96
  Sarah 96
Whinfell
  James 82
  Jonah 124
  Jonas 95
Whinsell
  Jonah 114
  Sarah 114, 126
Whitchally
  Jane 51
  Thomas 51
White
  Edward 167
  Kazia 116
  Nicholas 136, 152,
    167, 177, 194
  Sarah 37
  Widow 37
  William 79
Whitehead
  Charles 129, 218
  John 142
Whittell

Page 284

John 121, 141
Wilson
   (N) 143
   Alexander 218
   Elisabeth 95, 100,
     182, 186, 192
   Ephraim 217
   George 212
   Giles 57, 88, 118,
     210
   James 110, 116,
     121, 140, 180,
     206, 216
   John 65
   Joseph 65
   Mary 116
   Robert 95, 100,
     182, 192
Winchester
   Isaac 14, 152
Wincoer
   William 67
Wincoll
   John 199
Winder
   John 10, 18, 31,
     104, 135
Wine
   Daniell 46
Winfen
   Jonas 180
   Sarah 180
Winfield
   (N) 74
   Ellione 73
   Jonah 73
   Jonas 204, 213
Wingfield
   Jonah 58, 59
   Sarah 58, 59
Winley
   John 167
Winsmore
   Robert 132
Winter
   William 77
Winterbotham
   Jarvis 203
Winterbotom
   Jarvis 197
Winterbottam
   Jarvis 197, 203
Wintersel
   William 71

Winterson
   William 52
Wise
   Richard 177
Wiseman
   John 107, 132, 212,
     224
Witchaley
   Jane 191
Withers
   S. 187
   Sam. 215
Wood
   James 149
   Robert 48, 62, 67
Woodcock
   John 150
Wooden
   John 203
Woodnite
   Elisabeth 164
   Lawrence 164
Woodward
   John 76, 96, 119,
     128, 147, 164,
     165
Woolford
   Roger 5, 165, 223
   Stephen 104
Woolman
   Alice 9, 27
   Richard 9, 27
Workman
   Anthony 97, 102,
     105
Worthington
   Sarah 185
Wotton
   John 121
Wright
   John 38
   Mary 38
   Robert 49, 51, 102
   Solomon 86
   Thomas 29, 75
   William 159
Wroth
   James 19, 82, 83,
     84, 97, 109, 112
   Mr. 47
Wyait
   John 76
   Sarah 76
Wyet

John 48
Sarah 48
Wyner
John 71
Wythens
Samuell 6

William 10, 17, 20,
31, 54, 64, 75,
86, 115, 137
Younger
John 117, 152, 183,
206, 215

Yates
Rebecca 112, 142,
191, 192
Rebeckah 71
Robert 71, 112,
142, 150, 160,
191, 192, 201,
208, 212, 222
Yeedon
George 33
Yeo
John 2, 47, 89, 113
Yerberry
Elisabeth 180, 206,
216
Thomas 180, 206,
216
Yerbery
Elisabeth 129
Thomas 129
Yong
Mary 218
Samuel 188, 218
Yongue
Frances 63
William 63
Yore
James 124, 156,
169, 174, 178,
193, 197, 201
Patience 124, 156,
175, 197
York
William 47
Young
Ann 68
Frances 10, 17, 64,
86, 115
George 15, 169
Hannah 20, 31
Mary 141, 165
Samuel 165, 180
Samuell 141
Thomas 84, 111,
118, 183, 206,
215

INDEX OF EQUITY CASES

Lynes vs. Cooper 201, 222
Lynes vs. estate of Dennis 22

Mackall vs. Clarke 72
Mackdowell vs. Hambleton 62, 66, 93, 108, 126, 146, 156
Macklin vs. estate of Boyden 123
Macklyn vs. Clouds 48
Mahenny vs. Elgate 73, 74, 76, 107
Makamy et.al. vs. Elgate 126
McDowell vs. Evans 57
Meares vs. Holland 166
Miles & Duhattaway vs. Conant 97
Mills vs. James 49
Milstead vs. Serjeant 173, 184, 191, 202, 211, 221, 223
Moore vs. Cumber 202
Moy vs. Carvile 185, 191, 202, 211, 217, 222

Nichols vs. estate of Caswell 195
Nuthall vs. Bigger 36, 126

Proctor vs. estate of Cusick 17
Pye vs. estate of Toft 170

Rosewell vs. estate of Innes 2

Short vs. Bayne 209, 222
Smithson vs. Guither 34
Smoote vs. Yates 142, 191, 201, 208, 222
Sprigg vs. Bigger 6, 7, 64, 65, 66, 115
Sterry vs. Hearne 18
Sweatnam vs. estate of Mountford 52

Taillor vs. estate of Hedge 34
Taney vs. Dennis 112, 123, 124, 149
Tyrling vs. Orrell & Carvile 184, 191

Wheeler vs. Jones 128
Winsmore vs. Cooke 132

www.ingramcontent.com/pod-product-compliance
Lightning Source LLC
Chambersburg PA
CBHW061003280326
41935CB00009B/820